Gratitude
in Grief

Gratitude in Grief

FINDING DAILY JOY AND A LIFE OF PURPOSE FOLLOWING THE DEATH OF MY SON

Kelly S. Buckley

ISBN: 1543153976
ISBN 13: 9781543153972
Library of Congress Control Number: 2017902651
CreateSpace Independent Publishing Platform
North Charleston, South Carolina

For Stephen. From the moment you were born, to the moment of your death,
you have been my biggest teacher and one of my greatest creations. Thank you
for 23 years of joy and love, and for our wonderful story.
For Brady, who showed all of us how easy it was to love unconditionally. You
gave our family a love we never knew, and ignited a magic between all of us
that I will spend my life showing my thanks for. Your love allowed us to open our
own hearts, and to be present in that love for the last four years of Stephen's life.
For Brendan, the best boy a Mom could hope for, with a heart as big as the sun.
I have learned so much from you and your strength and grace amaze me. I am
the proudest Momma on the planet.
And for Rudy the Wonder Dog.
I llove each of you all more than all the sand on every beach in the world; more
than all the bubble gum on the bottom of all the desks in all the schools; more
than all the leaves on all the trees. I love you more than life, and more than
death. Thank you for being with me on this journey and choosing happiness.

Introduction

History will be kind to me for I intend to write it.

-*Winston Churchill*-

I would like to welcome you and thank you for choosing to read this story of Stephen, and my journey towards Gratitude. Rising from the depths of despair, this book is the story of finding goodness in the worst of situations. Through gratitude, humility, and quiet listening to my soul and to God, I have been able to work through the loss of my beautiful child. And, in the process, I have found purpose and peace.

I have loved to write. All my life, words have always flowed from my soul, and onto the page. I love to speak as well. I can remember my first Public Speaking contest in 7th Grade, with Mrs. Betty McHugh as my teacher and mentor, urging me on. The topic was "The Trials and Tribulations of Public Speaking." A tongue in cheek speech about the stressful aspects of speaking, I joked about being nervous, knees knocking, and mouth dry at the thought of getting up in front of a crowd. But, I wasn't. I loved to write words, and then practice reading them aloud until I could present them with excellence. It was so much better than the jumble of nonsense that otherwise came from my mouth on a day to day basis.

But for all the writing, and all the speaking I have done since that time, no words came easier than the ones that you will read in this book.

No words came as effortlessly as the words I spoke at my son's funeral, honoring the spirit and goodness that we should all work to have every single day. In fact, there have been times that, as the words flowed from my very being, I have wondered if it was even me writing.

I know that saying this story was easy for me to write must sound a little loopy; how could it be easy to speak and write after the sudden and heartbreaking loss of your 23-year-old son?

I don't have an answer, only to say that it is always easy to speak your truth. That is, when you realize what your truth is. My life has changed, but from it, I have been given clarity. Clarity of purpose, clarity of what is truly important; I've found my vision is no longer clouded with the blur of money, or position, status or ego. The interesting thing is prior to Stephen's death I was searching for purpose, feeling a little lost personally and professionally, feeling I was not living up to my potential. Thank God I was searching, as it allowed me to recognize the insight I had been presented with in the heartbreaking loss of my boy.

In many ways, I can see how all of this will be looked at as a great gift in my life. When people one day disassemble what I have created on this earthly world, I think they will see that this was a turning point for me. It was the moment that I let go of fear, and moved forward; allowed myself to move *over* the "cusp", instead of being *on* the cusp as I was for many years before. On the cusp of what? Enlightenment? Peace? Wisdom? Perhaps it was the moment I finally decided to trust, in something bigger, something mystical and unknown; to trust in myself and my own strength and abilities. I'm not sure, maybe they will simply say, "She finally got it."

That is not to say I don't hurt. My heart physically aches for my child, aches for my remaining son and his pain; it aches for what my husband and I and our families have lost, it aches with each passing day for the reality of this situation. It is not going away. But, for some unknown reason, I have decided to embrace it. I am embracing the ache, the pain, and I am seeing where it takes me, and how it changes me. I think my past has allowed me to see that resisting a change will only make it worse. And with change, comes true vision, but you must be brave enough to look at it. The true and only way through is to embrace it, let it happen, and learn. And, when you get to the other side of the grief, you pick yourself up, stick those lessons in your pocket, and become a better person because of it. I've promised myself, God and Stephen to live that purpose and be grateful for the lessons I have been given.

I write this book to honor who he was, and because I believe that we need to continue to talk about his spirit for life even in his death. I don't want the conversation to end. This is not because I need to continue to speak specifically about Stephen. Rather, I want to spark a conversation that talks about how we live our lives day to day, how we parent our children, how we relate to one another. I want to start a conversation that may help someone who has to walk this path of loss, in the hopes that my humble words may serve as a candle, a small but significant light in your own darkness.

And finally, I write this because I think the biggest learning opportunity we are presented with in life comes through death. It presents us with a flare in the night sky of our minds. It illuminates the truth about our individual lives, and what is truly important. I felt compelled to write about it before that flare dimmed back in the recesses of my mind and I lost sight of the simple truth. That Gratitude, even in grief, can uplift and transform your life; and how we can transfer that thankfulness to make all our days better. Gratitude is the one miracle that we can bring about through our own free will.

I write this from my perspective only. I know that some who played a part in Stephen's life may feel that their story is not found within the pages of this book. That is true. No disrespect, but it is not their story. This is the story of a mother and her son, the conversations I had with him during his time on earth, and the insight I have gained based on my reflection of his life. We were two children, who grew up together, and tried to make the most of every moment. This book is the purpose, the peace in all of this pain. Finding the reason, finding the meaning.

I have divided the book into sections, the first telling you the story of Stephen's death, what happened, the outpouring of love in some very unconventional ways, and how we have lived through it.

The next section focuses on my discovery of **"Gratitude in Grief-Finding my one little thing for the day."** Shortly after Stephen's death, I told my son we would need to find "one little thing" each day to hold on to, to help us when we felt sad. I knew that I needed to look for those little things to take comfort from in the dark days of mourning. And, to my surprise, I found countless things to be grateful for each day. It created a shift in my thinking, in my grieving, and in my life.

The Final section offers up some helpful suggestions for others who may be hurting as I am, and for the loving special people that comfort us in our time of pain.

Part of the proceeds of this book will go towards charities that support young women who find themselves with an unexpected pregnancy. I was blessed to be surrounded by love when I was a young girl, pregnant and afraid. That love, and those people helped mold me into the parent I needed to be, and shaped some of the best parts of Stephen's character. It is my hope that I can give back and through financial support and volunteerism, help young mothers grow their children into strong adults who live a life of honor, with kindness and courage. And finally, I will support young athletes such as the NC State Hockey Team, as I believe that participation in sport (particularly hockey) builds character that we need to see more of in this world.

Share this with whomever you like. Share with people who want to read it and people who don't. In fact, the people who don't want to read it probably need it the most. During his life, I told Stephen I thought he was destined for greatness, to change people and things for the good. My hope is that this book allows that to happen.

Part One

The Start of Our New Journey

I look at life as a gift of God. Now that he wants it back I have no right to complain. –

Joyce Cary–

"Hey you", I said in a happy tone as I looked at the caller ID and answered my cell phone. It was the evening of July 4th, and the night sky was beginning to light up in Louisville, with people celebrating Independence.

The "you" I was referring to was my baby, my boy, my grown man, my pride and joy; Stephen. Having fun with his friends for the day, he decided to spend the 4th at Jordan Lake. At 23, I had watched him blossom over the past few years, into this amazing man. A rising senior at North Carolina State University, Stephen was studying Political Science and looking forward to a bright future. My husband and I had discussed, just the day before, how happy and grateful we were, as he was having the time of his life. Good friends, happy with the progress he was making in his studies, things were good.

But, the caller on the other end was not my boy calling to wish us a Happy 4th. It was a Sergeant Reggie Barker with the North Carolina Fish and Wildlife Division for Jordan Lake, North Carolina. I can remember knowing, as soon as I heard his voice on the other end, that my boy was gone. Although neither I nor he would say it, I knew it. As he spoke those unbelievable words, I thought back to my days as a Nurse in Canada, working in the Emergency room. I witnessed tremendous loss, seeing a physician break the news, the RCMP officers carrying the heaviness of death on their shoulders as they walked through the sliding doors of the ER. I could recall working in the Oncology Clinic, talking to family, attempting to provide some measure of comfort when the gravity of their prognosis had been shared and hope had slipped away. I had a membership to that club, the group that, because of their chosen profession, carries the burden of bearing witness to the fragility of life. The full spectrum of life, with all of its joy and the equal measures of pain. Back in those days, I can remember being so affected by those moments, the passage of someone's life, and the people left behind. But I, like many in the profession, would be there in the moment of tragedy, and then would have to look away and choose to move on from it quickly. To carry all of that pain with you for too long, it was simply too much. It was far too grim to contemplate, too much of a burden to carry. That is why, when you watch reality shows about Trauma Units, you find that each employee has that edge, that dark sense of humor. It is a survival tactic, to get you through what you see and experience within the confines of a twelve-hour shift.

And here I was, on the other end of that message. The conversation was a blur of high level information, directions to the lake, and Sgt. Barker planting the seeds of reality for this child's mother. I wondered as he spoke, if he had ever had to make this type of call before, or if this was his first. I wondered if he practiced in his mind how he would say it. Once his directions had been given, and he had stated the facts, he paused, and then quietly said, "And, just to let you know, we have been searching for Stephen for 30 minutes now." Ka-Boom! My life as I knew it simply imploded. Everything that I knew as who I was had been blown to bits.

Somebody crack open my chest, take out my heart, and throw it away, because it is broken. "30 minutes now." That was all we needed to know, wasn't it? He was so respectful in the manner he presented that grave information, and, because I had been in his position before, I knew that he finished our call with me with a heavy heart. That phone call was the hardest part of his job, without a doubt. I thought about him, and if he had a family, if he went home that night, and kissed his children, held them a little longer, a little closer, as I did with Stephen after a particularly painful shift. I thought about his story, and how, in his career, this would become part of it, a notation in the chapter about his professional life. I had patients, who I still carry with me to this day. The man getting ready to be discharged after months in the hospital recuperating from an accident, only to throw a clot as he put on his shoes. He died, right there in front of me. He had worked so hard to recover, and in an instant, it was over. Another patient, a gorgeous teenage boy, one moment full of life and in the next gone, after a freak accident that left him with a broken neck and his friend without a scratch. I can still remember every detail about him, the smell of his hair gel, what his parents were wearing, the scent of his father's cologne, and the heaviness in the air as his family realized it was true, he was not coming back. I wondered if we would be a memory like that in the mind of Sgt. Barker, or if our story would fade away with time.

Thinking back now, it was almost comical how fast my husband and I readied ourselves to get on the road. Having just arrived home from a leisurely July 4th celebration, we were winding down for the day, stomachs full and hearts happy. Once the call came in, we sprang into action. Clothes thrown into the suitcases, things gathered quickly and thrown into the car, dog readied for the trip. Have you ever willed a dog to pee? It is no small task. Vaguely, I recall getting my father-in-law to start up his computer so I could MapQuest the fastest route. With Brady's parents standing in their garage looking at us with shock and concern, we left, to drive nine hours through the night to the lake.

They urged us to stay, not to drive off into the night in this emotional state. Thinking back, it was probably not the most sensible thing to do. But it was what we had to do, needing to get to him. The thought of sitting there, trying to find a flight, as they searched for him, was simply too much to bear. I needed to be in action, taking some steps, however foolish to bring me closer to my son.

As we drove through the night, passing one community after another, the fireworks filled the night sky on both sides of the Interstate. Beautiful colors bursting through the darkness, and cascading down until they disappeared into the earth. Much like his life, a burst of beauty, gone way too soon. I kept thinking that the fireworks were not for Independence this year, but rather to welcome my special boy into heaven. I can vividly recall having that thought, and then banishing it, not wanting it to be true. As we passed each town's celebration, I thought about Stephen's welcome into heaven, but would not verbalize my analogy to my husband, for fear I might will it into existence. The fireworks were coupled with rain, as if the heavens, celebrating his arrival, realized how many people would suffer once they heard the news and cried tears along with me for our pain. But, as the minutes turned to hours, I realized that no news was in fact the worst news I could ever imagine. They had not found him on some shoreline, dazed and confused and injured. They had not found him at all.

About 12:45 AM, we received a call from Sgt. Barker, explaining that for manpower and visibility reasons, they were calling off the search. They would resume in the morning. And, although I knew the reality of the situation, neither Sgt. Barker nor I could bring ourselves to say the obvious after hours of searching. The most he could utter to me was, "You need to prepare yourself."

I was thankful for that, thankful that he had not announced that his search had shifted from rescue to recovery. I had often watched televised reports at a crash scene, and wondered how families felt when that announcement was made on the evening news. Sitting on their couch, glued to the television, waiting to hear some news about a life altering tragedy. And someone, with perfect articulation and whitened teeth, takes all your hope away.

"You need to prepare yourself." But how does one do that? How does a mother prepare to be told her baby is gone? How do I prepare myself for what I will see when I arrive at Jordan Lake? How does a mother prepare to hear those words spoken, the words and thoughts every mother turns away from as they raise their children, too painful to even contemplate? Even as I write this, in the hopes that my story will affect change in the way only Stephen could, I know that most will have to look away, because it is simply too painful. I know that, because I was one of those mothers. I was one of those mothers who would never watch the Dateline episode about the death of a child, or rent a DVD with a plotline that focused on family loss. As a nurse in the Emergency Room, I would see things so horrific, and I would be weeks trying to recover.

Prepare yourself. So, we did. We called family in Canada, with more calm than I would have thought possible, explained the situation and told them to prepare themselves. Driving through the night, Brady and I expressed every emotion possible. We were silent and sad, chatty and anxious, crying and desperate, sentimental, and logical and planning. We planned the funeral, the memorial, to the finest details, knowing in our hearts how we wanted to celebrate his life, or rather, how he would want to be celebrated. Seems surreal even now as I type the words. We really did know what needed to be done. We just knew, without a doubt.

I turned on the stereo, to pass the time as we drove through the rain and dark night. And there it was, his mix of music, a playlist of his favorites, for us to listen to, to be comforted, almost speaking to us, as if he was sitting there with us. I believe that you know. He was sitting there with us for each long hour through the night as we traveled the loneliest road, where the destination was heartache and loss.

I felt him. The rain poured from the night sky for almost the entire trip, letting up only when we were on the final road leading us to the lake. But, I knew we would be okay, I knew that he was with us. For those who have not experienced a loss of someone you loved deeply, I know this may sound like the ranting of someone in grief, and I suppose to a point, it is. But he was with us. Hand on my shoulder, there with us to help us through. And, although I had never felt more distant from HIM, I knew God was with us too.

It was hard to know if the decreased visibility was due to the heavy rainfall outside, or the tears streaming down my face. I continued to listen to his deep, yet quirky music. I laughed, I cried. The haunting melodies running through each song, the words speaking of young love, lost, of going away, of loving in spite of the distance and time. Each song spoke of promise, told a story of who he was, and where he was as he contemplated on the next chapter of his life. And all I could think was, "God, it's me, Kelly. Take me. Please hear me, just take me. Leave him, and take me." I negotiated throughout the night, silently.

While still in Kentucky, I passed a car and looked at the license plate on the rear of the car. *"One Lifetime"*. Tears streamed down my face like a rainstorm on a window. One Lifetime, the words on the tattoo he had on his left flank. He decided to get the tattoo in his third week at school, a rite of passage as he embarked into adulthood. He and his girlfriend. She had announced it to me when I went to visit. I remember the look on his face as she told me, as she was quite proud of it, and had no reason to think I would be upset. Stephen, however, was desperately looking for an opening in the floor.

I have one eyebrow that rises when I am perplexed with a situation. That eyebrow has kept me honest through the years, and has let people know exactly what my position was on any matter. It did not fail me when she announced this tattoo. After the shock, I did not say much about it. He was after all, a grown man, capable of making decisions about his own life. After he and the girl broke it off, he said he was still happy about it. His younger brother asked frequently when the laser procedure would be scheduled.

One Lifetime. How absolutely poignant at this moment. How very accurate that this should be inked on his skin for all time. It was exactly how he lived. He knew he had only one lifetime, and he was the kind of person who made sure he fit as much in as he could in any given day. Was it a simple license plate, or a message from him? I will never know, but that car followed us through three states as we drove in the dead of night.

As the minutes ran into hours, I had some deep conversations. Not only with my husband, but silently, with God and with Stephen. I reviewed every minute of my time with him. From the pregnancy, to giving birth as a child, to growing up right along with him, to the hardships and heartache and stumbles in relationships, to new beginnings; to knowing that despite all of it, the depth of the love we had for each other was rare. I only had one true argument with him, ever. Sure, there were always some eye rolling, huffs and puffs and sighs as a teenager, frustration at times with choices, or discipline, but we only truly argued once. In his entire life. It was New Year's Day two years before, and it took me about six months to recover. And he would smile, and say, "It's okay Mom, it is over. It was just an off day. We both love each other right?"

Imagine that, only one argument. He had experienced a tough semester, and was struggling to find his way, and we both lost sight of the fact that we wanted the same thing, his happiness.

I questioned why I would have to experience the death of my own child, again, out of the natural order of things. I questioned the reasons, why God would give me two children in one womb, only to take them both away. I am a logical thinker, partly because I am my father's daughter, and because I had been conditioned to be strategic and logical. A tool for survival I suppose. I had to be able to, in short order, filter out the minutia, and see the truth of a situation, see not only the black and white, but all the shades of grey that exist between the two. I've always looked at this as a gift, but at times like this, I am not so sure. Because I can feel, like I have so many times before, the wheels of logic and solution turning in my mind and my heart. I don't have an answer why, but because of who I am, I will find some logic, some purpose to this. Even then, in the dark hours of July 4th, the last day of my son's life, I could feel it coming, some explanation being created that would allow me to survive, some logic. It frustrated me.

As the night turned to morning, we drove the last stretch of road, to the lake. I think driving would be a little inaccurate, as I remember us kind of flying over the pavement. Working on directions from Stephen's friend Ross, we managed to find the cove on the second try. As we drove along the shoreline, I realized just how big it was, a massive lake, and beautiful in every way; I surmised that thousands enjoyed this place every summer. Water blue and glistening, with wonderful trees all along the edge.

It looked to have a number of sandy coves around the perimeter. It was a perfect spot, and truly must have been a popular place for college students to come and blow off some steam.

We arrived at the spot at about 6:30 in the morning, before anyone else had arrived to resume the search. My husband and me, with our big brown dog Rudy. Walking ahead of Brady down the trail, I collapsed with grief in seeing the cove. Serene and absolutely stunning, it just didn't seem like a possible location for the end of someone's life, especially not Stephen's. He was an athlete, he ran for miles, climbed trees, pushed himself physically in ways I could only dream about. How could this picture-perfect setting be the place to take him? It simply did not make sense to me. After everything, being born eight weeks too soon, and all of the other struggles we had seen together. He is taken away because he went for a swim?

I walked the edge of the shore, inconsolable, crying from the depths of my soul, in the same way I did for his twin brother on the night of his birth. It was surreal, as I could hear the sounds coming out of my mouth, but they did not sound human. Wandering around with Rudy, I prayed we would find him ourselves, before any search party or stranger. The water was like glass, and the trees still, not a breath of air. It was as if God had asked everyone to be quiet out of respect. And then, I saw it. One spot in the water and for some reason, I could not take my eyes away from it. There was nothing to see, just still water and some gentle ripples from the fish moving below the surface. But I knew. I sat on a bump of sand in front of that spot, with Rudy by my side. As Rudy whined, he looked at the same spot as I did, and scratched at the water's edge. Were we right? I will never know why, but I knew that was where they would find him. And, on their very first dive, that is exactly where they found my boy.

Sitting there, I repeatedly said the same words, in my conversation with God. "Take me, please God, just take me. Please, please God, just take me." Over and over, I begged God to be merciful, and to take me and leave him on the shore to be found, alive, to continue on with the promise of his life. The world could continue to turn without me in it, and Stephen had so much to do. I thought about my other son, and how I loved him, but would be willing to sacrifice my own life if it meant I could bring back his brother. Oh, the ache. The physical and emotional ache that rocked me, well, I have never known anything like it, before or since. Because the more I said those seven words, the more I realized that God had made his choice, and there would be no negotiation.

I contemplated letting Rudy go in, but a Sheriff was circling in her boat, looking at me with concern. She was very kind, and came over to the shoreline and explained the plan for the search. She seemed young, so young, and I could not figure out if she had children of her own. I did not think so. If she did, her breath would have caught in her throat when she tried to speak to me. That was, at least, how I reacted in similar situations. She gently spoke to us about not being there when the divers arrive to begin the recovery operation. As she explained, it is not something a mother should have to see. As she moved the boat away from me, I could hear her talking to her colleagues on the radio, and saying "You guys, I understand, but this is his mother, this is her baby and she wants to be over here."

They needed me to leave for fear of what I might see when they pulled him out of the water. It was dreamlike listening to that conversation. I wondered if any parents had heard me have a conversation like that in the ER. To be discussed in the third person, your wellbeing and emotional state the topic, with everyone feeling they understood what was best, without you saying a word. The one piece of the puzzle they did not see or understand is what I had with him. They were being kind, I knew that, but did they really think anything I could see would make this situation any worse? Did they think anything I could possibly see could be any worse than what I had pictured in my mind for every hour of that drive? Did they think that anything that I could potentially witness could be more painful than the realization that my child was dead?

In any case, I surrendered to it. I am not a woman for dramatics, and so agreed to relocate to the dock where they were forming the search.

Driving into where the Search and Rescue group had set up their headquarters, I noticed that the police had closed the site to the media. We drove by the barricades, saying "We are Stephen's parents." Dreamlike. Can't be. Pulling into the parking area, I lifted my head, and there they were. His friends, a group of lost souls standing there at the shoreline, as the rain fell gently on each of them. As we pulled up, the tears flowed freely, both from our eyes and theirs. Just weeks before, they had spent the weekend with us, lying on our couch, laughing, playing Frisbee golf, drinking our beer, and eating our food. And we loved every minute of it. Now, the looks on their sweet faces spoke of so much pain and sadness. They looked older. Oh, how wrong, to have the joys and innocence of your youth taken away so quickly, and in this manner. I remember I was a little younger than them when my parents died, and it forever changed me. I could see that same change in their eyes this morning.

They stayed with us at the shoreline. Their parents stood with us, strangers showing up at a lake on a cloudy Sunday morning for no other purpose than to offer comfort. They brought food and water and chairs and umbrellas and love. Lots and lots of love. They stood right next to us during the most difficult time of our lives. And they did not look away.

I remember the warm summer rain hitting softly off the top of my head. It was the only thing that made me feel remotely alive. I watched the boats head off to the cove, and out of my field of vision. And we waited. I was enveloped by love. I had not one member of my family with me, other than Brady and Rudy, but I was surrounded by love. And then they found him. The paramedic came to explain to me that they had found him, and would be bringing him back shortly. She was an interesting sort. She had probably worked at her job for a few years, and had more seniority than the obvious green and inexperienced colleagues who stood over next to the ambulance shuffling their feet and having nervous conversation. When I looked over, they looked away. She, however, did not. She came and introduced herself and explained what would happen. She was professional and very kind, but somehow, I felt she was patronizing. She instructed me that they would need a moment to prepare him for us to see him. I explained I would give her seven minutes, and then I would come and help her. I told her I was a nurse, and I just wanted to see my boy. The tone, the tone of her voice. I will never forget the tone of her voice. I believe my sensitivity was related to her message rather than her personality.

And then the boat arrived and they raised a sheet to cover the removal of his body from the boat. This simply cannot be real, I thought.

Finally, we stepped into the back of the ambulance, and there he was. Sleeping perhaps, maybe it was just a cruel joke; I could take the punch line if he sat up now and said he was sorry for deceiving me. But alas, it was not a joke, it was all too real. His essence, his spark was no longer with us. The connection I felt with my flesh and blood, my baby was not there in the same way it had been since the first time I held him 23 years earlier. His spirit was gone, or was it? Or was it all around me, surrounding me like a warm sweater on a cold winter night, hugging into my chest, giving me comfort and hope. Yes, let's go with the second one.

Brady and I held our breath for a moment. Just inhaled and stopped. Time had stopped. The world stopped its rotation for an instant. And then, it was a real. It is hard to describe in simple words, so I will not try.

I will not share every detail, as I don't need to. But, it was the moment that I changed, Brady changed, our lives changed, and our view of the world and life was radically altered. We took some time to say good bye to his physical body, his sweet and handsome face, his perfect athletic physique. Good bye to the dreams of his future, of love and marriage and grand-children, and watching him continue to blossom into this amazing human being.

And so the journey begins.

The Story of a Special Boy

Making the decision to have a child – it's momentous. It is to decide forever to have your heart go walking outside your body.

–Elizabeth Stone-

Things were happening way too fast for me. Just weeks before I had finally told my family about my pregnancy. Two weeks later, an ultrasound revealed I was carrying not one, but two babies. And May 21, 1986, I was staring with shock at the OB/GYN resident standing at the foot of my bed.

She had bright red hair, cut very short, close to her head. I remember thinking that the haircut was not a matter of fashion for her, but rather because she thought she was much too busy to manage any other style. She wore hospital greens and a lab coat, and with her stethoscope strategically placed around her neck, she marched around the unit like she was the smartest person on earth. She immediately rubbed me the wrong way, perhaps from my own fear of the unknown, but more likely because of intimidation. She was a woman who seemed way too strong in the face of the weakest moment of my life.

I was lying in the same bed I had stayed in for the past 36 hours now, in a darkened room, with little or no stimuli, and hooked up to not one, but two fetal monitors. Preeclampsia was the reason they gave to me for this

14

solitary confinement. I would not understand just how serious that could be until years later, but I did know I did not feel right at all. I was alone when she arrived, and I wished that someone had been with me, to dull the abrasive tone in her voice, perhaps soften the impact of her personality on my weakened soul.

"I need to examine you." she said in a statement rather than in a question. I was young, but smart enough to know what she thought of me, a young girl in a hospital bed pregnant not yet 16. I could feel her impatience with me, when I asked why; her body language spoke loudly to me of her frustration. She did not have time for me, she did not see beyond my bulging belly. Because of her impatience, she did not see that I was an Honor Roll student, could sing in a few different languages, and had big plans that now sat on the unknown list. She chose to see none of it; I was simply a task in her day, not worthy of the respect she would later show the married professional lady in the adjacent bed.

Finally, when I realized I would not get a response to my inquiry for the rationale of this examination, I simply complied. Thinking back to that moment, I realize her treatment of me affected the way I treated people in my own nursing career, and in every aspect of the rest of my life. I would remember her distain for me every time I pulled the curtain closed prior to examining a homeless man who was ravaged by the affects of alcohol and drugs and needed some help; if only to get well enough to go out and do the same thing to his body all over again. I would remember her when I was tempted to judge someone on the basis of a first impression as something less than myself. It is said that the people who hurt and test you in your own life are actually your best teachers. And, although it is still difficult for me to give this person any credit, I have to agree with that statement. "You can't tell a book by its cover."

Following her cold and indifferent examination; she announced to me, "You are in labor. 2 centimeters dilated."

"No, I can't be." I said with disbelief. Still alone in the room with her, she rolled her eyes at me, bored with my ignorance.

"Well, you are. I will tell your doctor." And with that, she walked out.

I sat up and let my feet dangle on the edge of the bed, looking down and wondering where my ankles were vacationing, as I had not seen them in some weeks. My head was light and woozy, my blood pressure high. The shock of her words instantly upset my stomach. I was not ready for this. But I knew that she was right.

Even in my youth and inexperience, I knew that my body was telling me that it was time for these babies to come out, regardless of the fact that it was eight weeks too soon. Some days earlier, I had such a foreboding feeling, yet I was unable to articulate exactly what was wrong. Standing in my parents' bedroom, tears streaming down my face, I could only say, "There is something wrong with one of the babies."

It was an unusual feeling, both a physical feeling of being unwell, but a larger emotional feeling of dread, of unexplainable knowledge of something I did not want to know. I prayed to St. Gerard, the Saint of Mothers. I prayed this prayer for a sick and dying child over and over again.

Just hours after the resident's unfeeling declaration, there I was standing in the bathroom and looking at my very young reflection in the mirror as birth was imminent. The girl in the mirror did not look like a mother. She looked young and inexperienced, she looked very afraid.

And, despite the fact that the fetal monitors recorded and printed a steady heart rate for both babies hour after hour, I had a strange feeling that this would not end well. But, I did not say anything. I kept silent, thinking maybe that this feeling of dread was related to my overall uneasiness about impending motherhood. I feared if I verbalized this dread, it would appear I was not being motherly, or imply that I did not want the little ones inside of me.

Reflecting on these feelings years later, I realize that this was my first experience with the maternal connection between mother and child. And, although I did not feel motherly, my instincts were laser focused and I knew there was something terribly wrong with one of my children.

Labor progressed as labor does. Some of the memories of that time are clear, some are quite clouded, blocked out for my own comfort, memories judged to be irrelevant in the telling of this story.

I can recall the Gynecologist coming in with his parade of students to check my progress. Nice man, but hands scarily close in size to those of the Jolly Green Giant. That giant hand pushing upwards towards the ceiling as he put on the sterile glove in preparation for examination. Eyeballs, so many eyeballs staring, watching. My own eyeballs, wide with fear of the unknown. I've always marveled at the human brain, and how in times of great turmoil and change in one's life, you will remember the most random and seemingly insignificant things.

As I entered the next stage of active labor, I was aware of all that was happening around me. Muffled and hushed voices outside the room. I could hear the quiet conversations in the hallway, the preparations for the impending birth. I can remember all of it so clearly, as if it was yesterday.

My family physician entered the room, and I exhaled. A familiar face and someone who had been respectful, and had shown me a human kindness regardless of my circumstances. I trusted him.

And in between the cleansing breaths in a contraction, I said, "That resident, the one that told me I was in labor, she's not allowed in the delivery room. I don't want her in my room ever again."

You see, as young as I was, I was still smart, and I was still powerful, although I had no idea what my personal power was, and that discovery would span my lifetime. I understood that this was probably an exciting event for her in her residency, and would be something she could check off her list of experiences in her training. She had not taken this into consideration when she had marched into my room earlier that day. She needed someone like me. But, my fear and immaturity and weakness were not as strong as my desire to ensure she was not one of the first human beings to look into the eyes of my children. No, I thought, you must sit outside, you will have to go and sit in the cafeteria, and stew in your judgmental negativity. And I hope you understand that your lack of empathy, human kindness and dignity is the reason you were shut out of my experience.

Labor progressed, and before I knew it, I was being wheeled into the delivery room. Lying flat, prepped for delivery, I was overwhelmed by the lights, the people, everyone waiting for the arrival.

Thinking back on that night so many years later, I wonder if they quietly knew that Matthew would not live.

Matthew, born first, arrived to a deafening silence. Looking around into the eyes of the masked faces, I searched for some recognition, some hint of information. But, as I looked to each of them, they averted their eyes, quickly looking away. The room was full, this twin pregnancy with someone as young as I was a rare event I suppose. But, for as inquisitive as they all were, no one had the courage to make eye contact with me, or answer my questions. The only eyes that met mine were those of my doctor's and my sister's. My sister's were tear filled, her voice shaky, and all she could manage to say was it was time to deliver the second baby. My doctor's eyes, although competent and supportive, were lost and sad. I could see the sadness, no words were necessary. And even they could only look for a moment, and then had to look away.

Knowing in my heart what the silence translated into my life, I simply stopped; I simply could not do it. I could not bear the thought of delivering my remaining child, only to have him snatched away as well. I hesitated, although now, thinking back, I don't know if it was simply a feeling of hesitation in my mind, as birth is an event much like death. You are not in control; it is a higher power that calls the shots on scheduling.

So, life continued to move on, despite my silent protest and request for it to stop. And, a few short minutes later, Stephen Patrick Russell was born at 02:51 AM on May 22, 1986. And, there he was. No fanfare, so tiny.

Stephen came into life, giving me comfort, filling my heart with joy from the beginning with his tiny little cry. Through the oppressive silence in the room, Stephen was able to do the one thing that no one else in the room or the world could do. Give me a joy for life and some comfort in death all in one cry, in confirmation of his presence. "I am here! I am here with you, and you are not alone." Stephen announced to the world with a frail cry, and my world would never be the same after.

I was a young girl, a child in so many ways, when he was born. Naive, not ready for the challenges of parenting, I had no clue what was to come. But, there we were, together. As a pregnant teen, I had entered that hospital lost, at a fork in the road, unsure of which way to turn in my life. And, as if God had answered my prayers, my road map for the rest of my life had arrived.

Stephen spent a few weeks in the special care nursery prior to coming home. Having no strong sucking reflex because of his gestational age, and being such a low birth weight, he needed the special attention of the nurses and physicians before he could be released from the hospital. I, along with my parents and family, would visit him in the nursery, for feedings and for bonding. It was very overwhelming to go to the nursery for the feedings. Some of the nurses were quiet adamant that a successful feeding was what I needed to bond with my child. I don't think that the nurses understood that I had bonded with him from that first cry, and his existence was connected to me much like an emotional umbilical cord.

About three weeks of age, Stephen finally hit Five pounds, and was ready to be discharged. I remember packing the bag, with the tiny outfit he would wear for his journey home. As we dressed him, I noticed a fine coat of lanugo (peach fuzz often seen covering the skin of premature newborns); I had to roll up the sleeves of the extra, extra small sleeper. With his veins, visible through his paper-thin skin, I can honestly say I was completely overwhelmed. He looked very breakable. He looked very complicated. Between the life and death experience at his birth, a premature infant to care for, and my youth and inexperience, I did not know what to do. I was tremendously lucky to have the family I did, to guide me and teach me how to care for him.

Setting the alarm clock, we would wake him in the night, and slowly, encourage him to feed. And then, he started, to grow and to become the Stephen that would touch the hearts of many.

To call him an easy baby would be an understatement. He was just agreeable. Nothing fazed him, he understood when things did not go according to plan, and he rolled with the punches. Even as a toddler, if you told him not to do something, he simply didn't do it. I write that, knowing I sound like a completely biased mother, but it is true. I could not take any credit for such successes, no credit at all. I had no idea why he was that way, as I was on the other hand emotional and temperamental and learning this parenting thing as I went along. Perhaps it was the influence of key family members, maybe that was it. But it always seemed larger than that as well. He had this way, this way of comforting, of seeing the good in any situation, of finding peace in any circumstance, of knowing what people needed, and giving it to them, freely and without expectation of something in return.

He was a quiet but confident child. Many who met him thought he was painfully shy, but that was not the case. He was simply observing, and did not feel the need to be at the center of the conversation. In some ways, I think he was watching to see who needed him, knowing that you sometimes can understand more of a situation by standing at the periphery instead of right in the middle. He, even in youth, was rare to make rash judgments on people. He loved family. He was, even up to the moment of his death, both street smart and painfully naïve at the same time. I so admired that, as it seemed like he had made a choice to be naïve about situations, a conscious decision to simply see them with fresh eyes.

He was handsome, so very handsome, and athletic. But, he did not know it. After his death, I found not one, but several letters from girls who said they had a crush on Stephen, but he never noticed how many girls liked him. His athleticism came naturally and was accentuated by his willingness to try anything without the fear of stumbling as he learned and mastered new challenges. He was fiercely competitive, but the challenge was always within Stephen, not with others. He was athletic. Yes, in hockey, as he excelled farther than he should have for only starting the sport at the age of 12. But, in everything else too. I loved to watch him run, it was like watching the wind blow across a field of wheat. It was rhythmic and fast and beautiful. In everything that he did sports related, it was not that he was the best. It was simply that he decided not to give up.

He loved food, and he had an ability to put away more food than seemed possible for his physical size. His Grandfather joked that he had a hollow leg and his Grandmother always said she loved to cook for him. It was a deep and long lasting love affair with food, and it was truly something to watch when he sat to enjoy one of his favorite meals. He did not eat fast, but painfully slow, and ate things in order. So, he would eat the green beans first, then the potatoes, then the steak, and on and on. Never all together, but neat, tidy and orderly. And in massive amounts. He drank so much milk; I would get funny looks at the grocery store, as I am sure it looked as if I had a family of ten.

He did his own laundry from a young age. I never really understood it, he just did it. I oftentimes thought about being able to replicate that trait in other men in the world. If I could have figured that out, I could retire early. He also loved to clean. I would come home from work and the house would be spotless.

Children gravitated to him, and he would play with them as if he was seven all over again. He never had that ego, that feeling he needed to "act his age". The previous July 4th, I had watched him play in the sand with a four-year-old for an entire afternoon.

He loved the Power Rangers, and Mortal Kombat. But he also read Walt Whitman and wrote poetry. He loved music, all music and had an eclectic taste, and listened to everything from classical to hard rock.

He had a temperament that I could not take credit for. He was, in a way, a version of my Aunt Lorraine, who watched over him and loved him, harder than one would think possible. When I was in nursing school, and away from him, she showered him with her magic. And, it was a magic I will never be able to explain. She touched all of us with it. He was much like her, always had a smile, was never quick to anger, and had vision that always saw the good in people and situations; a gentle and old soul.

He was a gifted artist, although no one knew it. He, as my father had done so many years before, hid his talents and felt he was not good enough to be on display.

These are all random thoughts I know, but how does one describe their child and all the delicious and unique traits of a person that gave you so much joy?

Our life was not without struggles, but for the most part, we had decided to be happy. We had both, without words or conversations, decided to choose happiness through the nursing school days, when we were apart for extended periods of time. To also be happy when we had to move, several times during the course of his life, to prosper and climb the corporate ladder, starting our life in a new city, all over again. To be happy through hurt, a divorce, another move, a new beginning in a new country. Some days, it could not have been easy for him. I can recall carrying with me a feeling of inadequacy, wondering if my quest for betterment in our life was hurting more than helping him. I can recall, as I advanced in my professional positions and visibility, how vague I would be about my age, not wanting him or I to be judged because of his unconventional beginning. It was so silly really, looking back on it now, as I never saw the true power of our own resilience. I never saw that his unconventional beginning was the very reason our relationship was so very special.

In any case, all of the life events, much too many to mention, brought him to July 4th, 2009. A rising senior at North Carolina State University, excited about the possibilities of life, but still not sure what direction would provide him with fulfillment. Having had the fun I wanted for him since starting at the school, he had been playing hockey, had this amazing group of characters who had a bond of friendship that was so special. He was not perfect, no one is. But, he was close. And to see him, my resilient, beautiful Stephen, it took my breath away. To see him be happy, in the last few years of his life, it was the greatest gift a mother could ever receive. It is a gift I hold close to my heart today and comforts me in loss.

You often read those inspirational quotes about events in your life, challenges and trauma, and how you will reflect on them years later and see they were gifts. Gifts that allow you to grow into a richer human being, allow you to gain perspective, humility, compassion and grace. 23 years ago, a child gave birth to a tiny, fuzz covered, beautiful miracle. I thought life was over, thought I had no future or possibility. And years later, I would look back on that time, and say it was the best thing that ever happened to me. I always called him my fork in the road, and he was. As a parent, I tried my best with what I had, but he oftentimes offered more wisdom than I ever could.

The fact that something so challenging 23 years ago turned out to be a gift from God gives me the hope I need to move forward from grief. Because of what he and God taught me at his arrival, I know that something good always comes from the moments in life where you are brought to your knees with pain. I believe, I have to believe, that just as with his birth, his death will lead me to a greater purpose, wiser and stronger.

Part Two

Gratitude in Grief- Finding "Just One Little Thing"

*She was no longer wrestling with the grief, but
could sit down with it as a lasting companion
and make it a sharer in her thoughts.*

−GEORGE ELIOT−

I AM NOT SURE HOW my gratitude came about following Stephen's death. I
suppose I could say it had something to do with the lessons I had learned
previously through heartache and loss. Stephen's very birth taught me the
important lesson about the balance that exists between life and death. I
can recall, as a young mother, sitting in the hospital bed on the morning of
his birth and contemplating how I was supposed to navigate through this
complicated situation. I felt both tremendous sadness for the loss of one
child and happiness and excitement over the other, this tiny little creation
in the special care nursery.

It was not a smooth ride, those first few weeks. I had so, so much
trouble wrapping my mind around it, figuring out how to move on. Could
I allow myself to be happy even in the face of grief? Thinking back to
that moment now, I can see how it prepared me for my spiritual growth,
for my understanding and acceptance over the loss of my child. They
were two halves, and separated they showed me the physical and spiritual

connection between life and death. They showed me the lessons of life and death, all in one pregnancy, one womb. And, now, the two halves, once again together to make a whole, continue to teach me. Knowing that those two special boys are whole again gives me gratitude.

I watched Stephen be drawn to identical twins his entire life. It was always as if he was searching for something. From the brotherly closeness he had with his cousin Evan, to finding twins in many chapters of his life. At the age of twelve, he came to me to discuss two identical twin boys who played with him on his baseball team. "Mom, there is something about those boys, that is like me. I can't explain it, but I know that something about them that is the same as Me." he said matter of factly, as we munched on snacks and watched a movie, home alone together for the evening. He did not know he was a twin up to that point. I had waited to tell him, not wanting him to feel guilt about the demise of Matthew in the womb. I'm not sure if that was the right approach, but the best that I could do at the time with what I had in my parenting toolbox. There is no chapter for that kind of thing in any manual. And, once I did tell him that night, he honestly did not seem surprised.

Later in life, we would find that he would meet and develop friendships with boys, only to find out a few months in that the boy had an identical twin. And, I always wondered. On the day of his memorial service, my husband hugged into Stephen's close friend Nathan to thank him for his heartfelt words and all the work he did to give our son a wonderful send off. As Nathan stepped back, my husband noted that he had changed his shirt. And then it was clear, it was not Nathan. It was his identical twin brother. We never knew until that moment.

So, working from that early standpoint of gratitude, that my wonderful boy had been reunited with his brother, who he had sought on earth his entire life, I decided to build on it. If that gave me comfort, there must be other things that could comfort me during this time as well.

It started slowly. I could see things clearly, and I had a sense of clarity about life that I don't believe you can achieve until life stomps you into the floor, and then crushes you with its heel a little further just to make sure you can never be put back together in exactly the same way again.

And, because I was forever changed, I began to see things much differently. Things that once had tremendous importance fell away from my life. Things that should be truly valued were now illuminated. I still marvel at the fact that I could find some gratitude in the midst of the worst event of my life. Something bigger than me had led me to document this, and thankfully I decided to listen. I believe I listened at this time, because my heart, with its breaking ache was finally still. It was as still as the water in that cove on that cloudy Sunday morning. And with that stillness, came clarity. Part of the clarity that I received was a knowing. I knew that if I did not shift my focus and find my grateful life, I would not come through. I would be stuck, forever. Learn or die was the prevailing message.

On the evening of July 4th, God shot a flare into the night sky, and I looked around my life with wide open eyes. I could see. And, I began writing, trying to capture all of it, before the light of the flare dims. It has truly been the most freeing experience of my life. And, it turned out to be something of a life vest in my vast ocean of grief. I've held on to the fact that I could still find good in this world, despite the circumstances.

For this record, I originally decided to document my gratitude for forty days, but quickly realized that I needed to change that to the first two months. My grief was evolving with this focus on gratitude and I wanted to document that evolution as I allowed it to simply take me to places that were yet unknown. I simply surrendered. Beyond the documentation in this book, I will continue to do this for the rest of my life. Without a doubt. I know that without that gratitude, I have no place here; I cannot see my place in the larger picture.

Why the original forty days? I suppose it stems back to a conversation I had with my father about Jesus, and his forty days in the desert, no food or water, temptations from the devil. With everything stripped away, Jesus found clarity in that difficulty; it was a turning point of sorts.

Perhaps that is why I originally chose the forty days as my own turning point, the point at which I will turn the page to read on, in this book of life and love and grief. It was ambitious to think that I too, could have my own enlightenment in such a short period of time. But, no matter what the actual time recorded, and no matter how much time you take on your own journey, I felt connected to it as it was related to everything being stripped away from my life.

My parents and my Aunt Lorraine taught me many lessons. They were hard working people of faith, and they learned the lessons of service and gratitude early on. I watched them live those lessons each day. I am humbled by them now, as I feel my own life to this point has fallen short.

I can recall cold wintery evenings in the days leading up to Christmas, and three memories of my parents, my Aunt Lorraine being one of my parents, as I was fortunate enough to have three. First, my mother and Aunt Lorraine, always knitting or baking or doing something for others, to give to someone who needed it, to donate or to raise money for the church. These two amazing ladies showed me that giving and serving others was not about some elaborate gesture, or Mother Theresa moment; it was in the simple things, the simple gestures of sacrifice of yourself, your time.

Second, the life-sized statue of the Virgin Mary sitting on my kitchen table. Yes, you read that right. I can recall at least twice in my childhood, where my father would bring home the Virgin Mary and Joseph from our church nativity scene to repaint, so they would look their best for the Christmas season.

And finally, in the short days before Christmas, I would see my Dad, quietly and after dark, put on his long winter coat and hat, and head out into the night. His destination was goodness and kindness. Delivering Christmas Hampers to those who were in their own valleys of life. I will always remember his act of benevolence, but bigger than the act itself, I will remember how he approached that duty. Not with any desire to be noticed or glorified, but rather in the dark of night, masking himself and providing the receiver with much deserved privacy and dignity in their time of need.

They taught me the art of giving, of their life, their talents, their time. And now, as I rediscover those lessons in my adulthood and in my own valley of despair, I am humbled. I am quiet, realizing the simple truth. The strength of my parent's lessons lay not only in me learning to be grateful in life. The true lesson was that the truest form of gratitude for your own life can be found in the service of others. Oh, I have wasted so much time, so much time being wound up by my own story, held tight like a ball of elastic bands. But, I understand now. I understand that gratitude is something that is at the core of our human experience, and that happiness and peace can be found through gratitude no matter what your situation.

My parents were very firm on teaching me if you receive a gift, you should respond with thanks.

Stephen was a gift. This is my thanks.

July 4th: Fireworks, Pace Cars, CD Mixes and Rain

There are as many nights as days, and the one is just as long
as the other in the year's course. Even a happy life cannot be
without a measure of darkness and the word 'happy' would
lose its meaning if it were not balanced by sadness.

–CARL JUNG-

WHERE DO I FIND THE words today? Where would I find the one little thing in this day? I am not sure why I started with this, but I knew instantly that I would need one little thing each day as soon as I got the call from Sgt. Barker.

Earlier in the day, my husband and I had a glorious time. We toured around Louisville, Kentucky celebrating the fourth of July with his parents and Sister. It was just a simple and great day. We had been excited to get there, having let the pressures of business and life get in the way of past plans to visit. On our tour, I was surprised by the history and character of the city. I am still learning about America and always love new adventures.

After the call, life changed. Forever. As I type those words, it sounds negative. And, truthfully, the loss of my son will always bring me a measure of sadness. But, life changed in another way as well. The lesson I had not been able to carry with me from my youth had finally stuck. The fragility of life, and the need for reverence for the gift that is each day.

On this evening, I am thankful for the fireworks welcoming my son to heaven. I could not say those words aloud, for fear I would make something not yet confirmed true. I am thankful for my husband and his emotions. He cries, openly and freely weeping. He loves Stephen so. I am so grateful that I have a husband who can let his feelings show, who wears his heart on his sleeve, and who loves my children so hard. I am thankful for him, and understand that the only reason I have my footing right now is because he sits next to me.

I am thankful he knows better than to try and be the "man", and treats me like a shrinking violet. When we ran to the car, his parents looked and asked him if it was wise for me to drive as I jumped into the driver's seat. He simply said, "I am not going to tell her she can't drive." I needed to drive. I was a woman on a mission. I am grateful for the relationship we have together, and how we are partners, equal halves instead of the man and the woman.

I am thankful for the CD mix that Stephen left in my car. When did he leave this in the car? A CD of his favorite music, unknown and quirky artists, each song telling a story. It is funny, as Brady and I had such a long drive up here a few days earlier, but we did not even turn the stereo on. That's what I love about my relationship with Brady. We talked for the entire eight hours. We only turned it on when we were driving to Jordan Lake tonight. And it was primed and ready to go, almost as if Stephen had arranged it that way so we would know he was with us in the car. It was beautiful and soulful music, college music, rhythms that are only discovered in the years of transition between childhood and adulthood. That music, spoke to us as we drove through the night. It was as if it was guiding us to him.

I am so grateful for the feeling, the knowing that he was right there with us in the car. For one last time, I felt my sweet boy sitting in the back seat, as he had so many times before on happy trips or adventures. He was with us, hands on our shoulders, protecting us, making sure that we made it to the lake without harm.

Throughout the night, we were accompanied by what I labeled the "pace car." A small Toyota Camry, with California plates, that started driving in our direction in Kentucky. And, for a reason I will never understand, our pace car never left us until we were on the final road outside of Raleigh, taking the exit towards Jordan Lake. We would pass the car in the dark of night, and then, hours later, it would pass us. I never really got a good look at the driver or the occupants, but they drove with us, in the middle of the night, on lonely and unoccupied roads. And, each time we would pass each other, I would look at the California plate and smile. I would smile because I was getting a special message, one that was bigger than the simple things I knew and understood; one enveloped in the mystery of life and death. A message that confirmed that there is so much more than we can see or understand. The Camry had a vanity plate, which is not unusual in this ego driven society we live in. But it was what it spelled out. *"ONE LIFETIME"*. To most, it would not have been significant. But for us?

The same words that were inked into Stephen's left flank. The tattoo on his left flank, a true rite of passage in his first weeks at NC State, an independent act taken based on his want and not my approval. I can't say I was happy about that tattoo at first. I was not. I was disappointed, I was in reality frustrated that he and his girlfriend had decided to do this without, what I thought, was much deliberation of the long-term consequences. But, with time, I realized he was a man, and he had made a choice based on what he wanted. Now, the fact that those two words were what he selected seemed rather poignant. With a beautiful apple, his tattoo read *"One Lifetime"*.

Despite my logical mind, I could not help but think that the pace car was no simple coincidence. Through back roads, it crossed three different states with us that night.

And finally, it was God. I had not talked with Him in some time; I had been asking Him some pretty tough questions as of late. I had not been impressed with Him and His lack of answers. But, there He was. I could feel Him and the signal was loud and clear. He sat in the back of the Four Runner, with Stephen and Rudy, and on we drove through the night. I know it sounds crazy. I will never truly be able to articulate to anyone what the interior of the Four Runner was like for those nine long hours. But, we were not alone, of that I am sure.

July 5th: Conversations with God and Comfort and Kindness at the Shoreline

Deep unspeakable suffering may well be called a baptism,
regeneration, the initiation into a new state.

–GEORGE ELIOT-

WHAT IS THE ONE LITTLE thing that you can take goodness from on the day they pull your son's body from the lake? Unlike the other entries in this journal, I had to come back to this date, waiting for some perspective to be able to see fully what did get me through the day. And, believe it or not, there was more than one thing. There were several things that, looking back, helped us, to keep breathing, to keep on keeping on.

Pulling over to the side of the road, noticing the landmarks that we had been given by Ross, and knowing this was the spot. As I walked down the trail, I could almost picture them the day before, galloping down this hill, with the anticipation of an outstanding 4th of July. I could picture his smile, as he ran ahead, looking over his shoulders at his friends. He was like that, running ahead, anxious to get to the experience. On arriving, I paused, held my breath, and looked around, then collapsed with grief and pain. The dichotomous nature of life is quite something. This beautiful place was a paradise, and yet, the worst place on earth all at the same time. So, what would be the one little thing? I've listed them all out, for your information, but also to be able to marvel at how many I could actually find for the worst day of my life:

The place itself. The most beautiful location on earth. No one has a choice when it comes to death, but if you have to go, this is a beautiful place to be welcomed into heaven. I guess if I did not have a choice, and if he had to go, I would rather it be here, than on the side of the road in an accident, or from violence, or debilitating illness. The place of his death, on that morning, was almost like a glimpse into heaven itself. Looking around the serene cove, the water was still, motionless only for the few fish that would gently ripple the surface of the water with a turn of their tails. The trees were still, not a breath of air. It seems as if the world was quiet, except for a few birds here and there, almost as if God had asked for a moment of silence out of respect. The lush green trees reflected in the water and reminded me of my father's paintings from many years before. I loved it when he would paint those upside down trees.

Realizing my position in this. Sitting there and negotiating with God was an education for me. For many years, I have been fortunate enough to be able to affect change on things in my life. I have found, when I set my mind to something, I can usually make it happen. In the early morning hours of July 5th, I realized that the sense of control I had over my experiences was only an illusion. I realized that there is a power, a purpose, and a plan that is much bigger than me, so complex and intertwined I could never understand it. And, although that loss of power in the past would have stressed me tremendously, this time, for some reason, it gave me some peace. I had been let in on a mystery. So, once I realized that my negotiation with God, in the hopes of changing the outcome, was not going to work, I surrendered. And the sounds that I uttered in that submission were ones of pain, but also of peace as I let go.

My Maternal Connection. Mothers know about the connection they feel with their child. It is something that cannot be quantified, but it is there. A magical intuition, a knowing about the well-being of your baby. The knowing that comes from looking deep into their eyes in the quiet of a night feeding, or the connection you feel when you comfort their hurts, and know you are the only one that can do so. I had felt it when he was at school, and I would feel a sudden urge to call him, only to find he was not having a good day. On this morning, as I looked over the lake, I knew right where he was. Rudy the Wonder Dog and I sat at the shoreline and looked to the spot, and asked God to bring him to us. Knowing that as his mother, I was connected to him like that, even in death, made me thankful.

His friends and their parents. There are certain times in life where the character of human beings becomes very apparent. This was one of those times. Too often in life, we are bombarded by what is wrong in this world. The nightly news will tell you about the masses who don't care, who only want to take or hurt. But, the simple truth is, there is and always has been more good in this world than bad. I was reminded of that simple truth on this morning. I was amazed by his friends, the people he surrounded himself with in his life. His choices in companionship did not disappoint me; they were everything a mother could hope for in her child's friends. When we left the cove, and drove over to the wharf where the search was being coordinated, we were met by them, standing there, hearts on their sleeves, waiting for their friend. And with them, their parents, some strangers, who would not allow us to be alone in such a lonely and dark time. I should not have been surprised really, looking at the kids they raised, a testament to their character. They stood with Brady and me to support us, to be there to wait for the divers to find Stephen. Standing at the shoreline with us during the most difficult moments of our life. On that day, his friends and their parents became part of our family. They had coolers, with water and juice, muffins, fruit, chairs, canopies, hugs, and comfort. So much comfort. One mom in particular, she hugged just like my mom, with a tightness and intensity that made you feel for a moment, that you were protected and would be okay. And, for an instant, I did feel as if I had been sent one of my Mom's hugs from heaven. And, through it all, they did not look away. They stayed, when others would have turned and left, or not shown up at all. It was the greatest demonstration of compassion I have ever seen, a gift of kindness from people, some of them having never even met us prior to this morning. And, in my darkness, I could still see those who held a candle for me, so I might see a flicker of light.

The Rescue Crew. They are the nameless, the ones that quietly go in, and do the hardest job a human being could do. I know that. And, after they brought my son to me, I hugged them all and told them thank you for finding him so I could bring him home. It seems like a weird thing to be thankful for, but without them, I would still have a life of uncertainty, and not be able to move forward from this point. I'm not sure how they felt about me walking under the canopy, and hugging them, but I had to show them my gratitude just the same.

Saying Goodbye. This is a difficult one for me to type, but one that has to be on the list of little things for the day. Because, as difficult as it was to see him, I would not have changed a thing. I needed to say good bye, to count my baby's fingers and toes, to have my last moments with his physical form, in all its perfection. When Stephen was born, and his brother Matthew died, I was not given an opportunity to hold my baby and say good bye. I do not harbor ill will for that, I believe it was a different time, where the importance of this component of grieving was not yet understood. I am sure they did not think I could handle the experience. It is, to this day, one of the biggest regrets of my life. So, to be able to say goodbye, it was a gift.

The Funeral Director. At the shoreline, Brady and I had discussed the need for an autopsy. Looking at the cove, and hearing from his friends, we had doubts about him struggling in the water. We knew he had suffered a hard hit to the chest at hockey a few days earlier, had coughed up some blood, and he had complained of a "pain in his heart" earlier that day. We felt without a doubt that this was related to his death. This serene cove, with his athleticism should not have been an issue. But as the morning wore on, we realized that to send him to UNC Chapel Hill to get an answer really would not give us more peace, or change the outcome in any way. In fact, it would simply prolong this experience, and we wanted to move to the point of celebration of his life. So, after weighing out the options, we made the decision not to request an autopsy and asked that he be brought to a funeral home with a crematory service. This was the best decision. The Funeral Director, a local man from the area, operated the family owned business with his wife. His kindness and comfort were sincere. I could see his respect for us and our pain, for Stephen. It is rare these days, but once in a while you meet someone who is living their purpose, their job is not simply a profession, but a passion and every moment they are doing it, they are giving 110%. This was the man who comforted us on that day. Comfort we would not have otherwise had if we had decided to push ahead with the autopsy.

My husband. I was going to put Brady in the section about my family, but I needed to have my words for him separate. Because he carried me through this. Falling apart in his own right, he held himself together enough to be my one constant through that day. But, it was not only the hugs, comfort and love he gave me, or how he quietly handled the arrangements, the phone calls, the details I did not even notice. It was him, and who he was every other day as well. You see, every time I looked at him, I could recall every moment of joy he gave to Stephen in the last four years of his life. He had a relationship with my boy that my plain words could never describe adequately. He showed him unconditional love and acceptance and how to go after his dreams. Brady was the personification of positive energy, and he showered Stephen with it, showing him how to grab at life and get exactly what he wanted. I've often said that much like the lush foliage of the Carolinas, Stephen blossomed down here, and Brady was the fertilizer. And, on this day, the first day of life without Stephen, I could not help but look at the man I married, and know that Stephen had a better ending because of him. I could not help but be grateful for that, as so many people die sad, angry or alone. My child died happy, and we should all be so lucky to have people in our lives that help make that so in our last days.

My family. I am blessed with the family I have. To say we are close would be an understatement. Our parents died in the early 90's, and we are one of the rare families that kept the glue. You often see siblings fall away from one another in the loss of their parents, but that did not happen with us. In fact, I believe in some ways, we became closer because of it. On that day, my family, although many miles away, stood with me at the shoreline. I could feel it. On the phone with them, I could feel the pain, and I knew that they hurt right along with me. I spoke to everyone at some point throughout the day, but can clearly recall the conversation with my brother. Crying from the depths of my soul, he was telling me I was going to be okay. And, of everyone, he was someone I knew understood. He had lived it, losing his wife at the age of 32, two small boys to raise. I listened carefully to him, and I held on to his words, hoping that his expressions of comfort were true.

Priests and Prayers. We had driven all night, and stood all morning at the lake. We had not slept in about 32 hours, and physically we were exhausted. Everyone in Raleigh wanted us to stay, to rest. The kindness was overwhelming and they all wanted to do something to alleviate some of our distress. But, we wanted to just get home. And, I wanted to talk to a priest. I needed to, and Brady did as well. As I mentioned earlier, I had erratic communication with the Big Guy up to this point. There were some things from my past that I felt he had not explained adequately, not that He owed any explanations. But, on this day, the worst day compared to any of my other trivial life events, He and I were hearing each other loud and clear. So, before we went to bed, and cried ourselves to sleep, Brady and I sat with Father Cahill, and Rita, the Bereavement Coordinator, who were kind enough to meet with us at our church. We prayed, and I listened, intently. Reaching out to my church and God at that moment is something that I will always be grateful for in my life. Because, it would have been easier to turn away in the midst of the pain and loss.

So, for the worst day I have had in my entire existence, I did find things, little things to carry me through. Maybe they were not so little after all. Anything that could allow me to see the good in this day must be pretty special.

July 6th: Half Awake, Long Lost pictures, and One Cherished Email

What you leave behind is not what is engraved in stone monuments, but what is woven into the lives of others.

–PERICLES–

AT FIRST GLANCE, I THOUGHT the only thing I could really be thankful for today was that split second between sleep and wakefulness. At dawn, when, for an instant, all of this was only a bad dream. For a brief moment, I felt peace, knowing I would see him downstairs, eating his banana, and six to eight slices of toast, with about a half a gallon of milk to drink. But alas, that was not to be true. That lingering feeling of dread in my stomach returned with the speed of wakefulness. I turned to my side and looked at the floor next to my bed and saw his weekend bag and knapsack from the lake. I stared at them for what seemed to be an eternity. I am not sure why I brought them to my room, but I needed to be close to them. Gazing on them, I had my first cry for the day. It is a funny feeling, when you awake, and your eyelids feel puffy and large from crying yourself to sleep the night before. Then, you begin to cry again, and the new morning tears are almost cleansing, washing away the sleep, and providing some relief, much like tea bags but far more convenient. I think I am thankful for the tears. They needed to flow. I need to let them out, although I am not sure what volume of them I have on hand. It does seem endless.

In many ways, the tears I cry today are tears for Stephen, and the tears I have held in for twenty-three years for his brother. They are tears of sorrow, deep as the ocean sorrow, but also tears of happiness. Joy at the dream, the vision of him being with his brother, of meeting with him, of feeling that he was not alone that night. I'm not sure why I feel that way, but I do, and I am thankful.

As the day progresses, I busy myself with the minutia. The tasks are many, and I want to make sure that he is honored in a fitting manner for someone so special. So, I look for pictures of him. And oh, what treasures I find.

As a baby, so small, so fragile, I never thought that he would grow to be so healthy, so vibrant, and so athletic. I could not see beyond the delicate little one staring at me with eyes of ebony. The eyes seem to tell so much, even at a day old, it always seemed like he had experienced more life than I had. An old soul from the beginning.

Next, I found pictures of him as a toddler, huge smile, big eyes that would melt any heart. And, the greatest pictures of him as a participant in my father's parades. On Sundays, we would have Sunday dinner as a family after Mass. Whoever was in town would simply show up. Mom would be in the kitchen, and Dad would be helping. They loved having their children surround them. As the years passed, the places at the table grew, and little ones started to show up. Grandchildren were the single greatest joy to my parents. After we would push away from the table, stomachs full, Dad would take all of the grandchildren into his bedroom. You could hear them whispering, giggling, arguing and planning. The bedroom door would swing open, and marching out the hallway was the most fantastic parade! Each participant with an instrument in hand, they were the most fantastic, world renowned marching band known to man. Dad would be leading the charge, and the instruments ranged from a trombone, a tin whistle to a covered cup full of split peas.

More than the pictures themselves, I am thankful for the memories. Remembrances of how I was raised and the love that surrounded Stephen as he grew. Unconditional love enveloped him. As I matured, I realized that from a materialistic view, we didn't have a lot of stuff, but we had and appreciated what truly mattered. As I have moved and travelled and met so many different people, I have come to realize that the rare and precious gem I seemed to be looking for all these years was right in front of me, in my family.

Long forgotten memories to remind me of all that we had. That is certainly a "one little thing" for today, a very tough day.

But there was so much more. As I shuffled through the hours, trying to prepare for the memorial and funeral in Newfoundland, I came across an email. I have no idea why I looked for it or how I found it; rather it was presented to me.

I will return to this email often in the future to remind myself of what we had, mother and child; showing me that taking the time to talk about the real stuff in life with the ones you love is more important than anything. I am proud, as I read that email and others, that we were not satisfied to only have the mundane conversations in life, because of apathy or fear of the truth. We talked, at length, about the life changing stuff, the hard conversations; we spoke candidly, about our own strengths and weaknesses. I am most proud of the fact I was not afraid to tell him of my stumbles, my mistakes, and the lessons I learned. Somehow, I think it allowed him to see life for the imperfect miracle it was, and let him feel safe enough to share his own experiences with me. Of all the relationships I have had in my life, the one I had with him was the most honest. Perhaps because he had been with me the longest, and had walked the path right with me, hand in hand. It is difficult to explain the peace I felt in my heart when I read the email exchange between us. But, the hurt eased, if only for a moment. I still ache, but I know I have a gift, something that other mothers who experience this loss may not be as fortunate to find in their quest for comfort. I have, in writing, confirmation that all the lost moments and words I had been lamenting about were, in fact, said. And, this email and others will serve as a reminder of all the other times that we said I love you and thank you, and you mean the world to me, and I am proud of you, and on and on. In my grief and heartache, I know that this is a turning point. I know that finding this email will be part of my healing and part of finding a purpose in all of this. Now, to be patient with God and Stephen and let them lead me to that peace.

After reading this email to my husband, we quietly cried together. He felt that same comfort, and we thought it would also give consolation to our family. So, I sent it on to my siblings, in the hope they would also have some peace from it as well. The email exchange is below. Many things to be thankful for today.

Family,

I've been thinking a lot this morning about Stephen, and I wanted to send this along. More than a picture or an inaccurate news story, this shows you who he was and what we had. He, much like the greenery in the North Carolina sun, blossomed here, from love of family and friends, and from the success he created for himself. I am struggling minute by minute in trying to find some peace with all of this, but finding this email helps. Because as much as we had so much more to say, I know that we said what matters to each other, and we knew what we had together as a family.

The background of this email is we were talking about hockey and life. He was thinking about his future, and what he wanted for himself.

I can't wait to see you all. Feel free to share this with anyone you want. Knowing that I took the time to say these things, and how he responded helps me, and I hope it also helps all of you remember just how important it is. It is kind of like all of us saying we need to make copies from the picture copy box, and before you know it, 15 years have passed. Being present in our own life allows us not to miss moments like the one that I had with Stephen.

Anyway, I know it is deep but it helps me to share. Please expect more longwinded emails from me on the hour.
I love you,
Kelly

From: *Kelly Buckley*
Sent: *Monday, April 20, 2009 12:30 PM*
To: *Stephen*
Subject: *Re: Life*
Stephen,

I left you a phone message about this on Friday, but wanted to write a little note. I agree with what you have said below. Talk to coach and let him know how you feel. As for hockey, I completely understand your feelings about your senior year and academics. You have invested a lot of yourself and you want the team to do well. You are passionate and competitive. I will support you 100% whatever direction you decide to go in. But, whatever you decide, I know you will think it through and it will be the best for you. Let's talk more about it when we see each other.

*As for what you are going to do with your life, that is a tough one. The transition from full time student to all grown up can be a little intimidating. For me, I was kind of limited to my choices based on my nursing profession. But, I am still refining what it is **I WANT** to do with my life. I guess that is the important thing to remember. What you start off doing is and will be a stepping stone to the next place, until you find the right place for you.*

Once you finish with the pressures of exams, I want you to take some time this summer to really think about the type of life you want for yourself, knowing that you can do whatever you set your mind to.... you can. There are free aptitude tests online that could point you in the right direction, or at least suggest different options for you. I remember Brady telling me on the day of his graduation, he walked across the stage and did not have a clue what he would do with his life. But, he had a great work ethic and a wonderful attitude, he was ambitious, and it all worked out. It will work out for you too. I know that all your buddies have this very direct path with their chosen engineering professions, much like I did with nursing.. But believe me, someday about ten years from now, some may sit at their desk and wonder if they were too rigid when they made their choices. They may wish they had given themselves some flexibility.

The bottom line is this time next year you will be graduating with a great degree from a well-respected school. You are a very smart man, you are a strategic thinker, a great writer, a great athlete, you are logical (and believe me, there are less of you logical ones in the world than you might think), you are a giving and loving person, you are one of the hardest workers I know (along with Brady), and this will come for you.

As your mother, I am slightly biased, I realize that. But, I've always seen the greatness in you. Now, whether that means you will be a great RCMP officer, or a great journalist (You are a fantastic writer), or a great Political Analyst (you really seemed to like that course last summer, and we would be so, so excited to watch you on MSNBC's Hardball), a teacher, or whatever....you will bring greatness to it.

Sorry for being so longwinded with this, but I wanted you to know that I love you, support you, and believe in you.

Love you,

Mom xoxoxo

---- Original Message -----

From: <u>Stephen Russell</u>

To: <u>'Kelly Buckley'</u>

Sent: Tuesday, April 21, 2009 11:33 PM

Subject: RE: Life

Hi Mom,

Thanks for the words of wisdom......

I will let coach know what's going on, and I will draft an email that thoroughly explains the situation, as I want to make sure that he understands where I am coming from. Right now I am in the final push of the semester, but will draft one on the weekend or shortly after to let him know.....

As for hockey I will keep thinking about it because I love hockey. We have an exciting schedule for next year, like midnight games in Kentucky, games against Maryland (D1), etc., but I hate to lose....

I want more than anything to have some epiphany one day where everything is laid out for me and there is no more second-guessing or decisions to be made for my career path, but I can't force it I guess. I will think about it more when I have free time…..

I really appreciate all of the help you and Brady give me every day. If it wasn't for the both of you I don't know what I would do. I am very lucky to have great parents like you who care for me and would do anything for me I really mean it. It doesn't matter what the situation is, no matter if it is my fault or if it is dumb luck, you both always seem to be there for me and I can't thank you guys enough.

I love you very much, and I will call you tomorrow Love,

-Stephen

July 7th: Shouts From the Shower and Other Madness

I like nonsense. It wakes up the brain cells.

-Dr. Seuss-

LYING IN BED THIS MORNING, I spent the better part of an hour staring at the ceiling. I've been awake for some time, waiting for the sun to rise. I had some sleep, which is something to be thankful for I guess. Rising finally, I let my feet hang over the edge of the bed for a while. I just sit there for a minute, staring down at the hardwood floor. Sitting there is his knapsack, and his overnight bag. As I've mentioned, when we brought them home, I could not bear to put them into his room, needing to have them close to me. The last things he touched. Did he know, did he feel anything as he packed this bag for the last time? Those two bags have been the first things I have looked at in the morning and the last things at night. Tangible proof that he existed, he packed them himself, chose the clothes, planned his fun filled weekend.

I hold his cell phone for a while. I listen to his voice mails and was relieved to find out he had received our July 4th call, telling him we loved him. I think on that a while, as truly, even if he did not get that message, he still knew. **Note: *Important point of information for anyone who ever reads this. Tell people often what you feel. Say I love you, you're wonderful, and you've* *changed my life. If they are taken in an instant, it will make it a little bit easier for you to breathe.* **

Letting my feet fall to the floor, I shuffle to the bathroom, to shower, and to look reality in the face once again. The heaviness to my chest returns as I make my way from room to room. Yep, it's still happening. I did not will this out of existence in my sleep. It is still happening.

Looking in the mirror, I think, "Who is this old woman?" With dark circles under my eyes and a look of wear, I can hardly recognize myself. Far different from the young girl staring into the mirror on the night Stephen was born.

I make my way downstairs and grab a coffee. The quiet of the house is welcomed, and I hope that it stays that way for another while so I can set my course for the day. So much to do, and I want everything to be perfect for him. Tomorrow they will have his memorial. We will pick up his remains.

I've been thinking about what I need to say. I need to speak, and I am not sure why. Yet, when I think about what to write, fingers ready at the keyboard, nothing really comes. It sits in my head, but I cannot get it out. Instead, I read the memorial site, I read emails, and I look at flights. I simply sit and stare at the screen of my computer, and wish for this to be over. I struggle with the opposing forces in my head. One wishing for my own death so I can be with him, and one wanting God to give me the strength to still parent for Brendan and raise him in a happy home.

Brady's sister, and Mom and Dad are with us, having flown to Charlotte to be here with us, and it is a nice feeling having them here. Brady's sister Leigh rises and we have the best early morning chat. She has experienced loss, her husband having died of cancer some years before. She is a strong woman, and I have a great deal of respect for how she continued on, raising two wonderful children, and never complains, or has the "poor mouth" on. The "poor mouth" was a term used by my mother, to describe an individual who could not help but share with you all the mishaps and misfortunes that they had in life that made them worthy of your pity or help.

Here's another thing to be thankful for. Growing up in Newfoundland, where a descriptor like that could be used to sum up the entire need for the self help industry.

The chat was quiet and personal, and helpful. She told me things that she had faced in the immediate days and weeks following Chuck's passing, and it made me feel not so alone in this. I have to add this to the list of "one little things." Brady and his siblings, at first glance seem so different. But, the closer you look; you see they all have that tremendous capacity for love, huge caring hearts. And, looking at their parents, it all makes sense.

As the house started to wake up, the chat slowly ended, but I was thankful for that quiet time with my new sister.

Upstairs, Brady's parents were getting ready for the day. Brady's Mom was in the shower, and all of a sudden, we heard her calling from the bathroom. "Brady! Brady! Brady!"

Over and over, she screamed helplessly from behind the closed door. Oh my God, I thought. It's a broken hip. I was already calculating and planning how this would be handled, and where the closest hospital was located, who was the best in Orthopedics in Charlotte? The poor woman, it would be a long and difficult recovery.

"Brady, Brady, Brady!" She called in regular intervals, hoping to get someone to help her. Leigh and I were half way up the stairs when Brady made it to the bathroom door ahead of us. "What is it? Are you okay? What do you need?"

"I need some soap." She calmly relayed her request from behind the closed door.

I lost it. Standing at the base of the stairs with Leigh, I laughed a full and rich laugh at the hilarious situation. Huge laugh, snorts and all. Brady's mom had no idea, but she had just given me my first laugh since it all happened.

Later that day, I would make my way to the mall, for outfits and haircuts, and such. Now, this is not one little thing for the day, not at all. I hate shopping, and I had only been to this or any mall in Charlotte, three times before in almost five years! I think this is why my husband loves me so. Once I returned home, I had to continue funeral preparations, packing, taking endless phone calls, and other madness.

I also received a call from Marina, a former girlfriend of Stephen's. It was such a sad moment, as she was calling for Stephen from the airport. She was returning from Costa Rica, and was stopping in NC on her flight home. He was supposed to pick her up. I had to tell her the news, and it broke my heart. I could hear her own pain, and I wished I could be with her in person. She spoke the most beautiful words of how Stephen loved me, and how he loved Brendan and Brady as well. Through her own shock and hurt, she comforted me, and I could see what Stephen saw in her. I was thankful.

But, through it all, my mother-in law's cries from the shower kept me going today. Through all of the tears and the stress, they still gave me the smile I needed to keep moving. I am thankful that they are here.

July 8th: Gazebos, Gardens and Butterflies Galore

*What the caterpillar calls the end of the
world, the master calls a butterfly.*

-RICHARD BACH-

OKAY, TAKE A DEEP BREATH, because today is going to depend all on how you look at it. You can fall down and crumble up in a heap on the ground, or you can stare it in the face, and give him the send off he deserves. Those were my thoughts on the morning of his memorial, as Brady and I dressed quietly, in our black clothes. Black clothes and the sun of the Carolinas simply do not mix.

Maybe it was shock, maybe a little courage, maybe Stephen really was with us as we felt, giving us the strength to make it through this with grace. In any case, I kept moving, and kept standing. It was curious to me, as I had no idea where this strength was coming from.

Driving to Raleigh this morning, I knew I wanted to say something, I had put down some rough thoughts, but I had no plan. Brady, on the other hand, had thought about what he wanted to say, and was ready to go. I listened to him as he practiced in the car, wanting to have it just right for Stephen. Oh, how he loved him so. I have said before, and will continue to say, that the love he showered Stephen with in the last years of his life will continue to be one of my little things for the day for years to come.

And then, as if someone was whispering in my ear, the words came. They flowed freely, and I knew what I wanted to say, to both celebrate the special human being he was, and to comfort the young adults who quite likely were encountering one of their first experiences with death. The words, crafted on a yellow notepad in a moving vehicle, were more than I wanted to say. It was what Stephen wanted me to say. Right down to the part addressed to his teammates to play hard in the upcoming season. It was as if, I was speaking on his behalf. I cannot take credit for them, no more than I could take credit for the way that Stephen conducted himself while here on earth. And, I wanted to, if only for a moment, to speak to his friends about those things, to focus this memorial on those special attributes rather than on how he had been lost too soon. As I scribbled, I could see the faces of his friends at Jordan Lake that morning. Those sad faces, looking to each other, to their parents, and to us. No one had answers. I wanted to give them some comfort, something positive to take from this loss, something. I felt compelled to find the good. And calling it a compulsion seems like the most accurate explanation. I could not accept that was that, he was gone now, and it was time to move forward. I had to find something out of this that allowed his goodness to live on, if only in a memory.

The words, his words more than mine were one little thing for the day.

Leading up to the memorial, I deliberately did not ask Brady or anyone else about what had been planned and what was in store for the day. I wanted to see him through the eyes of his friends, those who he touched. I wanted to get a feel for the life he had built for himself, independent, starting the chapter of adulthood. I was not disappointed.

Arriving in Raleigh, we made our way to the Gardens. Pulling in, I could see his friends and teammates beginning to gather, dressed in the same suits they probably wore on game day. I held the pain in my throat. It was a large and uncomfortable lump in my neck, the pain only balanced by the gnawing feeling of utter despair in my stomach. Looking at them, it reminded me so much of Stephen. So much of the promise of that age, the enthusiasm and excitement of just starting out.

Opening the car door, I sat for a second, and soaked up the surroundings. I looked around at the lush trees, flowers, a beautiful pathway leading to the Arboretum gardens where the service would be held. The scenery reminded me of him, with its simple beauty.

Brady and I walked up the path, slowly and thoughtfully, drinking in every moment. Looking to the left of us, a beautiful butterfly fluttered alongside, the erratic movement in his journey looked as if he was trying to get our attention, to let us know he was walking with us. Brady and I held hands, squeezing tightly to both hold each other upright and to give comfort.

Walking beneath an archway of foliage, we were there, in the most picturesque place. Again, beauty much like the cove at Jordan Lake, peaceful and serene. I had to stop and appreciate it, as I could have selected no better place to remember Stephen.

A white gazebo was the center focal point of the event, with chairs all around. Pictures of Stephen were placed on a simple rock wall that encompassed the circular area. A banner with Stephen's picture was hanging in the front, and to the left, they had his NC State Hockey Jersey. On top of the hanging stand, was his helmet, strategically placed to look like the wearer was looking down in respectful reverence.

It was simple, it was stunning and beautiful, and it was so Stephen. I was thankful.

I was humbled by the attendees. Our dear friends, Mary and Pat, standing by us throughout all of this, quietly supporting us, were there with the kids. Brendan's hockey coach from the previous season and his beautiful pregnant wife, taking the time to drive the two and a half hours to pay their respects.

But, most of all, I was touched by his friends. They came from far and wide, some flying in from their homes all over the country to be here, to pay their respects to their teammate and friend. Professors, classmates, and friends. Being here today to bear witness to a life that had touched them in some way or another.

I mulled around the crowd and greeted people, kind of in a fog really. In thinking back to those moments, nothing is truly clear, but rather glimpses of things. Most of my morning was consumed with my thoughts of Stephen, looking around and having a quiet and private conversation with him. Once we were seated in the front, we waited for the services to begin, and Brady and I sat quietly, holding onto each other for dear life.

Deep breaths. The warmth of the day was amazing, the sunshine poured down on the area. I felt for the boys, with both their suits and hockey jerseys on in the hot sun.

I looked ahead. I thought a lot. And then, I noticed the butterfly. Flying around the gazebo, it came to a peaceful landing on the podium. I pointed to the little guy, sitting there for the longest while, as if it was readying to speak to the attendees. Butterflies. They were everywhere, flying all over the gardens. Dozens of them fluttered around, complementing this one magnificent white butterfly sitting at the podium.

As the service started, I listened to the kind minister speak to the group about the loss of someone so young. It seemed surreal to me. I thought back to a moment a few years back, when Stephen and I attended a funeral of one of his friends, who died at 19 in a motorcycle accident. I can remember marveling at the strength of the boy's parents. Back in the present, the minister spoke about some things that resonated with me, but said something about if Stephen could have known; he probably would have done more, said more. And, I disagreed. I could understand his perspective, but honestly, I believe Stephen said what needed to be said. I smiled to myself, feeling the Momma bear instinct come to the surface as it had so many times before in his life. And, as all of these thoughts, random and disconnected, flew over the synapses in my brain, I continued to watch that lone butterfly, sticking by the podium. The wonder of it all. I remember thinking that I must cement it into memory, it was a wondrous thing. I needed that gift at that moment, and for that I will be thankful.

Following the Minister, the "musketeers" approached the Podium. The Musketeers plus Marie. An eclectic group, these were some of the people he spoke most of when he told Brady and I stories of his college life. Nathan, a quiet and old soul, we had the pleasure of having as a house guest just weeks before. He was so kind, and as I looked at him, I was reminded of a conversation Stephen and I had about their friendship. C.J., gregarious and funny, with a smile that I am sure got him out of a few tight spots, with a simple flash of his pearly whites. Marie, once a girlfriend, then a friend, with a personality like sunshine and spring, a beautiful and tender soul, and someone I wished could have had more time with the kind of attention and care only Stephen could give a person. And Ross. I had met Ross at the Hockey Arena, as he was the other goalie for the hockey team for Stephen's first year playing with NC State. It was an unlikely friendship, two goalies competing for game time, but they bonded from the start. On road trips, they would drive together. They just got along, and a lasting friendship grew regardless of the fact they were competing for game time between the pipes. Years later, the friendship had endured, so much so that they were planning on living together for their upcoming senior year. The two Disc golfers, marching to their own drummers, planning another year of fun, with a little learning thrown in. Ross had arrived on our doorstep for quite a few weekends leading up to this day, to play Disc golf and hang out. We loved every moment of it. Ross and Stephen were a great combination. They were not exactly alike, but with big differences that complimented each other very well. I loved how I could sit back and watch how Stephen stepped out a little more, stretched a little more, grew as a person with the diverse personalities in his group. As Ross stood there with his hockey Jersey draped over his dress clothes in the blazing sun, I silently wept for him. They were all putting on a really strong face, but I could see the pain, and the hurt. I looked at Ross for a long time, and wished I could take away the events of the past few days. I wished with all of my heart that I could remove the hurt that he must feel, being the person who tried to save Stephen that day at the lake.

As they each spoke, their words told me a story of a Stephen who was enjoying life to the fullest. Each one had a different twist, but they all told of a Stephen who was fun, who knew how to take care of people, and who they loved as their friend. The butterfly responded to their words, fluttering and flying around their circle, pausing by each of them.

After they finished, many others got up to speak, and I was so comforted by the stories they shared about their "Canadian Steve." That's what they called him, or Canadian, for short.

The hockey coaches and the team stood and announced how they would be retiring his jersey. All dressed in their own team jerseys, it was beautiful and moving and heart wrenching at the same time. I looked in the familiar faces of the boys, and wished I could hug each of them.

Brady and I spoke. Brady told the greatest Tim Russert story. Stephen had often smiled at the both of us, as we loved Tim Russert, a respected host of NBC's Meet the Press and authority on all things political. We had talked to Stephen on the phone on the evening that Tim so tragically and suddenly passed away. We talked about him like he was our brother, or cousin or best friend, and we were devastated.

In the story, Tim called one of his dear friends to offer comfort after the passing of the friend's 17-year-old son. As the story went, Tim apparently had asked the man if God had come to him to make a deal 17 years before, what would he do. Would you take this wonderful and amazing boy for 17 happy years, or would you not take the deal? Of course there was no question. And, my wonderful husband said, "And, I am sure you all feel the same, just as I do. I would take the deal every time, for just a few years with Stephen."

I'm not sure how God works out things, but somehow I feel that He made sure this man was by my side before it was time for Stephen to go.

As I stood next to him, looking at him as he spoke, I knew that I was only standing because he was holding me up.

After Brady had finished, I spoke my words. It felt good to say them, and even though I could not take off my sunglasses, I did look into the eyes of many of his friends. One girl in particular, I noticed and watched her cry as I spoke, and hoped that I could provide some measure of comfort to her and others. My voice only caught once in my throat. It was at the point in my words where I want to tell the group that "I choose happiness", and I wanted them to do the same. Those three words stuck for a minute, and I had to make the determined effort to push them out of my mouth. I knew that was what I wanted, what Stephen wanted, but I just wasn't sure if it would ever materialize. As much as I knew in my heart I must speak those words, I will be honest in this record and admit I wonder if happiness will ever be synonymous with my life again.

In three short years at NC State, he had built a terrific life for himself. The momentum, Brady and I could feel it with every conversation he had with us about the future. He was happy, and today, as I look around, I could see why. I could see the kind of people he associated with, I could see that he had touched them. I could see, even though he was only 23, how he had affected people. I could see how his presence and his loss had affected me. Perhaps his happiness was not with anticipation of the future, but rather due to the unconscious realization that he had achieved his purpose. He was at the pinnacle of his life; he was living a life to the fullest, with joy. Isn't that what we all should aspire to do, no matter how much time we have on our own clocks?

I was humbled by this day, by the memorial, by the reception afterwards. I was humbled by the friends, the teammates, and the character of the human beings that he shared his life with.

Later, waiting in the airport, Brady and I would take a moment to view the DVD of the service. The coach's wife, taped it for our family, and had driven it to the airport after editing it the entire afternoon. Kindness that was above and beyond anything I ever thought possible.

We knew the day was magical, and we felt his spirit with us. But as we watched the DVD, butterflies flew across the screen in the most amazing display. When Ross and Nate spoke, when Brady spoke, Marie, Melissa, me; butterflies were everywhere.

As I said at the beginning, this day would be what I chose to make of it. I choose happiness. I choose magic and mystery and butterflies. I choose love. I am grateful, no matter how hard it is for me to say it.

July 9th: Air Canada's Sky Lounge and Going Irish on the Flight Attendant

Compassion automatically invites you to relate with people because you no longer regard people as a drain on your energy.

−Chogyam Trungpa−

THE GRATITUDE BETWEEN THE EIGHTH and ninth seem to merge together, as we were travelling all evening and into the night. So, my recording of these days is not clean and separate. Much like life, things bleed into other things. The gratitude for these days is mixed up, like my feelings of those two days; feelings of extreme sadness combined with gratefulness that I could not quite understand.

In any case, I see July 9th as the travel day. From the memorial in Raleigh, we drove to the funeral home to pick up Stephen's remains. Prior to leaving, Ross and his dad presented us with a special knapsack, embroidered with Stephen's name, with the dates of his birth and death. It had crossed flags, the American and Canadian, and the NC State logo. Small and compact, they had selected it and had it ready for us to take Stephen home. Again, I am simply speechless at the acts of kindness by those who knew Stephen for only a few years. They hugged us tight as we left for the funeral home.

Arriving at the place, I had to sit for a moment before getting out of the car. Just a few short days before, we had followed the ambulance here. A flood of emotions well up within me once again, as it has so many times today. The tears feel good. I read somewhere that the amount of grief is related to the depth of your love. Oh, I have loved deeply. I will be thankful for that today. I will be thankful that I know a depth of love that others may never experience.

In the funeral home, we expect to pay the bill, pick up the cremated remains of Stephen and head to the airport. But once again, we are shown that the world is full of good and kind people, who through their work or existence choose to give other people measures of comfort. The funeral home director and his wife are two of those individuals.

For, rather than making this a transaction with payment and pickup, he and his wife took the time and the care to make this about Stephen. Not a transaction, but a human interaction. A lone candle flickered on a small table. A picture of Stephen sat in a frame on one side of the table, and in a simple transport case, was my boy's remains. Tears ran down my face, for the reality that was becoming all too true. But they were also tears of appreciation, tears of humility. I was humbled by the level of kindness that was shown to us from so many others, who had no expectation of anything in return. Humbled and curious. Because, up to the moments prior to Stephen's death, my own gratitude and kindness was very personal, very shallow. It was based on the fulfillment of my wants and desires that would bring me what I thought I needed. These people, they were teaching me, that gratitude expressed by giving love to others was so much more. I wondered if I could be as good as the people who had poured out portions of their own soul to simply give us some peace. I did not have an answer, but knew that I was on to something here. Gratitude through giving.

So, back at the airport. Sitting at the gate, and waiting for the flight, with Stephen sitting on our lap. It seems funny to type that, but Brady and I placed that bag between us much like a new mother would hold and dote on her newborn.

We encountered many, whether it be in security, or on the flight itself, who approached, to either move or examine that bag, only to quickly realize that was not an option to be entertained. Perhaps it was my eyebrow, or the intensity of how I or Brady clutched on to it. In any case, most of our travels were uneventful.

In Toronto, a gentle and kind desk clerk talked to us as we checked in and found out the reason for our travel. She quietly left the desk, to make a call. Returning, she told us she had made arrangements for us to wait for our final leg of the flight in Toronto's Maple Leaf Sky Lounge. Again, a simple act that would not give anything back to this woman, only personal knowledge that she had been kind to someone who needed it.

Heading up to the lounge, we were thankful. It was quiet, without the endless announcements, crying children, and white noise of the usual gate areas. Fresh food was available, with drinks and big comfy chairs. It was a welcome reprieve from the real world, if only for an hour.

And, as I sat, I looked at the name of the lounge. The Maple Leafs, as in the Toronto Maple Leafs? I was not sure, but I could not help but see the irony in it all. Stephen, a lifelong die hard Montreal Canadiens fan, thought of the Maple Leafs in much the same way that most would think of a toothache or a tax audit. I smiled, thinking about how he would have laughed at our presence here. How very ironic that the Maple Leafs would give us comfort, and provide us with brief refuge from the stresses of our travels. Boarding the flight, for the last leg of the trip, I was anxious and tired. It was now midnight and we had been up since well before six the day before. I just wanted to bring him home. Stepping onto the plane, I managed a weak smile to the flight attendants who were assisting with boarding. They did not smile back. In my observations of people since July 4th, I had noticed how kindness changed how people reacted to you.

I was giving it a try. It did not work.

The flight attendant without any joy was focused on her own story. It was obvious that she was tired, and she was not happy about being on this late night flight to Newfoundland, a place in the middle of the North Atlantic. Her scarf was slightly skewed to the left, her makeup was not as fresh as it had been at the beginning of her shift, and her hair was beginning to fall from the up do. Had I had more on reserve, I would have smiled more brightly, but instead I quietly made my way to our seats. Brady and I settled ourselves for the flight, and placed Stephen between the two of us.

As the flight readied to take off, this same, frustrated, dissatisfied flight attendant made her way down the aisle. As she made her first pass, I watched her talk with someone a few rows ahead of us. She shook her head, her body language was, well, not inviting. She needed a day off. When she passed by us, she looked at the bag between the two if us. She paused and walked on. The desk clerk had indicated she would let the flight crew know we were travelling for bereavement reasons and I just hoped she would choose not to address this. But, she did.

"You are going to need to put that bag under your seat."

The typing of these words does not convey the tone adequately, but it was a mixture of condescension and just pure frustration that we were not smart enough to know this in the first place. My words caught in my throat, and Brady was trying to speak before me, to spare me the hurt of having this conversation. But he was also trying to help this lady, even if she did not necessarily deserve the assistance. Brady knew me. He knew what my razor sharp response would be. We had joked in the past when we would have heated and passionate discussions. He would look at me and say, "Don't go all Irish on me." Both proud of our Irish roots, this was a running joke.

Before Brady could respond, she pointed her manicured finger and said again, "You need to put *that* under your seat." There was no smile, not a hint of kindness; you could feel her unhappiness, oozing off her body like a heavy scent.

"I can't put *this* under the seat, I am sorry." I said.

"You are required to put *this* under your seat." she barked back.

"I am sorry, *this* is *my son*, and I will not be putting him under the seat." I replied, the tone of my voice escalating an octave with every syllable. In the corner of my eye, I caught a glimpse of Brady's face. Priceless.

I thought those words would be strong enough, poignant enough to make her back down, and get her the hell away from us for the rest of the flight. They did not.

"I know what *it* is, but *it* still needs to go under the seat. Do you know I could get fined?"

WOW. Did she actually say that? Did she really actually say that? Did she honestly think I cared if she was fined? "It" needs to go under the seat??? For an instant, I pictured the news headline about the grieving woman being escorted from the flight, with clumps of blond hair in both of my clenched fists.

"I'm sorry; my son will *not* be going under this seat." I said once again, making eye contact with her, so she could read between the lines of the simple words.

"Okay, well I guess you can keep *it* there. But I hope you know, I could get into trouble for this, I could get fined if someone found out." And with that, she walked away, moving on to the next inconvenient traveler who was put on this flight to make her evening uncomfortable. And, as she moved her way down the aisle, I listened to her conversations. She was in fact unhappy with everything. It was not just us, but everything. I felt bad for her.

So, why is this event recorded in my journal of gratitude? A couple of reasons. As I said, I believe those people that come into your life and create friction are your biggest teachers. Not your favorite teachers, but the ones who will give you lessons worthy of remembrance. This abrasive and unhappy lady showed me how destructive and hurtful selfishness can be, how much you miss in the care of others when you are self-consumed and focused only on meeting your own needs.

And second, I am grateful for this lady because she was a spotlight. Her actions did not diminish or hurt me, but rather illuminated further the depth of the kindness of all the others who had crossed our path on this night, or since the 4th of July.

Needless to say, Stephen sat between us for the entire flight. Brady and I held hands and touched the bag, keeping Stephen close. And, when we landed in St. John's, I exhaled. I was one step closer to bringing my boy back home. I flashed my pearly whites at that flight attendant when I walked off the plane. "Hope you have a great night, thanks so much!" I said. Let's hope that maybe, I was one of her teachers that night as well.

Family and friends stood waiting for us at the airport. They were there for nothing else other than to embrace us and to love us.

Our nephew had his truck, cleaned and ready for us, to use for our time in Newfoundland, so we would not have to worry about a rental car. Yes, Stephen, we were home. We were home to the place that we had longed for since the instant we had left so many years before. We were home, in the place where people knew us, and loved us, a place with our history.

We left in the dark of night, driving from St. John's to Grand Falls. I just wanted to get to my sister's house. It had been our family home before my parents died, and it was a place that could tell so many stories. Stories of my own life, memories of Stephen's early years. That house could tell some tales. Stories of family, laughter and love. Lots and lots of love. I just wanted to be there. To finish the journey.

Everyone was so concerned that we were driving at night. The moose. Newfoundland is known for its moose, and this year, they were out in full force. There had been a tremendous number of accidents or near misses. But Brady and I just wanted to go. I looked at it this way; someone was watching the moose for us, and if it was our time to go, waiting until dawn was not going to change it.

We left in the crisp cool darkness of night, after a pick up from Tim Horton's, a beloved coffee and donut shop that has become as much a part of the fabric of Canada as hockey and snow. Today, I am thankful for Tim Horton's, the best coffee and bagels on the face of the earth.

As we drove, the night sky slowly lightened with each mile, revealing a place that was much prettier than I remembered. A thick layer of early morning mist lay low over the water in the multitude of ponds that we passed. The landscape was rough, rocks, trees and moss mixing to become terrain that was both brutal and breathtaking all at the same time. And, as if God wanted to give you a coming attraction, every so often, the tree line would break to reveal an open view of the Atlantic Ocean, with the sun rising over the horizon. I love where I live, and North Carolina is the prettiest of places. But there was something about this place, the beauty was not manicured, but was the untouched version of magnificence from God, unchanged, unaltered from His original vision. It was cleaner and seemed more real to me. I am sure it is how everyone feels when they return home. I was grateful. As we drove, we passed a trail on the side of the road. It was the place where, two years earlier, Stephen and Brady had hiked with Sean, my brother in law for a fishing trip. That trip would be the topic of many conversations, and many laughs, for the weather turned and they had a terrible time. They had to hike for hours out of the woods because the winds were too high to put the canoe in the water. They had a fitful night of sleep in a tent, lying in water as the wind and the rain whipped around outside. Sean, Stephen and Brady would joke about it, telling the story of how they clutched on to each other in the dark of night, shivering and wet. We always told Brady that was part of his initiation and testing, to see if he was worthy to be married to a Newfoundlander. Even before this, our family had this way of turning a bad moment into a story, a memory.

I am thankful for that.

And, in that five hour drive, not one moose came to say good morning. Instead, it was a quiet drive, with Brady and me, and Stephen in the middle, on our last road trip together.

That night, I would be reunited with Brendan, who was visiting his dad in Alberta at the time of the accident. That was a big thing, the biggest thing in fact since all of this started. To be able to hold my baby, my only baby and to feel him next to me, alive and safe. Going to pick him up that evening was something I thought I would write about, as it was a moment worth recording. It turns out; it is not something I want to share in this forum. This book is my gratitude for Stephen. I was proud of myself and how I handled it, but that is another story, for another book perhaps.

The main thing was Brendan being the bologna in our "sandwich", lying together in bed, just talking and crying and holding on to each other, for dear life. Sweet, sensitive Brendan, the best little thing in my life.

July 10th: The Rock, Where it is Cold, But the People Keep You Warm

Call it a clan, call it a network, call it a tribe, call it a family:
Whatever you call it, whoever you are, you need one.

-JANE HOWARD-

WE ARE HOME, BACK ON "The Rock", a title Newfoundlanders use when describing our province. I feel surrounded by the love of my family. That is a big thing I am thankful for today. Home, it will always be home to me, no matter where I live, or how much time lapses between my visits. I am so proud I grew up here, and believe my roots are the reason for most of my strength.

About ten years before, I climbed into a cab in Edmonton, Alberta on my way to some meeting. The cab driver struck up a conversation with me, and instantly recognized the hint of a Newfoundland accent in my voice. "You're a Newfie?" he said, and laughed a rich laugh, peppered with character that could only come from smoking way too many cigarettes.

I braced myself. I had found that living in the West, being asked if you were a Newfie usually preceded a joke from someone about Newfoundlanders. Oh yes, if you were born in Newfoundland, you know all of them, and became accustomed to being a punch line from time to time.

But, instead, he said, "You know, I've traveled all over this country and I loved Newfoundland when I was there about 20 years ago. I tell people. Yes, Newfoundland is cold, but the people keep you warm."

It was the nicest thing that anyone had ever said to me about Newfoundland, especially since moving away some years before that. And his statement was so, so true.

Thinking back to that moment so many years before, I smiled and could feel those "people" keeping me warm already. One little thing.

Today, we were having a celebration of life for Stephen. In the planning stages, we had originally thought we would have the rosary and traditional wake. But, after some conversation, it simply did not fit. It did not fit who Stephen was.

In the same way that his friends had planned the memorial in Raleigh, his cousins and aunts and uncles planned the celebration of life for him in Newfoundland. It was so strange for me, to simply step back and let things just happen. I had spent my life working to ensure I was in control of my circumstances. To relinquish the need for power was freeing.

And, once again, putting my faith in others did not disappoint me. For the room was covered with so many beautiful pictures of Stephen from all stages of his growth. A slide show with photos of Stephen's life was played, his cousin sang, a childhood buddy came with two of his friends and played some of his favorite tunes. People mulled around and just talked, looked at the pictures, listening to the music. It was personal, it was simple and it was him.

It was a beautiful tribute to him. As I walked around the room saying hello to people, I could look at the different pictures and see how much joy he had in such a short life.

And, the people. So many people came, I was overwhelmed and touched. Classmates of his from elementary school, my own classmates from school, family friends I had not seen in years, teachers. His kindergarten teacher, who was also my kindergarten teacher! The doctor that delivered Stephen. Family I had not seen for decades. In all honesty, I thought I would only be surrounded by immediate family and some dear old friends. I did not expect to see the people who showed up, who drove for hours to be there for us. I was shocked.

It was light, people having conversations in quiet groups. People hugging one another, perhaps seeing each other for the first time in many months or years. It was social, with laughs and cries. It was real, and that is the best word I can use to describe the authenticity of the event. It was him.

And, as I moved from person to person, I noticed that in between those quiet conversations, people wandered the perimeter, perusing the pictures, seeing his life. Most of the people in this room had not seen Stephen for years, since he was a child, maybe ten or eleven. So, for many, the pictures around the room told a story of how he lived, the adventures he had within those short years. I was thankful, so very thankful for those pictures. Because Stephen had lived. He had lived a life so rich and full, and I wanted others to see and to know that. Looking around at the moments captured in Stephen's life, I was thankful for the adventures and for the good times. The pictures not only served as a remembrance today, but a reminder to me. He had a full life here on earth. He had lived. I also was reminded that sometimes, fear had prevented me from doing things in my own life that would allow me to live abundantly and full. I am thankful for that self-examination. It is another way I will change my life going forward.

There was a lot to be thankful for as I looked around. Even with Brendan, as difficult as it was for him to be here, to see this, I was glad that he had an opportunity to experience it. I wished he had been able to be with us in North Carolina as well. It was important, although painful to see the remembrance of someone's life, the passage between life and death. I had always thought it was a mistake to completely hide that reality from children. I believe that, rather we should choose to show them, to help them in their understanding that it is as much a part of life as birthday parties and summer vacations. I did not want my child to hurt, but also understood that through his hurt would come wisdom, and understanding.

As his mother, I had an immense and serious responsibility. To make sure that he, much like the choices I was now making, would also choose to learn from this instead of becoming bitter, to take the good from life, and not focus on the bad. I am thankful for that responsibility, but daunted by the task at the same time.

Two wonderful "little things" to note from the day.

One of Stephen's childhood friends, Katie, was so kind to us at the memorial. Katie, who was born just a month before Stephen, had Spina Bifida, and because of the tremendous spirit of her family and her own beautiful and determined outlook on life, has led a full and splendid life. In university now, she is showing all of us that our limits are simply illusions, and your life is truly what you make of it. In my younger days, I had looked at Katie's parents with such admiration, not only for the endless capacity for love they had for their child, but for teaching her that she could do anything. I do believe God puts you with the parents you need, and nothing was more obvious than in this case. Katie was one of the kids that Stephen and I talked about often when he was in elementary school, and she was truly one of the first people Stephen had known who had a physical challenge. I was always so proud, as the wheelchair was not ever what we talked about when we spoke of Katie. We talked about what a great friend she was, and how much he enjoyed her company. He simply saw a wonderful girl who was a good friend.

So, obviously, I was so touched to see Katie on this day. And, as I spoke to her, she gave me a great gift. She told me that when they would go ice skating with the school, that Stephen was one of the only ones she would allow to push her wheelchair around the ice. And he would act silly and dance around the chair and sing.

I remembered the weekly school skating sessions. Stephen did love to skate, and that was years before he even started to play ice hockey.

But I had no idea that he had done that. I had no clue that he had been such a good friend. It meant so much to me to hear that. It meant so much that after fifteen years had passed, that Katie would take the time to come out today and tell me that story.

And, my niece's husband, who I had not even realized had an experience with Stephen, told me a wonderful story as well. He talked about coaching Stephen in baseball. It was a crucial game in the season, and Stephen was up at bat. They had players on base and if they won this game, it would mean advancing closer to the finals for the season. Stephen made the hit, and was running the bases. But the runner ahead of him took a nasty fall, and was tagged out.

Jody said, "Stephen could have ran past him, and if he had, we probably would have won the game, and moved on, closer to the championship. But he didn't. He stopped to help his friend and teammate instead. He was tagged out and they lost the game."

I could not believe it. As I sat quietly later in the day, I thought about Stephen's competitive nature, and how he loved to win. But, in the analysis of his life, I've found some interesting facts. His favorite game of hockey that he ever played was, in fact a loss. The baseball game, because of his kindness, was a loss as well.

I am so, so grateful today. Because, through his death, I am learning that my son knew the real meaning of winning in life.

July 11th: The Priest, the Christian Brother, the iPod and the Funeral

Participate joyfully in the sorrows of the world. We cannot cure the world of sorrows, but we can choose to live in joy.

-*Joseph Campbell-*

As I LAY QUIETLY NEXT to Brady this morning, I stared at the ceiling. I've been doing that a lot lately. Staring at the ceiling and contemplating my existence. It is actually a good thing. Before Stephen's death, I recognize that I was, like so many others, on autopilot in many aspects of my life. Contemplative or reflective thinking was simply not a priority listed for the day in my planner. There was always a task or a chore, or a distraction that would prevent that quiet time with me. That has changed in my life, and I am happy and grateful about that.

On this day, I was reviewing over the moments preceding this one, and mentally preparing myself for a day that would serve as a turning point for the rest of my life. Today, we would have the funeral mass, and we would bury Stephen's physical remains next to his brother Matthew. As the sun would set on this day, we would close this chapter, and begin the journey of discovering and learning about our life without Stephen. It is difficult, having never, ever thought that I would have to consider how I would continue to live without another child.

But, as much as I did not think I would be in this place, here I sit. And I must continue to live.

I think about the day, and what will happen. Yesterday, I had quietly met with the priest who would be officiating the funeral mass. No one knew I was going there, and no one knew why. I had made an appointment with him to talk about Stephen, as he had never had the pleasure of meeting him. That and I wanted to ask him for permission to speak at the funeral. The priest was a wonderful man, quiet and thoughtful, with a similar personality to Stephen. We sat and chatted, and I shared with him some stories about Stephen, and what type of person he was. It felt really good to do that, and to tell him I wanted to celebrate the life of Stephen rather than mourn the loss. He listened quietly, and he shared with me, reflections from his own personal story. He had lost his mother at the age of twelve. His brother, also a priest, had officiated her funeral mass, and he was one of the altar boys. As I listened, I was thankful that this gentle man would be the priest for Stephen's mass. Everyone has their story of love and loss. No one goes through life without writing the story of their heart, full at one moment and broken at the next.

We had discussed and agreed to the plans for the day, and I was so thankful of how respectful he was, for me and my wishes, and I for the traditions of the church.

And now, it was here. In just a few short hours, we would be saying our final goodbyes.

Preparing for the mass quietly, I was looking over the words I intended to speak. A variation of the words spoken at the Raleigh, North Carolina memorial, I again knew that they were not my own. Sitting quietly, I could hear my family preparing inside, and I was thankful for the haven that my brother Gerard had provided us. A fifth wheel camper with all the comforts of home, Brady and I could be alone, Brendan had a quiet place. It was a blessing. In my solitude, I reached into my purse and pulled out Stephen's iPod. I had been unable to get it to work up to this point, but, on the first try this morning, the screen lit up, and it was ready to go.

Tentatively, I looked at the playlists, the music. I clicked on the playlist called "Marie." A soft melody played in my ear, and I began to cry. Brady, with his hands on my shoulders, comforted me as I quietly wept. I could feel him with us. I could feel his spirit all around us as we sat there, much in the same way as we did the night we drove to the lake. I gave Brady an ear bud, and we sat, listening quietly, weeping tears that were mixed with both deep unending sorrow and an appreciation for what we had with Stephen. It was a great way to start the day, and brought me closer to him if that is possible. I was so thankful for that quiet moment with him, prior to the funeral mass.

Dressed and ready to go, we were both quiet, consumed with our thoughts, but not wanting to break the silence and share them. It was a comfortable silence, and I was thankful for that.

My oldest and dearest friend Tracey came to see me before going to the church. Tracey had been a constant since the evening of July 4th, and for the 23 years proceeding that night as well. We had been best friends since the sixth grade, clutching together in survival when we were both placed in a class with a teacher that was, unique.

We connected immediately, and our friendship had grown over the many years of our lives, challenges and successes, hills and valleys, times when we thought we had it all figured out, and times when we realized we knew nothing. Our relationship is deeper these days, richer from the life journeys we have shared, from the perspectives we have gained in our transitions from being someone's child to someone's parent.

We have history. And if you are lucky enough to have a friend who has that much history with you and loves you just the same, you are blessed. Our friendship has stood the test of time, of differences, of disagreements, of life directions. It has endured, like a river rock that becomes more smooth and beautiful from the years of water rushing over it.

Tracey was Stephen's Godmother, standing beside me so many years before as we blessed the beginning of Stephen's life. Looking back at the pictures of his Baptism day, it is laughable, not only for the Flock of Seagulls 80's style haircuts and the eyeglasses as big as dinner plates.

But for the absurdity of the situation, as we thought we were mature and grown up, but as the pictures clearly show, we were children. It looked like a school play rather than a passage of life.

But, no matter what the humble beginnings, the friendship endured. And she loved Stephen with an intensity that was beautiful to see. As we both were starting out in our professional lives, we lived in the same city. Tracey would oftentimes pick Stephen up and take him for what they both called a "date". They would take off for the afternoon, take in a movie, or go to lunch. Hours later, they would show up, and he always had a smile. He so enjoyed those moments with her. And she would look at me in shock and tell me of the deepest conversation she had with him about life. It was the running joke between us; Stephen was far more mature than we were. And at that time in her life, Stephen looked to be the most mature man in her circle. This was before she met her fabulous husband, and she would say, "Don't you think I could just wait for him to grow up and marry him? Is that appropriate?"

She loved him deeply, and she stood here today with me, much like she had for so many years before. So, I sat her down and gave her an ear bud. As she listened, she cried, as I did. Listening to his music, it was like one final deep conversation with Stephen.

At the church, I held Brendan's hand until it was time to speak. Walking to the podium, I caught a quick glimpse of some of my family members, who had no idea I was going to do this today. Sneaky. I could not help but smile.

And then I spoke. My words were not fancy, but spoke the words that were Stephen. Much the same as the words spoken in North Carolina; it felt good to say them aloud. It felt good to tell those who loved him that, because of his choices, he had lived a full life. Somehow, it made me feel good to say those things. I knew there were those who would hear the words inspired by him, and absorb them. And there were others, who would not even listen. But it did not matter. The message mattered, as it was a synopsis of how he lived. Here it is.

Conversations with Stephen; the Wisdom of a Child
First, I want to begin by thanking all of you for supporting and loving us and celebrating the life of Stephen. It has been such a source of comfort for our family to read and hear how he touched the lives of so many.

I like so many of you, have been trying to find purpose and peace with all of this. I know the best way to honor Stephen is to continue to celebrate life as he did every day.

While looking for photos, I found an email exchange between Stephen and me from a few months back. Talking about hockey and life (those conversations always went together and were more closely related than you might think); we told each other what mattered. We talked about what we wanted from life, how much we had to appreciate, how we were so lucky to have this amazing family that loved without condition. As I read our words, I suddenly had peace in a raging sea of emotion. I realized that all of the important things had, in fact, been said. So, as a fitting tribute to my beautiful boy, I wanted to share some of the things we talked about in his lifetime. To be honest, not all of the insight came from the parent, but rather from this gentle and patient soul we remember today.

1   *As Stephen did, LIVE IT. Jump out of bed every morning and live the life God gave you.....to the fullest. Take chances, climb trees, don't put off your goals. Don't postpone happiness, just choose to be happy. Don't say you'll get it on the way back. Stop now, smell the roses, eat the ice cream, take the picture.*

2   *Wear your Rose Colored Glasses. EVERY DAY. See the silver lining. Laugh more, the out loud belly laughs, snorts and all. Find the good in every person and situation, EVEN THIS ONE. Don't judge others, accept differences and understand everyone has a distinct role in this dance called life.*

3   *Be Present in Your Life. The here and now. Don't hold yourself back because of yesterday. Don't tie yourself down with strings of fear because of the uncertainty of tomorrow. Don't miss the now, even a painful now like today. Drink it up, learn from it, and see what it makes for your tomorrow.*

4   *Bring excellence to what you do. On the ice, Stephen would skate out to the crease, tap both posts with his stick, and it was "game on". He gave everything, 100% of the time. He loved the spirit of competition. But his true excellence was most visible off the ice; how he loved his family, adored his little brother, nurtured friends in need, lived in the moment, and lifted people up.*

5   *Finally, don't let things go unsaid. Give love freely, even to those who are not easy to love. Say I love you and thank you as much as you brush your teeth. Wear your heart on your sleeve, and know that there can never be regret by doing so....*

Stephen would not want us to measure his life in years. Rather, I think he would prefer we measured his age by the amount of kindness he showed to others, the hours he listened and advised, the loads he lifted and carried for family and friends, the number of smiles, the number of people he loved without condition or agenda, or expectation for anything in return. If we measured those things, it would appear he died an old man, life rich and full, purpose on earth achieved. As my husband and I drove through the night to reach Jordan Lake, I watched community fireworks light up the night sky in celebration of the 4th of July. I could not help but think, for this year, they were welcoming a very special new addition to heaven....where...

The ice is always smooth, the refs are good, he's starting every game and his team is ready. And his worthy opponent will make him stand on his head before the third period ends with him victorious. Just as he loved it.

We could all choose to close our hearts at a time like this, be angry and bitter or confused. I stood at that fork in the road of my life in the last hours of July 4th, 2009. AND I CHOOSE HAPPINESS. I choose it, and I want you to do the same.

In that email, I told him I, although a tad biased, thought he was destined for greatness, on a path to change things and people for the better. Please help me make that true by honoring his spirit and living your life with the kind of joy he had.

Walking back to the pew, my heart felt light, no matter what the hurt. I was glad I did it, and I was thankful that Father Hearn had allowed me to have this personal moment.

As the mass progressed, Father Hearn showed me how closely he had listened to me the day before. His homily following the gospel was thoughtful; the readings he referred to completely applied to the life that Stephen had led. It was all like it should be.

I know that sounds funny. As life did not seem like it should be, life seemed to be very mixed up. But I found the little things to hold onto, to be thankful for on this day.

Following the completion of the mass, people mulled around on the church steps. I looked around. When I was a teenager, I stood on these steps after mass, hoping to get a glance from a boy I liked. I walked out on these steps, releasing the held in emotions following the burial of my mother, then my father. I stood on these same steps on my wedding day, with Stephen by my side. Today, I looked around and saw love, not pain. And, standing, assisted with his cane, was Brother Slattery. Things had officially come full circle.

Brother Slattery was one of my teachers at St. Michael's High School, but taught me so much more than the curriculum listed in the school agenda. Deep as the ocean, he made you ponder things in your life, and he came to me in a time when I needed some pondering. Advanced Literature. I sat there, with the weight of the world on my shoulders. Oh, I had it worse that the Lord of the Flies characters, I was suffering far more than The Old Man and The Sea. And he would ask questions of the group that made you pause. I remember one particular day; he was frustrated with someone's lack of performance in his class, and said, "You go through your life and you don't pay attention. You don't pay attention in my class, nor do you do so in your life. I bet you cannot even tell me how many stairs lead up to the senior side of this school. You walk them every day and you do not even know the answer." he said with his slow, cold molasses like drawl that left me with a feeling of anticipation for his every word.

I thought about that statement, and some 24 years later, I can still recite it. That day, I did not know the answer to the question about the stairs. But from that moment on, I counted every stair of every staircase my feet would touch. And I paid attention to a few other things too.

When I left school in the spring to have Stephen, I was very unsure of where I would go from that point in my life. After giving birth to Stephen and losing Matthew, I was farther from answers than before. My summer was a blur, of lifestyle adjustments, pressure, diapers, feedings, feelings of deep anxiety and inadequacy in my ability to succeed at anything. The last thing on my mind was school, and to be honest, I did not know if I could face people. One quiet summer afternoon, the mail arrived, and in the pile sat a letter for me, with the school letterhead on it. I paused and looked at it for a long time, thinking it would have to be something negative. Although I was an Honor Roll student, I somehow had instantaneously convinced myself this must be related to the fact I was not worthy of returning. But, instead of the correspondence of doom, it was a simple and hand written letter from Brother Slattery. In it, he told me that life's challenges sometimes turn out to be good teachers and God has a plan. He said I was smart, and I needed to come back to school, and finish and do good things in my life. That letter gave me the courage I needed to return after summer break, to go on and have a successful senior year, to believe I could be the Class co-president or the Valedictorian. He never knew, nor did anyone else, but I read that letter over 1000 times.

And there he was, standing there with assistance, having travelled over five hours from his retirement home to be here. I have to say, God has it all figured out. He knew what I needed today, and somehow, he gave it to me. For when I saw that sweet man's face, the feelings flooded me, filled my heart. Seeing him reminded me of the complete journey.

With the services complete, we congregated back at my sister's house once again. And, as my family often has done, we found strength in togetherness; we found laughter, even in our pain. Food poured into the house, the kindness of others displayed once again.

And, thinking of how much comfort I had earlier that morning, after listening to Stephen's iPod mix, we pulled it out again, and hooking it to a docking station, so we could share a part of him with everyone.

It was an amazing experience. It turned this post funeral gathering into a traditional Irish wake. It was personal, it was funny. It told me and my family things about Stephen that without it, we never would have known. It brought out feelings in people that otherwise would not have been expressed. It turned a very hard day into a celebration of gratitude. And do you know the most amazing thing? For a great part of the day, we were listening to the playlist called "The Lake". I tell you, that is resilience baby.

It was a gift. To see the reaction of his cousins, and of all us grown ups. It taught us that grief does not need to be mournful. It hurts, but it can be a celebration of a life worth honoring. Later that day, the cousins all stood on the front lawn, posing for pictures, with Brendan holding Stephen's picture proudly. They acted silly, posing in the most ridiculous fashion, flexed their biceps, and stuck out their tongues. All of them together, on the lawn, clutching the picture of the one lost from the group. The Resilient Russell Family. It simply amazed me.

Much like the 5th of July, I found so many things to be thankful for on this day, much more than I thought possible. I believe he would be proud of us all, singing well into the night, finding the good in the worst of situations. Thank you for a day that he deserved.

July 12th- Hometown Memories, Butterflies, Playlists and Weeping at the Cemetery

*What you leave behind is not what is engraved in stone
monuments, but what is woven into the lives of others.*

-PERICLES-

WELL, ALL IS COMPLETE.

Memorial in North Carolina, check.

Memorial and celebration of child's life in Newfoundland. Check. Funeral. Check.

As I lie in bed this morning, the finality of the whole thing begins to sink in, to seep into my skin like an expensive wrinkle resistant, Vitamin infused moisturizer I spent far too much money on in the hopes of cheating the destiny of aging. Funny, the frivolous and extravagant things that I both have enjoyed and sought after at times in my life seem very trivial and unimportant these days. My life has been stripped bare, and looks nothing like it used to. But, I am not sure if that is a bad thing necessarily. I actually think, despite how I got here, that my new simplified view of life here on earth is a good thing.

As I get up, I can hear the multitudes in my sister's house, talking and starting the day. Everyone sitting together and having coffee. They love me so much. I know it, I feel it. But I am not ready to be part of their conversation yet. I explain this to my husband, and with iPod in my ears, I dress in a NC State hockey t-shirt, my dark glasses and baseball hat, and set off to be alone with my thoughts. Returning to your hometown is an emotional experience in the easiest of times. Coming back to your roots forces you to look at those roots, remember all the good times, and the bad times as well. I've always found that each time I come home; I remember certain things about my youth that I am now old enough to process from a different perspective. Not that I had a traumatic childhood, I did not. At least not at the hands of others. My parents were awesome, I was surrounded by love. It's just funny how time away gives you perspective on things that seemed so wholly insurmountable so many years ago.

I take a familiar route, one that I used to walk to my Elementary school. Walking these very same streets as I did as a child, my thoughts were flooded with memories, both of my own youth and of my early beginnings as a young mother with Stephen.

I would walk this route, rain or shine, usually accompanied by my neighbor Mike, on our way to Notre Dame Academy. It was a wonderful school, connected to the Sisters convent and right next to the Cathedral. The old school is long gone now, torn down a number of years ago, but the school song still lingers in my memory.

> *Deo Duce, Let our Hearts Echo*
> *, That's the Key to victory day by day.*
> *All Hail to Thee our cherished Alma Mater,*
> *Notre Dame, the star to light the way.*

It was only five years ago that I looked up the definition of *Deo Duce*, and found it to mean *with God for a leader*. I like that.

I smile as I walk by a house on the route, remembering one early spring afternoon in fifth grade. I was "dilly dallying" as my mother called it, and it was taking me an extra long time to make it home from school. The sun was shining, the snow was finally starting to melt, and I was in no rush. As

I passed the house in question, there sitting in the melting snow bank was a ten-dollar bill. I was so excited, and quickly ran the rest of the way home to tell my mother, wet ten-dollar bill held between my soggy mittens and flapping in the wind.

And, then the bottom fell out of my excitement.

"Do you think that it might belong to the people who live in that house?" my mother said.

I already had that money spent in my mind. The comic books were purchased; Archie and Veronica had so much going on, and I needed the latest edition.

"Wait until your father gets home, and we can ask him." she said.

To this day, I think she knew what he would say, but wanted to make me think a little about the fact that the money had originally belonged to another person.

When Dad came home that evening, he informed me, "I think we need to put it on the radio, and see if anyone claims it as their own. If no one claims it in 24 hours, the money is yours."

And then, in Dad fashion, he took the ten-dollar bill, still wet from the snow, and placed it on top of the radio we had in the kitchen. "Now, come back tomorrow, and if it is still there, it is yours to spend."

I can't help but smile at the memory even though my mind is clouded with so much emotion. As I round the corner, a lone butterfly flits and flutters around me, following me for a bit down the road. Butterflies. They have been a constant companion since Stephen's death.

As I look at the butterfly, walking down the road with me, I am flooded with more memories. I am sixteen with a newborn baby. Walking down this very road with Stephen in the stroller, self-conscious and worried about the looks of those passing me, knowing I was too young to be a mother. Too young, but a mother indeed. Oh, what a beginning he and I had. I carried that feeling with me for many years in his life, feeling less than adequate in my role because of my age. It truly has been only in the last five years that I could see how rare and special our relationship truly was, and one of the biggest reasons was how we started. How freeing it has been to let go of all those hang ups, and simply love each other. How healing to see the wonder of it all finally.

Life is funny, as I think back on that. It seems like a lifetime ago, but at the same time, it feels as if it was only yesterday.

I continue to walk, past the corner store I used to go to for a bag of candy, when a quarter was enough to satisfy all of my needs. The name of the store has changed, but it is the same place. It is the place that, when I was in eighth grade, I would wander around during the entire Lenten season. My friend Lisa and I agreed to give up junk food for Lent. I can't help but laugh at the recollection, of Lisa and me wandering around that store for forty days looking for something that did not have the primary ingredient of sugar. Around day 20, we both agreed that Chocolate Milk was not junk food, and God would be okay with that.

The memories were everywhere.

Reaching Church Road, I looked at the Cathedral of Immaculate Conception. I always thought that was a mouthful, but somehow suitable for such a beautiful place. Just yesterday, my son's funeral was here. My first wedding was here. My children were baptized here. I was baptized here, along with all of my siblings. My parents were married here. The funeral masses for both my Mom and Dad were held here. Outside of the cathedral, the Christmas Nativity scene, in a log enclosure, sits, waiting for the Advent season. Inside, the same Mary and Joseph that spent some time on my kitchen table.

Most of my high school years, I would sing on most Sundays, being a soloist for the Mass. It was truly a glorious time for me, I do love to sing. One Sunday, in particular, comes to mind. It was a special Mass, Easter I believe. And, my friend Tonya and I were completely prepared, ready to put on a wonderful celebration with music. We had practiced, and we had our harmony perfected. In the minutes leading to the beginning of the mass, we readied ourselves. Dressed in our Sunday best, the church was full, and we could both see our smiling and proud parents in the congregation.

The priest motioned in the back of the church, incense in hand and began to walk the long aisle towards the altar. The organ began to play, and Tonya and I took our last breath before beginning the opening hymn. And, as if we had practiced it, we simultaneously burst out laughing into the microphone, our laughter echoing over the huge cathedral. We stopped, took a breath, and attempted to start again. Dianne, our accompanist, was looking at us with a mixture of horror and hilarity. Second time, same as the first. I looked up long enough to see my mother's eyes. I quickly looked away, as the look on her face was terrifying.

That was one of the longest masses I've ever attended, because things did not get better after the opening hymn. They got worse. I snorted. On the altar. Needless to say, it was a long drive home sitting in between my parents in my Dad's truck. It is one of my fondest memories.

This church symbolizes where the roots of my faith were planted, and truly, the roots of my family tree and personal history as well.

Across the street, is the Knights of Columbus building. I call it that, although it has been sold and has not served that function for some years now. My father was a Grand Knight here at one time. Every year, they had a huge softball tournament, and my father would draw cartoon character players for each one of their teammates. In the large hall upstairs, I as a little girl would not only color and cut out those softball players, but would help hang them all over the walls in anticipation of the out of town teams arrival. At the end of that tournament, I watched, as I grew, those players look around for their "character" to take home. Because my father had personalized each one, with their number and hair color, even their body shape. My father had no idea of his talent or how much he touched other people. To this day, his wondrous and huge spirit still awes me.

As I slow my pace to drink in these memories, Stephen's iPod does not fail me, playing some of my father's favorite tunes. Yes, Stephen had many of the tunes on his playlists. From Moon River to Etta James.

I am blessed you know. Even if I can't quite feel it just yet. I know it in my heart. I came from a family of wonder and giggles, of adventures and love, where special days were really special, where we went the extra mile for each other, where we handled adversity with grace and dignity. I had a son who absorbed every bit of that, and carried it with him throughout all of our travels, all of our ups and downs.

As I continue the walk, I pass by the mill, now a vacant and sad reminder of a busier time for our town. The mill closed earlier this year, and the town appeared to still be adjusting to the loss, and trying to find its new identity without something that had played a huge part in the entire purpose of the community. I could relate, as I was on a similar journey, although more personal. My father worked in that mill for his entire career. Back breaking work, long hours, to support and take care of his family. He had been injured in that building, his leg crushed in an elevator. They said he would never walk the same again. But he did not agree. And he walked just fine. That was the way with Dad; he always did what he set his mind to doing.

The butterfly, who had left me alone with my thoughts for a while, returned with me on my travels. I was thankful for sunglasses, because the waterworks were flowing freely by this point in the journey.

Mr. Butterfly stayed with me for most of the remaining walk, as if he knew I needed the support to make it to the cemetery. Arriving there, I made my way to Stephen's grave.

The temporary white cross stood like a soldier on guard. I sat quietly, next to it, and looked at the two graves, he and Matthew, side by side once more. Tears flowed freely, and were followed by deep and anguished sobs. As had been the case so many times in the past week, I could only say his name. I missed him so, so much. I had no idea how I could go on without him. As the tears subsided, I listened quietly to the music in my ears, feeling simply empty. And then, as if to serve as yet another reminder of the fact that there is a bigger plan and I am not alone, my butterfly returned. It fluttered around, the graves of my family, my parents. It pitched and stayed.

I am thankful. I am thankful because as deep as the wound is, I have faith that it will heal. I have surrendered, and I've decided to put my faith in God, and a bigger plan. I can look back over my life and see how divine intervention has played a part in getting me where I needed to be, to bringing people into my life that would forever change the direction it would take. I am thankful for the gifts of Stephen and Matthew. I am forever changed, for the better because of their impact on me.

Heading back to the house, I can smile. For though their physical bodies are together in the cemetery, they both rest gently in my heart, and will be part of my life in the days and years to come. I will see them in the random acts of kindness I show to others. I will see them in the people I love without condition or expectation. I will see them in the paths I choose to take going forward. I will honor them both, and will show my thanks for my time with them.

July 13th: Kelly's Tour of Memories, the Front Step of Poplar Road

Family faces are magic mirrors. Looking at people who belong to us, we see the past, present, and future.

~GAIL LUMET BUCKLEY

As I LIE IN BED this morning, awake once again with the birds, I am reflecting on the past few days. Brady and I took the afternoon to explore, just the two of us. It was good to have quiet time together, and I like sharing my memories with him. I am pretty thankful to be with someone who has such an appreciation for the wonder and possibility of life. I love telling him the stories of my childhood, my community, of Newfoundland. He seems to drink up and enjoy them as much as he enjoys a cold beer after a hot day.

We toured around, looking at the mill, now quiet. I told him stories of my Dad, of how this place played such a huge part in the town's history. Crossing the river, we looked down to see the salmon fishermen, vying for their catch of the day. Every time I come home, I am surprised by the beauty of this place. It is as if I file it away when I cross the border so I will not feel too homesick in between my visits.

We arrive at the Salmon Ladder Interpretative Centre, and I am excited for Brady to see the fish run. It truly is a marvel, and the centre has done a wonderful job in taking a miracle of nature and making it something that families can enjoy as a tourist stop. The place is full, sightseers snapping pictures and hanging over the railing of the salmon ladder to catch the best shot of the salmon on their amazing journey. I watch the salmon, swimming with all their might and energy, to make the jump over the ladder. Making this journey, it is not something they think about, but rather part of their being, their instinct. This is simply what they were made to do.

I think I am much like the salmon. When I received the call on July 4th, my instinct was to come home as well. I did not think about it, I simply knew. As I thought this, and as I type it hours later, I am laughing at myself and how deep I am. But this instinct, this longing for home will be something that I talk about more and more, I can feel it. Life has changed.

Leaving the Salmon Ladder, we head west, as I have to show Brady Leeches Brook, the best swimming hole on the planet. No, there are no leeches, it is a magical spot. We pull into the parking lot, and once again, I am inundated with memories. Of warm summer afternoons, kids from the neighborhood piled into Aunt Lorraine's car, to come for a swim. We had quite the neighborhood, all of us close in age, diverse in personality, but attached by geography. On those warm summer days, we would begin inquiring early in the day, moving our question from house to house, "Can someone take us to Leeches Brook? It is so hot!!" I would not know what hot was until I moved to the Carolinas. I thought it was normal to have blue lips after swimming.

And, on many an occasion, Aunt Lorraine, after a long day at work, would always be the only grown up to say yes. I think of those adventures today, remembering how she always teased us on the drive home, saying we did not have time to stop for a snack. Then, at the last moment, she would turn the car, and we would all be rewarded with a "Twirlie", otherwise know as a soft serve ice cream.

It is a marvelous thing, my life. Some face hardships, and run from their hometown, never looking back. There is no solace, no comfort, and no quiet when you cut your tree off at the roots, and leave it all behind.

But today, as I tour my husband around what was the most simplistic but wondrous of childhoods, I am so, so grateful. Being here, coming back here has reminded me of how good I have it, of how truly blessed I have been in my life, despite the pain.

And, because of that pain, I am here, and I am able to appreciate what others might call trivial or insignificant. Today, I see it is all very significant. I will parent Brendan differently from this moment, realizing that it is the simple memories that provide me with the most comfort in my grief.

Brady and I make our way up the trail, and it is all too familiar. No signage is here pointing the way, nor has there ever been any. People just seem to know how to get to the water. The roots of the trees, wrapping themselves around the rock makes up the terrain of the trail, and they serve as both foot holds and hazards at the same time. The trail is worn, having guided many a swimmer to this paradise. Oh, the stories this trail could tell. It climbs the hill, up hill we march, holding onto branches at times to keep our balance. Somehow, I think this may have something to do with the change in my center of gravity since the last time I climbed this hill. I remember running up this trail in my youth. I am not running now, but enjoying it just the same.

The sound of the water can be heard through the trees. As we approach the second falls, it becomes louder, and I can see the look of anticipation on the face of my husband. This suits his adventurous spirit just fine. He has raced cars, ran a triathlon, sailed and dived below the sea. He loves the experience of something new.

When we step out on the landing, he can only manage one word.

Wow...

Much like the morning we landed in Newfoundland, I am humbled by the natural beauty. Funny, the things we take for granted in our lives. I am thankful for my awakening, I see it now. It is a swimming hole straight out of a book; I imagine it would be what Mark Twain would have envisioned if he was to write about childhood in Newfoundland instead of adventures on the Mississippi River.

The physical terrain is rock, all rock. A few brave pieces of vegetation triumphantly break through the cracks in the rocks, but they are few and far between. And, despite their bravery and resilience to grow in this spot, I think they know their days are numbered. If an aerial picture was taken of the location, it would appear that God had made a mold of his cupped hands from stone, pressed it into the ground, and added water.

"This is where you grew up?" Brady says as his eyes survey this magical spot.

At the top of the hole, to the left, is a magnificent and powerful waterfall. The water flows freely; the tap is turned on full blast. The flow of the water showers the swimmers below with a mist that dances over their eyelashes, making their view of the world a little hazy, out of focus and sparkly. Wouldn't we all like to have that kind of vision every day?

Brady quickly heads towards the water, excited to swim. I laugh at the look on this Southern gentleman's face as he steps into the Newfoundland waters. But he is brave, and he plunges in, swimming towards the falls. It is glorious.

It is healing to take this journey, to review over my life, and pick out the good parts. I am thankful.

Later that evening, we return to Julie's house. Things are starting to settle down, and we all seem to congregate on the front step. The step is different than it was when I was a child, but the view is unchanged.

As a child, I sat on this step with my friends, playing Barbie dolls. When my father returned from the hospital after his leg injury in the mill, I was on this step when I pulled my rocking horse over to the bathroom window. I balanced myself on the horse that was only secured by springs, and wobbling back and forth, I looked in through the window to see what my parents were doing in the bathroom together. My mother was helping my father get dressed. I remember not understanding why he needed help. But, I could not think about it too long, because those darn springs were doing what springs do, and I wobbled a little too far to the left. My hand slapped on the window to gain my balance, and my father quickly looked up. He looked at me with those big blue eyes and he pointed his crooked index finger at me. That finger. He never needed to say a word; that finger always spoke volumes and elicited an apology without ever having to discuss anything.

It was on this step I would sit with my mother and watch thunder and lightening storms, marveling at the rain bouncing off the pavement. I sat on this step with friends, talking and giggling about life and love and plans for the future. I sat here with Stephen in my arms, holding him close, smelling the baby shampoo and powder freshness of his skin after I had bathed him before bedtime. I sat here some nights all alone, with my thoughts and the sound of the mill playing a soft melody in the background. That melody had serenaded my life for so long and now it was gone.

Tonight, I sit with my family, drinking it all in. We laugh and tell silly stories. We talked about our youth, we talked about Stephen, and I let their love wash all over me. Looking into their faces, tonight, and over the past few days, I can see their pain, their hurt. Not only for the loss of Stephen. I can see how they love me, and how they want to carry some of this hurt for me. Their pain comes from the fact they know they can only comfort, but never carry this burden.

Once again, lots of little things have weaved this day into a beautiful tapestry of memories, and love, and family. Lots to be thankful for today.

July 14th: Badger Lake, Brendan and Good Friends

I get by with a little help from my friends.

- John Lennon-

With Brendan by our side, we head off for Badger Lake today. Our plan is to spend the night with Tracey, Chris, and their kids Liam and Alana. Tracey's sister has graciously opened her cabin to us. We welcome the reprieve, a break from the world, if only for the night.

Driving to the Lake, I am again reminded of happier times and I hold them as a child would clutch a sugar laced lollipop. I cry openly and often, even with this approach of gratitude. In some ways, as I analyze how I am doing, I feel as if I am a third party, looking on, outside of my own body, sizing up the situation. And here's the big thing I see. I am surviving, and I don't know how people do it without focusing on gratitude. Honestly, I don't know how I would breathe. It does not lighten the load on my shoulders, the shawl of sadness I wear. But, it does give me hope I will be able to, someday, shed it and be happy again.

Arriving at Tracey's parent's cabin, we are greeted by my second set of parents. Tracey's Mom and Dad have been an integral part of my life, and helped shape my view of the world. Think about it, three in my own house, and another full set right here. They have known me longer than most; have travelled the path with me through heartache and happiness. But, through all of it, the changes, the years, and the distance, they still hug me just like I had visited yesterday.

Tracey's father personifies joy. His rich laughter, and warm smile warm my heart, and you just want to hug him. Tracey's mom is protective and caring, wanting to make sure everything and everyone is okay. I love them both, and I am thankful to see them.

If this cabin could talk, oh boy. We've had some good times here. I look out over the water and think about Tracey and me, 13 years old, and caught in the middle of the lake, over confident in our abilities as sailors, and requiring rescue.

Or, riding the dirt bike, ending up in the ditch instead of down the road. Shoulder dislocated. We were, over confident again, which seemed to be a theme for some of our most colorful adventures.

Imagine losing someone without this love surrounding you. That is what I think, over and over. I am empty, absolutely gutted by this reality, but I still feel loved.

Later that evening, settled in at Pauline's cabin, Tracey and I munch on snacks as the boys ride the dirt bikes, and explore. Brendan is smiling, and so proud of himself as he takes off down the trail. Thankfully, he has more talent and skill with a clutch than his mother.

This is exactly what we need, to be away from civilization, surrounded by people who love us, who view life as we do. I feel protected, and safe. It is good to see Brendan smile. And we all get a huge laugh at Brady trying to fit his head into a helmet that is two sizes two small for his melon. He will be the first to admit his head is large, but will also tell you it is because it encases a very large brain, or rocks, I am not sure which. As I look at him, he smiles gently, never one to be afraid of looking silly if it gives someone else a giggle. I laugh again, and think Stephen would have enjoyed that moment as well.

With the boys playing, Tracey and I chat, and listen to Stephen's iPod. Should I write to Apple/iTunes and tell them what this little piece of technology has done for me, has helped me to heal, to get to know my child after his death?

It is quite something. As we parent our children, you give them the lessons and the pieces of magic you want them to carry with them through life, and essentially, you hope for the best. You hope you parented with skill, and the glue of your words sticks with them on their journey. But you never really know. As I listen to this music, I know. I quietly listen, and I know. I can feel him; feel his spirit and his heart, his passion and his whimsy. Thank you Apple people.

As the afternoon turns to evening, we sit down to a fabulous meal with the dearest of friends. Tracey and I are, of course, two peas in a pod. But the beautiful thing is Brady and Chris, Tracey's husband, also really enjoy each other's company. The four of us had formed our bond before, meeting in Boston to see The Police in concert at Fenway Park. Chris and Brady had no choice but to form a lasting friendship as their wives were too busy drooling, crying, and swooning over Sting. It was a fun filled weekend, and one I will carry with me for a lifetime.

It is all very comfortable, like a good pair of slippers, or your favorite quilt on a cold winter's day. The kids, so different in personality, are also simply comfortable. They are kind kids, all three of them.

Brendan, is witty, and comes up with the funniest analogies. His intelligence helps him with his humor, and I watch him feed off the responses of his audience. But, underneath, he is a tender soul, with a huge heart.

Liam is kind and thoughtful. He, in many ways, reminds me of Stephen, as he is a person who takes care of the needs of others. It is in his bones. He is curious, and sweet.

And Alana. Sweet Alana. She makes me smile, which is quite a feat these days. She is five going on thirty five, and has things all figured out. She is her mother's match. It is fantastic to watch her expressive face as she calmly explains the rationale for not doing what her mother has requested. Not that she is disobedient, she is not. She is simply a strong woman, who will live her life on her terms. World, prepare yourself, because this girl has some things to say.

It is difficult because I feel like someone is missing from the table, and I am right. But, as I look around, and I feel the love in the room, I realize that he can't be far away.

July 15th: Goodbyes, Gander, Good Food and Gerard

The family is one of nature's masterpieces.

−GEORGE SANTAYANA−

THE TITLE OF THIS ENTRY is one little thing for the day, as I am beginning to enjoy the quirkiness of my personality. I am strange, weird, and different. I march to my own drummer, and finally, after all these years, like the beat.

I know it seems that having goodbyes as something to be thankful for seems a little odd. "Don't let the door hit you on the way out", or however that saying goes. But it is not like that all.

Today, I said good bye to my sister Julie, her husband Clyde, and her kids, Aunt Lorraine, my beautiful grand niece and nephew. It was so hard, for all of us. Brendan told me he wanted to stay; he liked it at Aunt Julie's. It is hard to leave the embrace of family.

So, why would I be grateful for it? Couple of reasons. First, Brendan's response to leaving. It served as confirmation for me that he absorbed the magic of Poplar Road. I wanted him to feel it, to drink it in, be enveloped by the love that is as much a part of the foundation of this house as the concrete.

And the other reason is simple. Our tears, the embrace, they served as verification of the depth of the love we feel. They were a reminder, tattooed on my heart that I was not alone. I was never alone, and there were people who would love me in this world, no matter how deep the valley.

I am blessed.

Arriving later that evening at my brothers, we were once again welcomed with open arms.

Gerard's wife Karla prepared an absolutely magnificent meal, and it was nice to sit with everyone. I keep watching Brendan, and how he is drinking up the love of family. Conversation was light at first. And then, somehow, we got on the topic of Brother Slattery. I told the story of his attendance at the funeral, and why it meant so much to me.

Although I had talked about it with my friends, and some knew the story, others did not. And, as I spoke, I could see Gerard, at the end of the table, and he was emotional. He told us that Brother Murphy, one of his high school teachers, had written him when I was pregnant with Stephen. The memory touched him deeply.

It has been a curious thing to see my brother in this light. A beautiful thing really. Not only him, but my brother-in-law as well, and what they have shown in the loss of my boy.

At bedtime, I am thankful for my quiet time with Brendan. I love our hushed conversations at bedtime. Some begin in an effort to work through our feelings, and some are the result of Brendan wanting to stay awake just for a little while longer. Tonight, we have silly chit chat about things, hockey, and life. I tickle his back, which is our routine, as he drifts slowly to sleep. And, mixed in with our light conversation, he asks little questions about Stephen. I answer simply, to the best of my ability, but any questions about why this happened, I stumble over, and feel horribly inadequate as his mother and protector. Those questions make me cry.

But I am thankful for the exchange nonetheless. I am reminded that I have an honest relationship with my child. We talk about everything, and he knows he can ask the hard questions. He is an amazing boy, resilient and wise beyond his years, and I am blessed. As much as we hurt, we will work through this together.

July 16th: Wisdom, the Scenic Route and Fish Chowder

One can overcome the forces of negative emotions, like anger and
hatred, by cultivating their counterforces,
like love and compassion.

~*DALAI LAMA*

I AM FOCUSED ON GRATITUDE, and I know I am on the right track. But sometimes, in life, you will be faced with people and situations that will drag you into the mud; that will shift your focus on things that can do you no good. Sometimes, no matter how much you swing those old pom poms, something or someone can and will get under your skin and make you look towards what is wrong rather than what is right. And, no matter how hard you try, they will not see your point of view, nor will they try to compromise. Sometimes, that lava will start to bubble in the pit of your stomach and you will feel yourself, readying to erupt. Simmering like a thick sauce in a pot, with slow bubbles, here and there, rising to the surface of the sauce; the frequency increases until the entire surface is a mass of bubbles bursting forth from the heat of the flame beneath the vessel. That is how I feel this morning.

For many years, I tried and tried to affect change or compromise with those people or situations. It never worked. It ate me up inside, that I could not get someone to see my point of view; that just as I was sure I was right, they were positive I was wrong.

So, how can I be thankful for that? Why would I include such a thing in my recording of gratitude?

I list this as something I am thankful for because of the lessons it brings me on this beautiful sunny day. The first lesson is one of love and patience in times of frustration. I am still learning this lesson, and will probably still refine my expertise throughout the remainder of my lifetime. But, I am getting better at it, not reacting to something that I cannot affect change on, but rather observing it, and continuing on my path. The path I know is right for me and the people I love. It is quite something, as I would have lamented about so much five or ten years ago, and now I simply chalk it up to life. I still become frustrated, and get hooked like a fish, biting at the bait, but I am a smarter fish these days. So, a big thank you for that one.

Second, this particular situation has reminded me of an important conversation I had with Stephen about life, love, and happiness. It is a good memory, and I am glad it was sparked by this situation. Because it is important, and will help me going forward. It will help me continue my work on forgiveness, and I have promised myself I will work on it every day. I remember reading about the Buddhist faith, and how it is believed that the purpose of our time here on earth is to learn how to forgive. I have thought about that a lot. Because, it is truly one of the most difficult things to master. People go through life and still have not forgiven others for things that happened to them in childhood. They carry these hurts year after year. They pile them up, putting them on like sweaters each morning, wearing the cloak of bitterness throughout their life. And, with each layer of that anger, that inability to forgive, to move on, to love, they move further away from themselves. They become identified with the hurt, defined by the wrongs instead of their own soul, their purpose. I have been one of those people at points in my life. But not anymore. I am shedding my sweaters, and it feels good to feel the breeze on my bare arms. I feel more alive without the burdens of it all.

And finally, this situation reminds me once again of what I do still have in my life. A husband, who never waivers, protects and loves without question. A beautiful son, who is wise beyond his years, with a heart proudly worn on his sleeve; who talks to me and tells me what he is feeling. Family that loves me and a son whose spirit both surrounds me and sits in my own heart. I have so much, and others will never know this joy, and for this I am thankful.

Okay, that is all I am going to say about that.

Following that moment of clarity, Brady and I left my brother's house, to drive out to St. John's, and decided to take a scenic route. We stopped at a lookout, and stared out over the beautiful landscape of Gambo, the community where my mother grew up. I am reminded as I gaze at the ocean reaching in to touch the land, of happy times, picnics and camping and my father's erratic driving. I am reminded of joy. I have moved from place to place looking for it, and it was always right here.

Driving down the winding roads, and seeing my husband's expressions as we pass tiny towns, communities that persevered in the harshest of times, I am happy. I am desperately sad, but I am happy all at the same time. I laugh as he takes off his shoes and tips his toes in the North Atlantic, thinking the waters will be as warm and welcoming as those at Kiawah Island, South Carolina. They are not. But, they are clear, and clean and sparkling, and if you really squint your eyes and look closely at the horizon, you can see the other side of the world. Magic. It is magic.

Another beautiful day, and I am thankful.

Arriving at my sister's house in St. John's, we are welcomed with the smells of fish chowder. But it is not just any fish chowder; it is not the Campbell's variety. It is amazing, and has been prepared as a result of a very firm request by Brady.

So, today, I am thankful for wisdom, the scenic route, and of course, fish chowder.

July 17th: Trails, Jigg's Dinner, and Friends and Family Who Love Me...

Home is not where you live, but where they understand you.

–Christian Morganstern-

Well, this is the last day. The last day in Newfoundland. As I lay awake in bed this morning, I can't help but feel a slight dread for the travel portion of this event coming to an end. Not only because of the great comfort of family. But, I know, when the flight touches down in Raleigh tomorrow, we are back to reality. When we walk out of the airport, we begin the next part of our journey. And, I could pretend that I am ready for it. But I am not. I am scared, frightened like a child, and I am not sure if I can do it. But time marches on right?

That very thought, "time marches on" reminds me of a birthday card I gave my brother. The cover of the card had this great marching band, and the caption "Time marches on..." Opening the card, it said "Your face" on the inside. I laugh quietly in bed as Brady sleeps next to me. Random and quirky. I am thankful for those random thoughts, injected into my brain when I need them the most.

Brady and I had the most fantastic time seeing the sights the day before. Just the two of us, we took off to see the classic sights of the city. Downtown

St. John's, The Rooms, Signal Hill with the Tattoo. We ate lunch in a neat pub on Water Street, drinking in my culture, savoring every moment.

It is such a rich place. And I believe it has provided not only Brady, but me with some insight into the origins of my own resilience. As we walked around the museum exhibits of the Rooms, there was story after story of the people, and what they endured, how they lived, and still managed to be happy. Truly amazing history, of people overcoming the climate, the hard knocks, to not only survive, but thrive. The Newfoundland people have found the secret to life, that it is not about how hard you hit the ground; it is all about the bounce. And now, they are seeing the rewards for the perseverance, the hard work. I am so proud of my roots. One little thing.

So, today, we hiked up the Manuals River, looking for the perfect swimming hole. A beautiful spot, I took pictures of my brother in law Sean and Brady sitting under a waterfall of sorts in the river bed. The earth's stones positioned perfectly to create a swimming hole that no builder could create. We find a perfect place, and Brendan is like a fish and is in the water immediately. I am thankful for that, and I am also proud of myself. We did not hesitate in getting back in the water. I thought about it, but we just kept moving forward. I am thankful as I watch him swim, with such abandon and joy, diving under the water to get a look at a passing fish.

Now, let's talk about Jigg's Dinner. It is one of my favorite meals. Salt Beef, with all the vegetables, I have heard it described "like corned beef and cabbage". I need to confirm, clarify and rebut. It is nothing like it. It is 300% better. Is it dietician approved? I suppose it could potentially receive approval, if the vegetables were steamed instead of cooked in a large pot of salt brine. But, every once in a while, it is a meal that will bring you joy. Tonight was the night. Dinner and the company. Family, and friends. I am thankful.

That night, we said our goodbyes. To Tracey and Chris, crying in the driveway, and vowing to be together again sooner rather than later.

Hugging family, we prepared for the trip home. I am thankful for the healing elixir of family and friends I have sipped for the past number of days. It is a mixture of love and unwavering support, and I hope it will get me through the coming weeks.

July 18th: The Miracle of an Uneventful Flight, Neighbors, Pajamas, and Home

Joy and sorrow are inseparable. Together
they come and when one
sits alone with you, remember that the
other is asleep upon your bed.

-KAHLIL GIBRAN-

FLYING HOME. BUT WAIT, I am home. I have mixed emotions on this dark morning, as we drive to the airport. In some ways, I do long to be back to my own space, with his things and with my privacy. In other ways, I am afraid and I don't want to leave. In any case, we are going.

The flights home are unremarkable. Not much to say about it, unlike our flight to The Rock. And that is something to be thankful for, and we all know it. I think the three of us are kind of shell shocked. We are all sort of subdued, as if we know what awaits us when we exit the arrivals gate in North Carolina. Reality. I am pretty sure I am not thankful for that, at least not right now.

The plane touches down. I look out the window and see the heat, hanging in the trees. I can't quite describe it adequately, but it was something I noticed when I first moved to the south. You can see the heat, or at least this North Atlantic girl can.

It is curious when you are so hurt that you feel like a spectator in your own emotions. I suppose it is a protectionist tactic of the brain, to disconnect you so you can survive and get through the worst of it. You see so much more this way.

Back at the car, I take a deep breath. Home. As we begin to drive, I quietly weep. Thank God for the sunglasses. Yes, I suppose if I am committed to this gratitude thing, I will say thank you for the sunglasses. They have covered my eyes from the blazing sun, from the curious looks of people passing by as I openly bawl, they have covered the Samsonite baggage that sits below my eyes, and they shield my eyes now as I weep.

I don't want to be here, this reality is too painful. We continue to drive, and we are all kind of quiet. No words spoken, but I know we are all feeling the same. We drive past the exit for Jordan Lake. I sob. Yes, it is all still happening, it is all still very real. As we zoom past the exit, I think about that morning, and I cry some more. I am broken, and I don't know if I can be fixed. I don't know if I want to be fixed.

So, this does not sound very thankful does it? Let's regroup.

I am thankful for the sunglasses as I said. I am thankful for an uneventful flight home, which is rarer than winning the lottery. I am thankful for my boys, and how they love me, and how much joy it gives me to love them back.

I am thankful for arriving home, and seeing the enthusiastic and somewhat desperate greeting from Rudy the Wonder Dog. He missed us so, and I know he is hurting too. I am glad that we are all back together.

I am thankful for the love. Our neighbors, who cared for Rudy and for us. Terry who is always with a smile and a helping hand. Janet with flowers and dinner prepared, never a question, they are simply always there. And the rest of our neighbors as well, with food and cards and support, have eased our pain. I tell you, if people truly understood what should be valued in this world, they would determine property values by the character and kindness of the people living in them. And we would proudly be able to say that we live in the most affluent neighborhood in the country. I am thankful.

I am thankful for my pajamas, my bath tub, and my bed. I am thankful for the exhausted cuddle that I had with Brendan this evening. I am not sure who needed it more, but I am pretty sure it was the mother. I am thankful for Stephen's bag, still sitting on the floor by my bed. I missed looking at them. And yes, I know at some point I have to move them, to unpack them, the last things he ever packed. But not yet. For now, I am thankful I have them, and can look at them and be close to his spirit.

I've been thinking about how others grieve and feel an attachment to places where they lost a loved one. Some feel close to where their loved one is buried, and make a ritual of visiting the place where their earthly remains sit, serving as a reminder of their lives. Others return often to the site of the loss, a crash site, or a lake. Perhaps they feel that the spirit of their loved one could be found at that spot, or they would at least be closer to them. I can see the value in both. But, for some reason, I am not tied to location in my grief. He is just with me, wherever I go. And, for that, I am thankful.

So, the list is simple, but we are still grateful. The day was rough, no doubt about it, but we made it. And life will go on, not in the same way as before, but it will continue nonetheless. With my baby in my heart, my two other boys at my side, and Rudy the Wonder Dog, we will live.

July 19th: The Scent, the Wallet and the Condom

There are stars whose light only reaches the earth long after they
have fallen apart. There are people whose remembrance gives
light in this world, long after they have passed away. This light
shines in our darkest nights on the road we must follow.

-*The Talmud*-

WE ARE HOME, BACK TO our routines. But, nothing seems normal. Nothing in this life seems quite the same. In fact, when I do get a flash of the familiar, it really hurts. I mean real, tremendous pain. It causes me to stop in my tracks, to feel a tightening in my throat, a loss of breath for a moment. And, slowly, the clock starts again, and I begin to move forward. These moments of agony come quickly, and without warning, without rhyme or reason. I can be brought to my knees by a meaningful memory, or by something that appears to be unrelated to Stephen in any way, shape or form.

I am thankful for the hurt. I know it sounds strange, but I am thankful for the pain, as it is my teacher. I am thankful for the moments when I lose my breath, because it gives me gratitude for the moments I breathe easy or laugh with my son or my husband. I am gaining wisdom, and I never thought I would say that about myself. I ache, but I am facing the pain, the truth, and so, I am grateful.

The bags still sit by the bed. Brendan arrives in the room, and picks up one of the knapsacks that have served as a shrine for some weeks now. He immediately opens it, and starts looking through the contents. My breath and my voice catch for a moment, but I quickly exhale. This is right. This is what Stephen would want, for his brother to look through his things, to be comforted by them. It does so much more good than having them collect dust and sit on my bedroom floor.

I love Brendan. I love him because he has a huge heart, and I love him for his matter of fact approach to life. He is a pragmatic thinker at twelve, and just as his brother was, he is my teacher.

He dumps the contents of the knapsack on the bed and begins to go through them.

Simple things really, nothing earth shattering in the lot. And then he takes Stephen's wallet and asks me if he can go through it. I tentatively say yes, knowing that my son was in fact twenty-three. He pulls out Student ID cards, his driver's license, and seven dollars. He pauses, and says he would like to donate those seven dollars to the NC State hockey team, and I agree it is a fantastic idea. He goes back in for more, and pauses, only to say, "What the heck?"

He pulls out a condom. The look on his face as he extracted this amazing find from the worn wallet makes me smile.

"Mom…"

That is all he could say at the moment. "Can I open it?"

Once again, my breath catches. But, what am I to say? They have talked about and discussed condoms at school, but this is a little too close to home.

"Yes", I say impulsively, not quite thinking though the implications of that decision.

He tears it open and pulls it out, examining it much like the frog in biology class. He asks questions, I stumble over answers, and I mean stumble. And then it comes to me. A funny memory of "the talk" I had with Stephen about the birds and the bees. I was working in the Emergency Department at the time, and the poor guy received an ER nurse's guide to puberty. It was one of the family jokes. He would laugh with Brady when describing it, saying he was so scared, and so traumatized by my graphic and scary version of the birds and the bees, it took him years to recover. He would laugh and tell Brendan to prepare himself.

So, as I fumbled with my hands, and stumbled over every word, I could sense Stephen's amusement. I could sense that he was with us, and having the greatest laugh, at this very uncomfortable and awkward situation his mother found herself sitting in, brought to us by the condom in the wallet. I am thankful that I was honest with Brendan, and focused on the memory of the "talk", rather than on the fact we were looking through my dead son's wallet.

Brendan, feeling satisfied that I had allowed him unlimited access, had enough and off he went, to play with Brady and the dog. I sat on the bed, for a long time, looking at the pile of cards, the contents he kept close by, in his back pocket. I stared at his battered passport that he took everywhere. Brady and I were always pleading with him not to take it out with him, to parties and such, to just use his driver's license. But, he never listened. He always had it, and it showed. It looked like it had been wet previously, and the edges of the cover curled up in the shape of a C. I somehow think there was a story about that. He carried it everywhere. But, he did not need it anymore. He was in a place where everyone knew him, and his character. For that I am thankful.

Reaching down, I picked up a T-shirt from his bag. Crumpled into my hands, I brought it up to my nose and inhaled. And, for a moment, he was here. With my eyes closed and smelling him, I could feel one of his hugs, the greatest hugs. Tight and intense, his hugs spoke emotion to you without words. He hugged me like that when we clung to each other after moving across Canada, he hugged me like that when our lives changed and we moved to another country, and he hugged me like that when I married Brady. And many other times in between. He would joke, say something funny, or a touch sarcastic, and then hug me tight and laugh a rich laugh. And for a moment, he was here with me, hugging me and telling me it was going to be okay. It was going to get better, and one day, I may even be brave enough to move his knapsacks from my bedroom floor. One day, but not today.

Tears flowed freely as I held on to that shirt, and I simply let them. There is so much inside, and I can't hold it back, I don't want to hold it back. I want to grieve for him as he deserves.

I am thankful.

July 20th: Speaking Out, Holy Medals, and Friends

*The guardian angels of life fly so high as to be beyond our
sight, but they are always looking down upon us.*

~Jean Paul Richter-

It's the little things isn't it? That's what I keep finding, in my search for the gratitude. It is the little things that make all the difference. For example, finding a great quote for the day, that captures where I am, or gives me strength and resolve to carry on really helps me. It is one little thing for my day, guaranteed.

I am beginning to understand this more as each day passes. I cannot focus on the colossal bad stuff, and I can't see all the good around me just yet. So, I focus on the little things. The simple little things that get me through. Today, it is righting the wrongs, the contents of a knapsack pocket and an email.

First, I am working on correcting some things that are not right. One of the things I noticed following Stephen's death was the media interpretation of the events, as well as the comment sections that are in place for online articles. This is a different world we live in, and people's need for information and for their own voice to be heard is growing faster than it has at any other time in history. I have watched the approach of the media with some distain for a number of years now. Not all media, but certainly a great proportion that focus on the negative aspects of an event; who look for the sensation in any story and then cycle it incessantly for days on end until we become desensitized to the story. It is disheartening, to see someone's pain be publicly displayed and speculated, with no consideration for those who are actually suffering. I saw and was disappointed with this trend far before now, but it has been magnified for me as of late. The news coverage, with its inaccuracies and downloaded pictures portrayed Stephen and the event as a drunken miscalculation in the distance of the swim. It did not tell the story of a great kid, student, who suffered a medical emergency, resulting in the drowning. They quote that alcohol was at the scene, but cannot confirm if Stephen consumed any. As my friend, who has been in the PR business for some time said, it is just an inflammatory statement. They do not say, "There were hot dogs at the scene, but no one could confirm if he ate one." It is so true. And the comments sections for these articles is no better; with the anonymity giving the posters courage to say anything they like, to pass judgment when they were not informed or qualified to do so.

So, I am righting the wrongs. My friend sent a better photo than the one they downloaded from facebook. I have written to the news organizations, and requested that items be fixed for accuracy purposes, or removed entirely. I have reported posters, who wrote things about my son's death that no mother should have to read. I am making it one of my missions. I will not only speak out for the articles about my own son, but for others as well.

I know it is insignificant, and perhaps I am only one voice in a crowd of naysayers. But somewhere, somehow, maybe I can get someone to listen to me or change their perspective. The media frames how we see things, and we are parroting their "breaking news" mentality on discussion boards all over the world. For, instead of sending out love to people, we are looking for the dark back story, and assuming the worst. We are losing our compassion for others, and it has to change.

I am thankful for my new mission. I am thankful because I never want to have any other mother read what I read about my son, from people who displayed such insensitivity and cruelty.

And, I am getting braver you know. I am strong and powerful and I actually took something out of the knapsack! Okay, I am not so brave, but a step forward is a step forward, no matter what the size. I have started, much like Brendan to be curious, to feel strong enough to look at some of his things.

Going to the knapsack, I found an interior pocket I had not noticed before. I opened it, and inside were some wonderful gifts.

First, the Declaration of Independence. I could not help but laugh. The boys had presented it to him on the 4th, and I had been told that they were all reciting it at the lake. So, I am thankful, for those were my son's last moments on earth, and they were joyful.

Next, a guardian angel medal I had given him. Cue waterworks now. As a child, being tucked in for the night, my parents would say a prayer with me before kissing my forehead. When Stephen was born, that same prayer was taught to him, and actually, to all of the children in my family. Somewhere in my travels, I found a small medal, with the prayer inscribed. I gave it to him, years ago. I always thought of that prayer in times of trouble or uncertainty in my own life. It comforted me. To this day, if I wake from a nightmare and can't get back to sleep, I say that prayer. It reminds me I am not alone, even if I am scared.

Oh Angel of God, my guardian dear.
To whom God's love commits me
here.
Ever this night, be at my side.
To light and guard, to rule and guide.
Amen

Just as finding the email from him days after his death gave me comfort, finding this medal gave me solace. I was joyful, knowing that it meant something special to him, and he had it with him at the lake. I am thankful.

And, with that medal in his pocket, was another one; his St. Christopher medal. Given to him by his cherished grandfather, Poppy Boyd, it meant a lot to him. I felt thankful, so very thankful to find it here. St. Christopher has historically been known to be the patron saint of those on a journey, so it seems fitting it was with my beautiful boy on the biggest journey ever. I knew that it would mean so much to Poppy Boyd, to know that he had it with him. I looked forward to emailing him to tell him, hoping it would give him some comfort.

Finally, my final little thing for the day was an email from a dear friend. It's funny how you have these friends in your life, who give you different gifts. Treena and I worked together in Canada, and quickly formed a trusting friendship in what was a very stressful time. The power of our effectiveness in all matters work related was based on our genuine respect for the other person. That and our smarts of course. After I moved, she and I kept in touch, and I miss having her as part of my day to day life. I have such admiration for her with her faith, and she has provided me with great comfort. The following is part of the email she sent after reading the words about Stephen spoken at the funeral.

Kelly, this is a beautiful tribute to Stephen…it shows that both of you are committed to GIVING to life – not taking whatever you can get out of it for your own selfish gain… he was a lot like you from what I know and I remember being in awe of your relationship – you obviously had a great bond and you really purposefully raised him to be such a great and beautiful boy. He was a gift to everyone around him.

I have been praying for you Kelly, that you do have those moments to breathe…it's funny that you write that, because that's how I feel when I pray for you – that the grief must be suffocating and I find my breath catching…so I ask the Lord to help you breathe… and to every day or hour to be refreshed in your choice to be at peace …because you are absolutely right – we cannot let that anger get a foothold and life is too precious to waste it on those negative feelings (even though we feel we are justified in feeling them sometimes!!!) God is God, and his ways are not our ways and it's really impossible to understand sometimes. But He is there to sustain you every step of the way...Isaiah 26:3 says "You will keep in perfect peace him whose mind is steadfast, because he trusts in you." So keep your eyes on Him and not the anger...let Him be your anchor.

I am thankful for her words, and her friendship. Through her, and so many others, I and my family receive comfort.

July 21st: Meditation Revelations, Hallmark Moments, and Courage

Things don't go wrong and break your heart so you can become bitter and give up. They happen to break you down and build you up so you can be all you were intended to be.

-CHARLIE "TREMENDOUS" JONES-

I FIND THAT I LIE in bed for about ten minutes in the morning before I get up. I'm not sure how it started; perhaps it was the initial pause I took to catch my breath, or the minutes I waited to see if the pain would leave my chest. In any case, I have started to be thankful for it. It is a meditation of sorts, some time with my soul, in which I gather my inner strength to go out and live another day.

It is through this meditation I am finding myself. Sounds funny to say, as prior to July 4th, I never really thought I was lost. I felt a little unfulfilled, or perhaps thought I was not living up to my true potential, but I thought I knew myself. Through the course of my life, the challenges and opportunities that I have been presented with have afforded me success and lessons, and I've always felt I was a fairly evolved person. Boy, am I learning. I have only begun my journey.

So, as I lie in bed, staring at my ceiling, I think two thoughts. First, I missed a spot when I painted the ceiling. There is a ridge there, and now that I have noticed, it, will irritate me until I fix it.

Second, I am liking the Kelly I am finding in all of this hurt. I don't like how I found her, but I like her just the same. I am releasing so much pain, hang ups, and minutia that did nothing but overwhelm and stress me. I am shedding it because I have no room for it. In the past few weeks, I have grieved and let go of things that happened years before. I have grieved Matthew, Stephen's brother, I have let go of the pains of poor decisions, and so much more. I am letting go of the negative, whether it be thoughts, fears, mindsets, or people. I am releasing them all, and wishing them luck. Because when I get caught in their story, I start to move away from my own. It is hard to explain really, but that clarity that I spoke of, that came to me that morning at the lake. I know that magic, that knowing, that wisdom, that PEACE, will leave me if I let myself slip back into old habits of thinking.

And, with that clarity, and that wisdom, I feel Stephen. I can feel him with me, every step of the way. And, when I slip back into a negative thought, or speak with a negative person, he feels far away. I want him with me, if only it is in my heart, his spirit around me. So, the shift must continue.

I am thinking a lot about what I am going to do as this new Kelly. When I try to tell others about it, I can see a slight raise in their eyebrows. Not as pronounced as my own, but it is there. I don't think they know what to say to me, and I think they think I must be a little wacky. It just does not make sense that I am talking about the future. It does not make sense that I have a sense of calm or acceptance of my reality, and I am not in the fetal position in my bed.

And my answer to them? I know! It does not make sense to me either! And it does not mean that the hurt is any less intense. I have no explanation for it, only to say that I have put my faith in what God has in store for me. I knew from very early on after Stephen's death I needed to write this, without a true understanding of why. And, with each passing day, I am being given the answers.

And that, my friends is a huge thing for a Type A girl like me. Going with the flow was for rivers, garden hoses, tap water, but not me. I made my flow. Or at least that is what I thought. What I now know is I was not making my way through the world; I was swimming against the current of my life. I was making things way too difficult, too stressful, and focused on an incorrect theory of success.

I have changed. And for that I am thankful. Life has slapped me "up the side of the head", and it stings. But I feel alive.

This is something I feel tremendous gratitude for in my life today. And, my acceptance of this surrendering makes me feel like I am doing right by Stephen and honoring his spirit in the best way I can. I accept what is, and I choose not to suffer because of it. I choose to learn from it.

The rest of the day is filled with more writing, emails to friends and family, reading and just being with my two boys. We spend some time reading the posts on facebook, and reviewing everything that his friends said about him. What a tremendous gift it has been. In the blink of an eye, we were connected with all of his contacts from every corner of the world. And they were able to connect with us. A gift.

Brendan and I spent a little time in Stephen's room today. We go in for short spurts, and then quickly leave, feeling as if we may suffocate, and that the air has been taken out of the room. It is funny, as one of us will say, "Okay, that's enough." And we simply leave. It feels good to be strong enough to go in there, but it is difficult. We are taking little steps.

So, on our visit today, we found a couple of treasures. First, a collection of all the cards we gave Stephen. He kept them, and put them away in a special spot. It touched me, and looking through them, I again was reassured that we had loved him as hard as we could. Oh, the power of words, written on a greeting card or in an email, or in this journal I type in today. The words made all the difference, to him, and now to me. I could smile through the tears, as I read one particular note, telling him how special he was, how we believed in him, and knew he could do anything. I thought back to the moment I wrote those words, the day he was leaving for college. I wanted him to know, that I was so proud of him, and I was humbled by how wonderful he was, as I felt I was such an imperfect parent. I gave the card to him as he was getting into his car to leave for school. I was standing in the garage and I slipped it into his hand as we hugged tightly and said goodbye. I was trying to be strong and told him I loved him and was so proud of him. I told him he was going to do so well at school, and this was his time. He kissed my cheek, told me he loved me and turned to walk towards the car.

And as he turned, to begin the next chapter of his own life, a chapter of my own was concluding. And I was not ready for it, I wanted to protest it, and have him come back in the house and unpack his bags. He needed to stay, as I could keep him safe here. I wanted to tell him that because of my youth, that we had not had enough time together, as I had been busy with school, or immature, or not old enough to understand the swift passage of time that adults seems to know all to well. But, I could not say that, nor make that request. It was time, and I could see how eager he was to begin this journey. He jumped in the car, and I tried to give a supportive wave, but the tears started, the face contorted. I am terrible at crying. I don't look like the people in the movies, who can cry and still look ravishing. I snort and sob, and it is not at all glamorous.

And, sitting in the driver's seat, he looked up and saw me. And he put the car in park, and jumped out and came towards me with his arms extended. He hugged me, deeply and whispered in my ear.

"I love you Mom. We will see each other soon. I love you very much, and I am not far away."

Looking down at the card, and reliving that memory, I am touched deeply by the words. For, just as he said those words in reference to his move to Raleigh and beginning university, he could say the same words to me if he could speak to me right now.

I love you Mom. We will see each other soon. I
love you very much, and I am not far away.

I am thankful. And I do believe he is not far away, he is with me. Brendan finds some game footage, and we take a moment to watch Stephen playing university hockey. I am thankful we have this record, and we can see him, playing, with a gracefulness in the net that did not seem to match with the sport of hockey.

So thank you. I have gratitude for insight, for memories; good and loving memories, and for courage and resilience. I am learning.

July 22nd: The Weight of Sadness and the Letter

Beauty that dies the soonest has the longest life. Because it cannot keep itself for a day, we keep it forever. Because it can have existence only in memory, we give it immortality there.

–AUTHOR UNKNOWN-

I KNOW THAT EVERY DAY is not going to be a good one. I am realistic, fairly intelligent. I understand it, and as I have said before, I am accepting of the pain. I cannot change it, and I will not fight it. But, it does not mean I have to enjoy it. Today is a painful day.

All day, I've felt like I could not move. I am tired, exhausted actually, and I just can't get out of my own way. I look at things around the house and I cry. Brendan is sleeping late, and I am thankful for that, as I don't want him to see me completely falling apart. I am feeling that I was incorrect in my assessment of my personal resilience. I don't think I can actually move on from this. I was delusional in thinking I could because I had survived all the other struggles in my life, bounced back from things stronger and wiser. Not this time. Today, I feel like the best course of action would be to lie down and just give up.

I type this with a feeling of shame, and I don't know why. I am allowed to feel that way; it should be no surprise that a day like this would come. But, for some reason, I know in my heart that wallowing is not part of the path. This is not how I get through this; this is how I get stuck. I am not saying that these moments are not part of grief, but I am saying that I cannot let myself be in this emotional place for a prolonged period of time. This dark space can only breed anger and bitterness for me, and I promised myself that would not happen. But, I can't help myself.

I lay there; quiet for well over an hour. The story of my misfortune replays in my mind over and over. There is nothing good that can come from this, only bad. Maybe what I've been reading is true. Maybe I should be asking the same question that others ask on those grief message boards. Maybe I should be asking why God wanted to punish me, why did he let this happen?

But, that does not seem right. That question does not fit. Because I don't think God did let this happen. I don't think this was done to punish anyone.

Thankfully, Brendan wakes from his slumber and drags me away from my dark thoughts. So, on this dark day, I am thankful for Brendan. He is a gift. He has an ability, without words, to realign me with the real view of the world, and with the goodness that exists within it. He, much like Stephen has done that since birth. He serves as an important reminder for me, so I will say thank you for that today.

But, despite his smile, and the sparkle in his eyes, I cannot shake the shawl of sadness from my shoulders.

It is a quiet day, and I busy myself with the mundane, but find myself sluggish. And with each passing hour, I am more frustrated with my outlook, and wish I had more power over my emotions. I feel like I am falling down a deep hole and I can't stop it, nor did I bring a shovel to dig out.

I walk outside to get the mail, and the warmth of the Carolina sun hits my face. I usually celebrate this fantastic gift, but today, it is too hot, too humid, too far away from my family. I look quickly up and down the street, not wanting to see anyone or talk to any of my neighbors. Thankfully, it is quiet, and human interaction will not interrupt the pity party I am throwing for myself.

And then it shifts. In the mail, a plain envelope, addressed to Brady and I. And inside, is a gift from Ben, one of Stephen's friends. This gift will not only shift my perspective for the day, but is something I will carry with me for months and years to come.

This boy, hockey player, busy engineering student took the time to type a five page letter to Brady, Brendan and me. The content was personal, and funny, and heartbreaking all at the same time. It told me stories of his relationship with Stephen that I had not known, and added strokes to the pictures of my boy I had painted in my mind. Just as the words of those brave enough to speak at the memorial helped me see the Stephen they saw; this letter told me a beautiful story. It was a story of Stephen, fun and goofy, living life to the fullest, enjoying every minute of the university experience, and touching the lives of people like Ben. It was honest, and I found myself at times laughing out loud while crying at the same time. It did not paint a picture of him as a saint, because he wasn't. It was real, it was not an obituary, or a speech, or a greeting card, where someone is glorified. It was a simple picture of a friendship, and what it meant.

I will write to him to thank him, but I am not sure if he will ever truly understand what his letter did for me. He will never understand how his words gave us strength; how his words to Brendan helped him understand that he still had a connection with the team and with his friends. He will never understand how his words to Brady about his relationship with Stephen not only provided comfort, but provided Brady with a validation that others saw how remarkable and special their bond was, having only known each other for a short period of time.

With his permission, here it is:

Dear Kelly and Brady, I would like to say I'm very sorry, as losing Stephen is a big loss to everyone. The reason I am writing this is because of my lack of speaking at Stephen's memorial service. I did not speak because I knew I would get through saying "Stephen" and then start bawling and I wouldn't be able to get out what I really wanted to say. I know this cause even walking into the house was tough. Everywhere I looked I saw

Stephen. Whether it was where he always parked his car to the Christmas tree that stayed up till like March to the "artwork" we got at Goodwill, or late nights in the kitchen. Everywhere I turned in that house I would think of a good time I had with Stephen. So I wanted to share with you guys those good stories that I have about Stephen and the joy he brought. I also want to share what Stephen meant to me and everyone around him. I would like to tell you that this could get pretty long because there are so many stories, so take a seat in a nice and comfy chair. I also want to let you know that I am an engineering student so I have bad grammar and jump around a lot so bear with me.

I guess I will start from the beginning of knowing Stephen, which was obviously his first year on the team. That first year was a year of learning about him and all the goalie quirks he had. He was quiet the first year and I thought he was just one of those quiet and goofy goalies that just want to be by themselves. Let's just say I was way off on that.

I remember the road trips that year when Phil and myself would usually follow Stephen and Ross in a car to wherever we were going. I could never really understand how two goalies battling for playing time could be friends, but who knows. Anyway on the road trips, I had to do all the driving in my car, and Stephen doing the most with him and Ross since we both had stick and no one else could ever figure out how to drive stick. We would try to lose each other and do stuff like faking an exit and what not. The thing I remember most though is this. It was about 2 or 3 in the morning after the game. We were driving home and I noticed Stephen started to weave from side to side, but he kept on going. Finally, we stopped at a rest stop, and I asked him about it. He said, "Yeah, I'm a little tired, but I figured it would help you stay awake, worrying about me." That first year, I also remember how serious he was and how important hockey was to him. You could not say the wrong thing to him on game day because game day was his day. By the way, who got him the roller bag? Let's just say he got a little heat for that in the locker room.

The next year we started to hang out a lot more. I think it really started after one morning practice. Stephen was one of the last ones out *of the dressing room, like usual, and I was hanging around. We started talking hockey and what not and came up with a brilliant idea to take our conversation to IHOP. We got there and heard they had a $4.99 breakfast, so we were game. But, for some reason, we felt that something that cost only $4.99 would not be filling enough because we just came from practice. So, we got two each. On top of that, Stephen orders the biggest Apple Juice they had, which was a carafe of juice. We got all of our food, and then realized what a mistake we had made because on the hockey team, we have a rule that you have to finish what you order. We set out to finish our meals. Three hours, two bathroom breaks and one waitress later we both finished our meals. That whole time I think we talked about hockey. We also decided that going to class that day was not going to be an option, as we were going to spend the rest of the day on the toilet.*

Going to IHOP after Thursday morning practice quickly became a tradition for us. We always had our same waitress, Teresa. She would have our drinks waiting for us and was always excited to see us. We even carried that tradition over to Florida Gulf Coast University because after Stephen stood on his head we decided to go to Denny's. While there, a guy came up to us and said some girls wanted to give this napkin to us. It had their number on it and they recognized Stephen and they wanted to talk to us. We were completely speechless and needless to say that made our night. We did in fact have to call them the next day. Our bus broke down so we were able to convince them to drive thirty minutes out of their way to come pick us up and drop us off at our hotel. We never talked to them again, but they did love Stephen's Canadian charm. Stephen also got a facebook friend request a month later from some girl at FGCU, and she would send him messages and write on his wall. Stephen left quite an impression, not only on the coaches and players that game, but also on the females watching as well.

That game was one of the best games I had every seen Stephen play. It took him at least a half an hour to get undressed because he was so tired. Two other games that come to mind that season were when we played Kennesaw State and Liberty. In those games, Stephen knew what he had to do, and that was basically stand on his head if we were to have a chance to win. He took that challenge and stared it right down and played better than any other goalie in the league. While in one of those games, I may not have been very helpful, but I was always extremely proud to go talk to someone and say, "Yeah, that's my team's goalie and he is one of my best friends."

Another thing Stephen and I did that year was to go to the State Fair, just the two of us, which may seem pretty lame, but it was by far the best time I have ever had at a fair. We played all the games and spent close to $50.00 a piece on silly carnival games like break the glass bottle. But we each came out with a playboy bunny pillow. Those were probably the most expensive playboy bunny pillows out there, but they are also the most memorable. Stephen was able to come out with a little something extra though; an admirer. Her name was dawn and she was in her late 40's. Somehow she started talking to us, and we talked to her about hockey and what not. One thing led to another and she grabbed Stephen's butt. I'm not sure Stephen was ever the same after that experience. Apparently, grabbing Stephen wasn't enough, because she came to one of our games. After the game, we were terrified that she would be waiting for us, so we made sure we went out in a group.

We also played racquetball all the time. Stephen started out slow, as he did not receive his training from the great NC State Racquetball classes yet, but he still put forth his best and would run after balls that seemed unachievable. I have never seen someone dive onto a hard wooden floor as much as I saw Stephen do it. It just showed how much he cared about what he was doing and how much he wanted to win. By the end of the year, he was starting to beat me, and I did not know what to do. The only thing I could think of was to hit him "accidentally" with the ball. It would sting him a little, but he would still pull out a victory and also re-spond with his own "accidental" hit. So we would end up with bruises and marks all over and they were not from playing hockey. Those games got so intense that one day I was able to win and celebrate my victory. I decided to drive all the way to Toys 'R' Us to get a wrestling belt that said I was the champion. Stephen was in the car with me and had no clue where I was going but was cool with it. Once we found the belts, Stephen decided that if I was going to be the World Champion, he was going to be the Intercontinental Champion. Then we decided that while we were at it, we should get tag team belts, as we made a pretty good team too. At the end of it, we had four kids' belts and more fun than any kid could ever have.

Another great memory of Stephen is the Christmas party. As you guys are well aware, we had some pretty sweet outfits including pipes (thanks Brady). You guys probably also knew that Stephen was my Secret Santa. He got me some funny things and some thing digging into my past, but it was Stephen so I couldn't be mad for long. We had a lot of fun that night. Stephen and I made it home but lost Phil. I told Stephen to sleep in Phil's room. The next morning, I walk into Phil's room and Stephen is sleeping in his closet. I asked him why and he said he didn't want to sleep in Phil's bed and the closet looked comfortable. Another moment I will never forget as Stephen did things that you could not explain but put a smile on your face.

Here are some random facts about Stephen: Favorite Song: Mortal Kombat Theme Song Helped create a drink called the CanUSA Late night Taco Bell was a favorite

Known to Sing in the Shower

A very skilled Mario Kart 64 Player

Great at thinking of Secret Santa Gifts

Ate any food given to him, no matter how burnt it was.

Could jump really, really high.

Hockey has been interlaced through a lot of these stories so I think it's time to talk about it. We all know how much it meant to Stephen. When the team found out about this goalie from Canada, we thought he better be good, and he lived up to it. I think we would have lowered those expectations if we knew he only started playing hockey at the age of 12. Most of us have been playing hockey since we were 5. For him to start so late and still be as good as he was just was amazing. We would tell the coaches and players on any team we played that he started that late, and they would laugh at us and say you can't do that. But Stephen did do it and he cool to see him do it.

One of the reasons that Stephen was able to be so successful was the fact that he was so intense and cared about what he did. He always wanted to stop the puck, no matter if it was the 200th shot he faced at practice, or a one goal with one minute left in the third. He was going to stop that puck. The preparation that Stephen went through was also amazing and quite entertaining. On game days, everything had to go to plan. He had to eat the right things, watch the right videos, drink his red Gatorade, and make sure his clothes were ironed. All of it had to be just so before we left for the rink. Once we got to the rink, it was Stephen's time, no matter if he was starting or not. And nobody minded because they knew the results that his rituals produced.

Stephen also made other people better because even though he was a goalie, he would get on you if you were not working hard or taking bad penalties. I got my fair share of scolding from Stephen. I didn't mind them because I knew Stephen cared and that he had one of the best hockey minds on the team even though he never played out. As you know, Stephen was not very happy with the number of penalties that I took and he probably got pissed at me more than anyone, and it was deserved. But, for some reason, I could never change my bad ways. This season it is my goal to lessen my penalty minutes dramatically because I know how much Stephen hated it, and every time I go in the box he will be looking down and shaking his finger at me. I want to say I will try my best, but I will not promise his finger won't be shaking at me a few times. My game will not only be different in less penalty minutes, but it will also be a step up. Because I know Stephen will be right there along side of me telling me exactly what to do or not do, as he will be with every other player on the team. So, when you see NC State Hockey have one of its best seasons, know that even though your son is not on the roster, he is the reason we are winning.

Our hockey talk was not just limited to NC State Hockey. The Bruins and Canadiens was usually a daily topic. Depending on whose team was doing better, that person would always bring it up. If both teams were sucking, our conversation wouldn't last too long. But, as much as I hate to say it, I intend to carry on some of Stephen's passion for the Canadiens, as long as they aren't playing the Bruins.

There are so many more good stories with Stephen, it's hard not to think of all the good times we had. Stephen became like a brother to me. I was able to talk to him about anything, joke about anything, and I was always having fun when I was around him. Stephen would not let things get him down even if they didn't go his way. He wouldn't let anyone else around him get down either. If the situation looked bad, Stephen would find a way to turn it around, and make sure everyone was happy. As crazy as it sounds about quiet Stephen, he was the life of the party and made sure he enjoyed his life every moment.

Stephen was fiercely competitive no matter what we were playing. Whether it was Jeopardy, Bocce Ball, NHL '96, Racquetball, or hockey, Stephen always wanted to win. But what made him really unique was despite his competitiveness, if he lost, he would be just as happy as if he won and would celebrate with you....which would kind of take the thrill out of winning. But it made it really good to be around him.

It was a real pleasure to spend a few years with Stephen and he is a person I will never forget and will always keep in my heart. Stephen was one of the best people I have every met and you should be proud of how he was raised. Kelly, he loved you so much and he knew you were always there for him and how much you loved him. The relationship you guys had is something every mother and son wants to achieve. Brady, Phil and I were talking and we had to stop and think that you were not always with Stephen, in his life. The relationship you two had was amazing, it was like you had always been part of his life and the two of you were best friends since he was born. Please also let Brendan know that he was so

important to Stephen and how much Stephen loved him... Tell him that
he is always welcome to skate with the NC State Hockey team anytime he
wants. Stephen touched everyone he met and he will be missed dearly, but
know what a great affect he had on everybody and what a great affect
you guys had on him.
Love,
Ben Dombrowski

Just as things always seem to happen, it came to me at the very moment I
needed it most. As if someone was watching out for us, and had a bag full
of comfort, to hand out at just the right moment, when we could not see
the goodness and needed some help. I think someone may be watching out
for us. Just maybe.

I am thankful. Because the magic and mystery of life, even when I lose
faith in it from time to time, is still there.

July 23rd: "I Am Who I Am"

Be yourself. Above all, let who you are, what
you are, what you believe, shine through
every sentence you write, every piece you finish.

-JOHN JAKES-

NEVER JUDGE A BOOK BY its cover. I am reminded of a reflection on that topic I had some time ago as I stare at the unpainted spot on the ceiling this morning. I am thinking a lot lately, and my brain hurts. At least that is how I describe it.

In any case, I am thinking about judgments. How we judge ourselves, our families, our friends, strangers, products, commercials, TV shows, sports teams. We all need to be given gavels at birth; we are so good at passing sentence on anyone who crosses our path.

I write this knowing I have been one of those people. And, I may, despite the work I have promised myself to do, be one of those people in the future at moments. But, today, I am thinking about it and promising to change.

As a parent, I have told my children not to judge people for their differences. The obvious things being race, religion and economic position. I feel good about my own feelings on those fundamental and core issues when it comes to judgment. I came from an island that lacked a great deal of diversity in either of the categories. But yet, when I moved to different areas, I never thought of the differences I encountered in people to be a big deal. In fact, it was something to learn from more than judge. I am proud of that. And, I think I instilled that feeling of equality into my boys, which is one of the accomplishments I am most proud of as a parent. Both Stephen and Brendan would often have long conversations with me about injustices in the world, and tell me passionately how they felt about them. In particular, those conversations grew deeper when we moved to the United States. Don't get me wrong, I love my home. But, the focus on the differences in people rather than the similarities was quite a shock to the system for me. I never really used the word prejudice in conversation much before. All of a sudden, it seemed like it was a more regular word I heard in conversation.

It was curious to me. Not because I suddenly noticed those differences. But because I did not understand where everyone else was getting the time to spend thinking about them. And, why could one not look at the similarities?

In any case, I am thinking about all these random thoughts this morning. In particular the old man in the scary house. About two years ago, there was an old, and somewhat run down house on the corner of an intersection not far from my neighborhood. Adjacent to my son's school, the house was sheltered from view by a number of large trees. The look and feel of the property did not match with the newly built dwellings surrounding it. This house had been here long before developers surveyed the area, with dollar signs dancing in their head.

Brendan and his friends would talk about the house, and how it was scary. They would speculate about the man, as he was rarely, if ever, seen. And, I will admit, when I noticed the house peeking through the trees one fall evening, I wondered myself.

And then he died. And his family cleared out the contents of the house, the property was sold and the house torn down. And, on a summer day, I was at that same intersection, and I looked at the now vacant and overgrown lot and thought about him. I had judged him, based on the outward appearances of his lodging, but I did not know him. And, in the corner of the lot, I saw the most beautiful arrangement of various daylilies, blooming in spite of their owner's absence. Planted long ago, perhaps when he was younger, or happier, or maybe with his wife by his side.

It was a life lesson for me. Walking through life in the hopes I would be accepted without expectation, only I was not paying it forward to the rest of the world. Stephen was one of my teachers for that lesson, and that is humbling for me.

And, as I looked at the spectrum of color peeking out at me from the overgrown foliage, I was reminded not to judge a book by its cover. Just as that resident did to me on the night Stephen was born. Being judged was a fear of mine, for my unconventional approach to motherhood, my successes and failings, of who I was.

How many times have I done it, made an assumption, and always in a negative light? How many times have we made a remark or rolled our eyes to a friend as someone who marched to their own drummer walked by? Why do we do that? Why does someone have to be wrong for us to feel right?

But no more. I no longer carry that burden. "I am who I am", said Popeye, and I agree. I may not be able to pop open a can of spinach, nor am I inclined, but it feels good to finally, after all these years, be comfortable in my own skin.

And, as for the rest of ya, be who you are too. I don't know about the rest of the planet, but I feel I've held myself back for far too long, in fear of what another would have to say about me, when I could have been stepping out and living to my potential.

God, I am a slow learner. But, today I promise to try and not judge others, and I promise to put on my shield of protection when others judge me and keep pushing forward. Maybe I will wear my cape too.

I am thankful for the lessons taught to me by the resident, the scary man, and Stephen. I am thankful that I am who I am. And I am thankful for who I am becoming.

I miss Stephen, but I am grateful, as he is still my biggest teacher. He continues to teach me and to surround me with his love, and for that, thank you.

July 24th: Taking the High Road, Faith and Butterflies of Ink...

The unthankful heart discovers no mercies; but the thankful heart will find, in every hour, some heavenly blessings.

−HENRY WARD BEECHER−

FOCUSING ON GRATITUDE HAS ALLOWED me to get out of my own head. And I welcome the break. I have spent far too much time in there, defining reality according to my perspective alone. I can't tell you the weeks and months I have had closed door sessions in that head of mine, reviewing over and over not only real situations, but imagined ones as well, based on my fears or past experiences, or emotional baggage. It has held me back.

But now, with this loss, I am no longer afraid. I have nothing left to lose in a sense, and it is making me fearless. So, even though I am hurting, I am happy for the break from that constant strategy session in my cranium. To be honest, I hope I never go back to the way it was.

But life does go on, and I know I will be challenged by the outside world once again. Let's face it, not everyone out in this great world of ours is happy. In fact, a startling number of people are very, very unhappy. And I think they like it that way. So, I know that I will have to work at staying in this place of gratitude, and I know that some days it will be hard work. Today is one of those days.

Today, I am faced with a situation that brings it all back. All the fears, the anxieties, the feelings as they relate to my self worth, the feelings of being judged or defined by someone who really does not even know you.

And, as I sit quietly at my desk, I am pondering how I want to handle them. It is tempting to fall back into the old patterns, of anger, sarcasm. It seems much too soon to have to deal with this. I am still hurt, so very, very hurt.

But, life still awaits my response.

The wheels of my mind turn and creek and I imagine a "factory worker" looking for a large can of WD-40 to get things moving in there. But here's the good news. I paused. I did not react, as I have in the past. I paused. I took some time, and I reframed the negative situation. I looked at it for what it was, not for all the potential outcomes, or fears, just for what it was. And, in the moment of pause, I took away its power.

Unlike before, I am not sitting here making a mental list of all the things I feel will affect me in this circumstance. I am simply observing the situation and watching. Sounds like I should be wearing a robe and meditating doesn't it? It is curious to me, how I have evolved to this place through hurt and pain.

So, today I am thankful for the new pattern of thinking that this loss has brought to my life. I am grateful, as I am more present than I have been for a long, long time. I am no longer angry, or anxious, or self righteous, or insecure. I just am… How marvelous.

But, I have to be honest. I do it for somewhat selfish reasons. For when I stay positive, I feel my precious son with me. I feel him. And when I let myself get caught in the minutia again, I feel he is gone. There is no choice for me.

I deal with the situation with my new found wisdom, and it feels great to take the high road. It feels more than great. It is freeing, and gives me more peace to show mercy and kindness instead of anger and conflict, even to a person or situation that may not deserve (according to me) that mercy or kindness. It feels right. How did I not figure that out before now?

I wonder why life is that way. Why is it we need to be jarred out of our existence by pain or hurt to change how we see things?

Moving on with the day, I watch as we keep moving as a family. I can see we don't lift our feet as high when we walk, or smile the full toothed grin we did on July 3rd, but we keep moving. We hug, we say I love you. Can I ask for more? It makes me proud, because we are doing it. I feel like this is what Stephen would want for us. I am thankful.

And to finish off the day, I look at a wonderful picture sent to me by my sister. A beautiful butterfly tattooed on my sister's shoulder. It is colorful and beautiful, and it represents Stephen. It is touching to know how she loved him, and how she carries a piece of him with her, in her heart, and in ink.

Butterflies. I am thankful for butterflies, as they have played such a huge role in our grief. From the moments following his death, to the memorial, private moments for me and my family, butterflies have surrounded us and comforted us.

The whole thing fascinates me, and I have no explanation for their consistent presence in our lives since Stephen's passing. I have read a little more about their presence after death, and found there are a number of sources that talk about it. There is a story from Dr. Wayne Dyer on the topic that I found particularly comforting.

Butterflies have been identified for thousands of years as a creature that plays a role in bridging the gap between life and death. Many of the ancient civilizations believed that butterflies were symbols of the human soul. There are variations in the interpretation, from the Irish to the Maya, but the theme is similar and the relationship between life and death undeniable. The Aztecs in particular, believed that the happy dead in the form of beautiful butterflies would visit their relatives to assure them that all was well and they were happy on the other side.

I can't explain it, but I believe it. I guess it is kind of like faith. I've learned a lot about my faith lately. What I, through my own independent choice, decide to believe. Faith is choosing to believe in something, even if you can't see it or explain it, even if others tell you something different, or doubt. Faith is believing in something, even when the circumstances of your life present a far different and easier option to you. My life circumstances have presented me with an option with my faith. It would be so much easier to be bitter and angry and blame God for taking my son from me.

But, just like my choice with gratitude, I am choosing to look towards the goodness of life. And I believe, in gratitude, in butterflies and God. And no matter how rough the day gets, I will still be stronger with that faith than without.

I am thankful.

July 25th: The Wisdom from the Bags on the Floor

*Gratitude bestows reverence, allowing us to encounter
everyday epiphanies, those transcendent moments of awe
that change forever how we experience life and the world.*

–John Milton-

Saturday mornings. One of my favorite times, next to Sunday mornings. The quiet of a Saturday morning, where the only agenda you need to worry about is your own. They don't come often, and I never see them during hockey season, but during the summer, they are all mine.

Waking before anyone else, I once again spend some time with my thoughts, and looking at the bags on the floor. Yes, I know I need to unpack them. I need to move them from my bedroom floor. I need to put them away. But not yet. I am not ready yet, and I am okay with that. Where his hands touched, his mark on the world, I somehow feel it is evaporating like the morning mist. The bags are confirmation, a piece of him, and his touch on the world. I am not ready to undo that.

I've looked through the contents, and I've thought a lot about his thoughts as he packed the bag in anticipation. As I did with my father's death, I wonder if he had a feeling, an unconscious knowing, that this was it, it was his time. Did he feel the angels circling? All the thoughts rush through my brain and it is much too early to think about such deep things. Especially deep thoughts for which I have no answers.

In that email exchange I have written so much about, I remember him saying:

"I want more than anything to have some epiphany one day where everything is laid out for me and there is no more second-guessing or decisions to be made for my career path, but I can't force it I guess."

I've thought a lot about those words, about how they relate to life. Is it that he could not see things laid out before him because God had a much bigger plan? I will never have an answer, but I wonder about things like that these days. I wonder if he did not press the questions, because on some level, he was aware the answers were not necessary, or had been taken care of.

In my own life, as a consequence of my ponderings since Stephen's death, I am looking at my own life questions that I have not yet answered. We all sit here in this life and plan to do things, plan to be happy, plan to achieve all those goals and dreams on our list, plan to right wrongs, call that family member. With the exception of those who lay on their death beds, ravaged by disease, their expiration date confirmed by medical specialists, aren't we all walking though this life of ours like we have infinite time? Time to be happy, to lose the weight, write the book, make a mark on the world, to feel good about yourself, forgive those who've hurt you. For most of us, we look away from the things that truly are most meaningful, and instead, obsess about the worthless, and the details that will be of no consequence when we are faced with the end of our life here on earth. I have to take responsibility for doing all of the above in one way or another at points in my life. I've thought a lot about that lately. How much time did I waste in my life lamenting, not moving on, being afraid to take the risk, hiding my true self for fear of judgment? How much time did I waste when I could have been focused on being happy with Stephen when he was here on earth? That is a painful thing to contemplate. For, although

I know we had an exceptional relationship, filled with love, I still have an uneasy feeling for those moments where I did not see all that I did have in my life, only what I did not have in my possession.

Those bags, sitting on a now dusty floor teach me lessons every morning I look at them. Every day, having them in my field of vision sparks a different thought, a new point to reflect. They are my inanimate teachers, and I am showing up every morning for the lesson.

I am thankful for those lessons.

So, rather than dwell on my past mistakes, or moments of time I missed with Stephen because I was not living in the present moment, I will choose to take the lesson and change how I move forward.

I have some emotional work to do, so much so that I believe there should be a "Woman at Work" sign on the front lawn. But, I am going to heal, and when I do, I am not going to just talk about this life thing anymore. I am going to live more each day, be more present, make peace with the "stuff" I have carried with myself for way, way too long. I am going to let go of hurt and anger, the anxiety and the worry and I am going to drink up every moment. And, when I am finally at the end of my time here on earth, and when I see Stephen again, I want to tell him, "You were my epiphany."

Thank you God for the insights given to me by a Roots Knapsack. Thank you for the epiphany of Stephen. Thank you for allowing me to finally be ready to learn the lessons.

July 26th: Dreams, Church and Words of Love from Friends

Though dreams can be deceiving, like
faces are to hearts, they serve
for sweet relieving, when fantasy and reality lie too far apart.

-ANONYMOUS-

I AWOKE AT THE EARLY hours, well before seven. My wakefulness was bittersweet, stepping away from the greatest dream, talking to Stephen. In it, he was speaking to me, but his voice was muffled and I could not hear everything he was trying to say. It is funny that I would dream about this, as Brady and I always joked with him how hard it was to hear him when he called us. He was a "quiet talker" and I spent many a conversation adjusting the volume and saying "What?" It was a running family joke.

And wouldn't you know it; I continue to have my hearing issues, even in my dreams. The dreams are random, and have stories that are jumbled, like a big stew of different components of my life. In this particular dream, he is telling me that if good fights evil, good becomes evil. As I ponder this message, I am humbled by the fact that he really was so much wiser than me. Even in my dreams, he was the wise counselor.

I can't remember what topic we were discussing, dreams are like that. But I do remember the feeling. It was glorious, and if I could bottle and sell that feeling, I would not have any financial worries for the remainder of my lifetime. It was the feeling of contentment. As I sat with him in my dream, and listened to his muffled voice, my heart was full once again. It did not ache, I did not feel sad. It was what I had longed for! But alas, I woke up and the feeling dissipated like break of day mist once touched by a rising sun.

The feeling left me, but remained as a sweet memory in my mind. But the lesson stuck. I rolled the words around in my head as I read my book in the bath. If good fights evil, good becomes evil. I always thought my strength was in my ability to convey my viewpoint, to sway the masses. But, in my attempt to do so, I would sometimes argue a point so much that I would lose sight of my initial vision of progress. Even when I knew I was right, and someone or some situation was wronging me, my resistance and fighting in that situation, made me no better than those who had offended. Yes, the true strength I need to work on is finding the courage to not allow that to happen. I need to think on this one a little more.

Later that morning, we readied ourselves and went to church. I tried to be strong, I really did. I walked into the church with a feeling of peace, and I was glad we were there. But, as the mass started, I felt the lump in my throat grow. As the songs were sung, it increased in size. It was roughly the size of a bowling ball by the time the Gospel was read. I literally shook in the pew, holding back the tears. Brendan held my hand, and squeezed it every so often. Such a kind hearted boy, I am thankful for him. I prayed for God to help us, prayed for Stephen's spirit to stay close to us for another little while, as we really need him. Monsignor McSweeney gave a great homily about the attitude of gratitude and finding something to be thankful for no matter what the circumstance. How very timely he would speak about this today. And the crazy thing is, I can find things to be thankful for, each day. I never thought that would happen. I am also grateful for my husband, who made goofy faces at me and kicked me under the pew to make me smile, preventing the loud sobs from escaping from my throat.

But, I did it.

I wonder when I will be strong enough to go out in public without completely losing it. It is funny, as I can sit at the computer and the words simply pour from my soul. But ask me to talk to someone, and I simply can't do it. I suppose it will come with time. I just need to be patient. For now, I am thankful that at least the words are flowing, even if they are not spoken. Later that day, I take the time to open a letter from dear friends, Mary and Patrick. Having met at a hockey arena, our friendship has grown right along with our children. From friends to business partners, my friendship with Mary is one I cherish. Again, I am reminded that this world is filled with more kindness than evil. And maybe that was the message from my dream. Focus on the good stuff.

The letter is personal, and again tells us a story of Stephen from another's perspective. It is hard to explain how much joy it gives me to see that others saw what I saw in my boy. It makes things better, even if only for a short while.

The words are beautiful, and, sent without fanfare quietly in the mail. Mary has been a great comfort to me, and I am thankful.

Dear Kelly, Brady and Brendan,

I hope it goes without saying how much you all mean to us which makes it all the more difficult to articulate our deep sorrow and sympathy to you over the loss of Stephen. We feel very fortunate to have known him for the brief time that we did because Stephen was such a unique, memorable and kind person, that brief friendship was filled with more brightness than many others we have known or will ever know.

You know how sometimes you just have a feeling about something. Well, I've been thinking a lot lately and I believe our lives were destined to be intertwined although, just four short years ago, we did not know each other. And it is somehow fitting that it all began with Stephen, making such an impression on Patrick, not just for his incredible goalie skills, but for his quiet unassuming demeanor in light of such potent talent.

Over the last two years, we have had the unique perspective, as your friends, to watch Stephen with all three of you.

With Kelly, I have never seen a more devoted, loving son in a grown man. Especially at the beach last year, I could see how important you were to Stephen. Or, on hockey travel weekends when you and he would steal away from the crowd for a long overdue mother-son talk. It was obvious that your happiness and fulfillment were of the utmost importance to him and I hope that as each day passes the memory of all that Stephen was provides you with some measure of both.

With Brady, we watched a relationship that was filled with so much laughter and love. Catching an ironic roll of Stephen's eyes when Brady would say something completely inappropriate and then his quiet laugh knowing there was nothing he could do to stop Brady, but all could tell, nor would Stephen ever want to stop him. The mutual acceptance of each other exactly as you were was ever apparent and the greatest gift you could have ever given to each other.

With Brendan, I remember the first time Stephen brought you to the rink for a game. I didn't realize who he was at first but it didn't take long to figure out that he was the proudest big brother that ever lived. I think it meant the world to him that you follow in his goalie footsteps and he loved watching you play, as he always will. Even though you won't be able to see him, which I know is hard, he will be watching out for you, clapping the loudest when you make that great save, and giving you the courage to get back up when one slips by you. And I don't just mean hockey.

At the Memorial Service in Raleigh, Patrick and I considered getting up to say a few words, but we didn't want to intrude on the special camaraderie of his college friends and teammates. However, this letter serves as our memorial to Stephen, so here goes.

Of all the times we spent with Stephen and you all, my favorite was our cook out over Memorial Day a few weeks ago. It was the epitome of Stephen. I remember saying to Kelly at the time, how I loved watching Stephen and Ross toss the Frisbee in our backyard, realizing that although they were grown men, they were still young enough to enjoy the simplest things in life like a great friendship, a beautiful day, and good chocolate chip ice cream sandwiches. The laughter and the frivolity between Stephen and Brendan throwing things at each other as Ben and Ross joined in. Of course, hockey was part of that evening too as we watched an NHL playoff game, some of us with much more intensity than others, i.e. Kelly and I talking up a blue streak in the corner as we basked in the happiness that game seemed to provide to all the young men in the room. And finally, of Thomas jumping on and off Stephen's lap as Stephen accepted this little worshipper with the humility, grace and love of someone well beyond his twenty three years.

If I could, I would stop time for you in that moment, in that evening, in that happiness.

Unfortunately, I'll have to settle for keeping that moment alive by reminding you of it and all the other wonderful moments we spent with Stephen on the days when his loss hits the hardest. Destiny brought us your tremendous friendship and Patrick, Ben, Thomas and I are here for each of you.

With much love and great sadness, please accept our contribution to the NC State Club Hockey Team in Stephen's honor.
Mary

July 27th: The Dreams of Clarity, and Being the Favorite Aunt...

Gratitude unlocks the fullness of life. It turns what we have into enough, and more. It turns denial into acceptance, chaos to order, confusion to clarity. It can turn a meal into a feast, a house into a home, a stranger into a friend. Gratitude makes sense of our past, brings peace for today, and creates vision for tomorrow.

–MELODY BEATTIE-

I LOVE MY DREAMS. IN them, he can still be here with me, and I have had the greatest dreams now, two nights in a row. Him talking to me. They are weird and disconnected, as dreams go, as in it I am planning his funeral, but yet, at one point, we sneak away to talk about something, just the two of us. Last night, here were the words I took, "Mom, what I've learned is that many people go through life and miss 9-1, completely. Over half of their day, gone." A weird and random thought, but true nonetheless. These dreams come to me, perhaps from my exhaustive REM sleep, the past few weeks are catching up on me, and I am really tired. Both from the travel, but mostly from the simple act of grieving. I have opened myself to it, and it takes all that I have. But the fatigue is welcomed, because I am facing the truth, and learning from it.

In the dream, missing half the day resonates with me. I have spent many portions of my life distracting myself from what hurt me. I've missed so much time running from the truth, the pain. But now, I feel softened, and vulnerable, and open, and I am allowing the truth in, even though it hurts terribly. I am awake for each moment of the day, and I am giving thanks for all that I am learning.

With my new awareness, I have things to say. I want to share my thoughts with others, and no longer limit myself with the illusions of self doubt. I simply put it out there. I have let go of the worries that not all will understand, or agree with me. I am not running from myself anymore.

In some ways, I think it is Stephen guiding me to this place, continuing to be my teacher.

So, today I am thankful for my words, my wakefulness and the clarity I have received from my hurt.

And from this clarity, I wrote the following email. Sent to all of Stephen's cousins, I felt the need to circle back with all of them as they, like us, resume life as usual after an unusual summer. They are all so different, but similar in so many other ways. They all are walking different paths in life, and at different stages. But no matter, I see in each of them a similar spark, a light that reminds me of Stephen.

From: Kelly Buckley
Sent: Monday, July 27, 2009 7:28 PM
To: The Cousins
Subject: The Russell Cousins are the best....
Hello Cousins...

I've had this email on my list for a while now, but had to wait for the right moment to send it. Things hurt pretty bad right now, for all of us, and I feel very thankful that we Russell's are made of the tough stuff. You may not know it yet, but as you go through life, and you meet more people, you are going to realize just how rare a family like ours truly is. I never thought too much about how special we were, and actually never even realized it until my own parents were gone. But, it is true. More families than not would shy away and retreat from one another in a time like this, most families would not be able to stay all together, 25 or so deep at Aunt Julie's. It just would not happen. But we did, sticking together through this, just as we have for so many other things in our lifetime. Just as we will for anything that comes our way in the future.

But, maybe you all sense that, and maybe you know it much better than I did at your age. Because, I saw everything you all did to make Stephen's memorial and funeral so special, so much like him. From the music, to the video, the pictures, getting everything ready, the stories, the stuff that went on back at Aunt Julie's, taking care of us and bringing the 5th wheel in and backing it in on the first try, the mass and all that was associated with that, some of the logistics stuff with the funeral home (yes Amy, I mean you, our family strategic communications expert) And, I know, in my sadness, I did not even see half of it.

So, Brady, Brendan and I want to say a special thank you. I wanted to put it in a mass email, instead of sending a thank you note, as I am the hip aunt. I would have texted all of you, but that would have taken me months. And, even though I am on facebook, I don't know what the poke thing is, and was a little nervous about doing that.

Thank you to all of you for each little special piece you brought to the event. As his cousins, you all knew him in a special and unique way and how he was remembered really showed that. I know he was looking down and smiling on each of you. Most of all, I want to thank you for the heartfelt hugs and chats, and for you all to share your emotions freely with me. You have no idea how much your Aunt Kelly loves all of you.

I've attached the words I spoke at the funeral. I also attached them to the memorial site on Facebook and sent them to your parents. In some weird way, it makes me feel better to share them. I think it has something to do with honoring who he was by spreading the word about how he did it when he was here on earth. I wish we had all been closer (same country at least), as the past four years were an amazing period for him down here, and he was grabbing at everything life had to offer. That is why I attach the words. Because I want each of you to do the same, and know that many of you are...

You all have that same "special" in you. Don't be afraid to take the risks you need to take to let that special out....think of things you are afraid of as sheets of tissue paper and burst right through them. FEAR= Fearful Emotions Appearing Real...

If you wake up one day, and decide you want to change, do it. Just like the Nike slogan, "Just do it". We are like cars, and need realignments sometimes. Many people get caught in a rut, living a certain way for so long, they think there is no way out. But that is an illusion, nothing more than your mind making mental roadblocks. The reality is you can do ANYTHING......so, if you wake up one morning, and decide you don't like how things are going. Change....I do it all the time.

Now, I am admitting, and did when I spoke, not all of the wisdom came from the Mom. For you family, as long as you keep it confidential, I will tell you......in fact, most came from Stephen. He was a lot smarter than me.... Again, thank you all. We love you tons and tons. I leave you with a thought from Joan...

You don't get to choose how you're going to die, or when.
You can only decide how you're going to live now.

-- JOAN BAEZ

Love and Kisses,
*Your **Most Favorite Aunt** Kelly*

July 28th: Taking Care of Each Other, Dad's Whistle, and Faith

There is sacredness in tears. They are
not the mark of weakness, but
of power. They speak more eloquently than ten thousand tongues.
They are messengers of overwhelming
grief...and unspeakable love.

–WASHINGTON IRVING–

SO MANY BAGS. 3000 PAIRS of socks. Stephen had so many socks. As Brendan and I rummage through a few more boxes, we find more treasures from his life. At moments, it is comforting, and others it is not. Rather than comfort, I feel like an unknown force with a big hand is clenching my heart beneath his strong fingers, squeezing the life out of it. The joy dripping from the ends of his fingertips.

I cannot help myself and I smell one of his shirts. And, when the olfactory senses kick in and spark memories from his scent, my face contorts, squeezes up like I am a raisin, and the tears flow freely. The good news is Brendan seems to have made peace with my crying periodically. He tells me he loves me, or hugs me, I compose myself and we continue on with our day. I am thankful for that. I am happy that I can weep in front of him, and he understands it is a normal response to losing Stephen. We talked about it, and he is not alarmed. He does not leave the room to get away from it, he stays, close. I am glad that we are working through this together, instead of alone, behind closed doors, hiding our pain. I believe it helps him as well, and he knows what he is feeling inside is a normal response.

We talk quietly as we find things. Some make us laugh, others make us quiet, and we quickly move on to the next thing. It is an unspoken understanding between my boy and me about how to handle this. We are the keepers of the other's heart, and we step tentatively while in this room, to protect the other. Today we stayed here for about an hour, other days it was mere minutes. And some days, we don't even have the courage to open the door, but it is all good.

I am thankful for those moments with my boy. I want Brendan to drink up the parts of Stephen's personality and spirit that sit in these boxes. I want him to hold on to them, and have his brother in his heart as he grows. Perhaps, in some way, it will comfort him when he can't have that conversation after a hockey game or that big brother support when he faces those tough teenage dating scenarios.

In the side pocket of one of the bags, Brendan pulls out a Sambridge recorder. I smile. It was my father's, and for some reason, Stephen had it in this bag, carrying it with him back and forth from school. How curious, how comforting. The "whistle" is black and white in color and has seen better days. Brendan asks me about this new found treasure, and I explain it belonged to his Grandfather. He asked some questions about the overall condition of the find, and I explain that many years earlier, my dog Boots had decided it looked like a pretty good chew toy. The marks were from his teeth, but for whatever reason, we kept it instead of throwing it in the trash.

When my father died, it was something that was important for me to hold onto, as part of my memory of him, and it was also important for Stephen as well. I love that he carried it with him. Much like the medals in his knapsack, his respect for those unspoken bonds of love and faith give me peace.

Brendan starts to play it. Now, if you need to experience unbridled joy, watch my son play any whistle or harmonica. It is the epitome of joy. It is glorious. From the time that this boy was a toddler, he would walk around the house playing a harmonica, and singing. And now, even though he is much older, you can still see the delight when he picks up an instrument that allows free expression.

I am reminded of a funny memory of those earlier musical escapades. At the local music store, a three year old Brendan was so excited when his first harmonica was purchased. So proud, he played it endlessly at home, walking around the house and making music. And, when anyone would come and visit, he would proudly enter the room and announce, "Hey, would you like me to play you a song on my **Hormonica**?" Yes, you read it right. I smile, thinking back to those moments, this tiny three year old, with the clear articulated speech, announcing to company, that he wanted to play the instrument named after the ladies of the night. Stephen would laugh, and it was so innocent and so funny, we did not want to correct him. But we did. Stephen took so much pleasure from his little brother. The eleven year age difference helped with that, and they did not have the typical sibling rivalry you would see in children closer in age. It was good for both of them and for me as well.

I am thankful for this exercise in grief, as it is allowing us to revisit moments from our past, and relive the good and the bad with a new perspective. I am thankful, for the truth is, I have mostly good memories. I am thankful for each item in these boxes, as they give us an opportunity to take a journey back to those moments and be thankful for the life we did have with a wonderful boy.

July 29th: Falling to Pieces and Being Put Back Together by Faith

Perhaps love is like a resting place, A shelter from the storm, It exists to give you comfort, It is there to keep you warm, And in those times of trouble, When you are most alone, The memory of love will bring you home.

-JOHN DENVER-

IT MAY SOUND WEIRD, BUT my one little thing today was having a couple hours to myself where I simply fell apart. Crying as I did on the shoreline that day, from the depths of my soul, chanting Stephen's name. Letting some of the "ache" out of me. Because boy, do I ache. I am focused on the present and finding peace and the purpose. But, that doesn't mean I don't feel the pain. In fact, because I am facing it head on I feel in some ways I am "feeling it" even more than most, not looking away from it. I've made the decision to see it for what it really is, to walk through the valley and not around it as such, but it hurts.

My heart throbs. I keep talking about the good things to embrace in my life, because I am trying to convince myself that they are not just figments of my imagination. I am trying to convince myself, and I suppose whoever reads this journal that good can still exist in the middle of such pain. Through my tears, I feel if I could convince myself and others of this, that I would be honoring the life of Stephen. I am human, and have wondered at times how I will go on, wanting to see him again, desperately. If God would only be merciful, and let me see him one more time. Stephen was my child, but he was also with me for over half my life. Imagine that, I was a child and so was he. I've had more of my life with him than without, and of all the people in my life, he and I had the most history. And now, I have to figure out what my life means without him in it. My life without him physically in it at least.

I believe my tears will tell me. With each drop that flows endlessly from my eyes, rolling down my cheeks, I am figuring it out. For that, I am thankful.

As I had some alone time, I quietly went to Stephen's room, wanting to spend some time looking through his belongings. Being alone with his things aided the flow of tears from my eyes. I found papers from school, projects from the fifth grade, silly things that sparked memories and more tears. I don't know what I am looking for, some sort of message, some "moment" or communication that will confirm that part of him is still with me. Perhaps some note that outlines everything that he felt and thought about. You know nothing too elaborate, just the secrets of the universe. And, I suppose I found it in a school paper from 2003.

The paper was simplistic, and from the length and writing style, I am pretty sure it was completed about 30 minutes prior to the due date. Nonetheless, it was poetry for my soul, and exactly what I needed. Life is funny that way. It gives you what you need, if you take the time to notice what has been presented to you. Most times, in life, we just don't notice. The paper was about resilience, which has always been one of my favorite topics. It talked about finding the good in things, even in bad times. Okay Stephen, I get it. Your eleventh grade interpretation of resilience is exactly what I needed.

This paper being presented to me at just the right moment leads me to think more about my faith. Thinking so much these days about faith, and life. There must be smoke billowing from my ears from all the rusty wheels turning in there.

I feel hardly qualified to write about faith. Not because I do not have faith, because I do, more now than I have ever before. But, because of my on and off again relationship with my faith leading up to this life change, I certainly don't feel like the expert. But, the more I think about it, the more I realize I really am qualified. Sure, I would lose terribly if I was in a theological discussion with some of the respected religious leaders of this world. But I now believe I understand faith, at least in a personal sense.

The reason? On July 4th, 2009, I stood at a crossroads in my life. I had lost everything, my baby, my beautiful son was gone. In my mind and my pain, it had all been taken away from me. And, even though I had questions about how God had handled things in the past, I had wondered if He truly had forgiven me for my own shortcomings as I had asked for, I held on to my faith in Him. And, not only did I hold on, I clutched my faith for dear life. With everything stripped away, it was truly the only thing that remained. Nothing else could give me comfort or peace. My faith was the only thing I still believed in. I say that, knowing I had a loving and stupendous husband holding me up, a beautiful younger son who loves large, and family and friends like no other. But truly, at that moment, and for many moments after that day, my faith is what has allowed me to accept reality with a peace in my heart.

It was as if God said, "I know it is pretty bad, I know a lot of people will find it too painful to be around you because they don't know what to say and it hurts. But I love you and I am not going anywhere." In my heart and mind, I did not feel that anyone really knew how I felt, only God.

Since that time, I have explored so much within my faith. I have looked at what I believed prior to my loss and what I believe now. My beliefs have given me peace, and a gentle knowing that my child is with God, and is part of a bigger story and plan I do not yet understand. My faith allows me to have patience to wait for the plot of that story to be revealed to me.

July 30ᵗʰ: Old Friends, The Grief Lady and Taking the Leap

Friends are angels who lift our feet when our own
wings have trouble remembering how to fly.

-AUTHOR UNKNOWN-

I AM FORTUNATE. I GREW up in a small town. I lived in the same house my entire childhood, we never moved, and I never changed schools. I have friends who have known me through all my phases and stages. These are the "peeps" who have watched me shine when things were good, and who have dusted me off when things went drastically off course. They love me now, and they loved me then. These are the girls who played with me on the playground, and who giggled with me at high school dances. I have been with some of these girls through changes, in my own life and in theirs. Changes in relationships, in death and life.

We have all grown up and have very different lives. But the fabric of our being was woven together long before today, and the bond stays. I am blessed in my life, as these women know me, all of me. And, they knew Stephen. They knew Stephen from the moment of his birth. If you have people in your life who know your story, who have history with you, you are beyond lucky. You have been blessed.

Marlene is one of those friends. I've known her since I was knee high to a grasshopper. I played square ball with her; we went on field trips in the summer with the playground that was right next store to her house.

My purple banana seat bike was run over in her driveway. We hung out together in high school and we lived together in university.

When I flew home to bury my son, she was there. I had not talked to her in some time, not because of any rift, just because of life. But she was there. And, since that time, we have shared some emails back and forth that have softened the rough edges of my grief, and have reminded me of my past and my humble beginnings with Stephen. I am thankful for her and for the other friends who just showed up, without a word to be there for me when I needed them the most. Here are her words.

Hi Kel,

I knew I had to be in Grand Falls for you and Stephen and your family. It's wild how there are times when you just know you have to do something and that was one of them and I think that it came from somewhere deep inside me that was stripped bare when I got the call about Stephen. It is that special bond that exists between friends that have known each other for so long. A friendship based on pure innocence and just a simple idea of liking each other. Not because of children, hockey, work, neighbors, and on and on....

I have no idea how you are coping but I am very proud of you. The strength you are demonstrating for your family and for Stephen will make him proud. You are a Leader Kelly, you always have been, and leaders do great things. You are teaching me to improve my life, can you imagine what your strength and grace is showing Brendan. You may not see it now or even any time soon but this gift you are giving in Stephen's memory will play out for lifetimes.

I know you may not feel like moving some days or talking or eating or breathing, but that is okay too, we must hurt to heal. And although your heart will never mend completely you will make it out on the other side some how. Getting there will be tough but know that there is a heart up here in NL holding you in it each day with a prayer for you to keep going. Like you said, for Brady, Brendan, Stephen and for you, for Kelly.

Thank you for sharing your words about Stephen with me. I have been sharing it with those whom I know need it and with those who will be grateful for receiving it. I am reading it over and over.
Take care,
Marlene

If I was to go back over my life since July 4th, one thing is becoming very clear. I hope for those reading this you are seeing the pattern. Every day, I have been presented with goodness. It just keeps coming. And, it comes when I need it the most, when I don't feel I can take another breath. I am thankful.

Today, I also had my first appointment with Clarisse. She is a gifted counselor, and her practice is connected with our church, which makes it somewhat more personal. I've never been one to ask for help with things. I have walked my path alone for many of the hardships in my life, and most times, it was to my own detriment. People need to be able to ask for help and to lean on others in times like this. That has been a hard lesson for me to learn, but I am glad I finally get it. I knew from the beginning that, unlike other things that had happened in the past, I was going to need some help with this one.

As I drove to the appointment, I laughed to myself, wondering if this poor woman knew what she was in for with me. The plan was to have me meet with her first, and then Brendan would see her in the afternoon. My initial thought was I would meet with her and fill her in on how the family was coping, how we were doing, what things I was hoping to achieve from the sessions. I even took the time to draw out a chart, explaining all of the family dynamics and our vision and goals for the sessions. Yes, I did that. Typing that makes me laugh at myself.

Being completely prepped, I arrived at her office. Meeting her for the first time, I felt immediately at ease. What a kind person. You know when you get a great vibe from a person, and I was so happy with our decision to come and see her.

The session began, and basically, my agenda went out the window. Any hope of intelligent conversation based on my family dynamics chart or the goals fell by the wayside as I cried, sobbed, snorted, and blubbered. I told her the story of Stephen, from beginning to end. And it was healing. To just let it all out. To just let it flow out without me feeling I had to control the message, or keep strong, or follow an agenda. It was nothing like I planned, but it was exactly what I needed. And the most beautiful thing? She, at points, cried with me. It was the most empathetic and beautiful thing I have ever experienced from someone. She was professional and kind all at the same time and there are so many who could take a lesson from her.

I am thankful.

Later that afternoon, Brendan had his first appointment. It was a big step for both of us, and we felt good after it was over. Without prompting, he said "I like her" as we walked across the parking lot. And, it was at that moment, he first used the title that would make me smile for weeks to come. "The Grief Lady." He titled her, anointing her with a name that described exactly why we were seeing her. I love twelve year old minds. I am not sure how she would feel about it, but I have a hunch she would be fine with us injecting some levity into our difficult days.

Thank you for The Grief Lady.

That evening, we decided to go for a swim, just Brady, Brendan and I. I had promised Brendan I would jump right in, from the high part on the pool. And, because a promise is a promise, I did it. It was not a typical thing for me, but I've been taking leaps in my life all over the place lately. I may as well stick with the trend in the pool.

I am thankful.

July 31st: Bathtub Reflections and Time

Nothing valuable can be lost by taking time.

-*Abraham Lincoln*-

WOKE EARLY AND READ FOR a while in the bathtub. I've always loved that time, the quiet, early in the morning, when it is just me and my thoughts. I have contemplated many things in my life from the comfort of my bathtub. There is a great window over my bathtub that looks out onto the backyard, and we just have the best backyard. Private and inviting, the yard has a little of Stephen at every corner. Our *inukshuk*, built from leftover stone used in our landscaping, designed as a marker for our family. The Inuit used it as a tool for navigation, a point of reference to communicate it was a safe place to camp, or a good hunting ground. We built it to remind ourselves that this was our haven, our safe spot to return to where you would always be welcomed, nurtured and loved. Looking around, I see the flagstone patio we built together as a family, and had no idea what we were getting into until we were too far into the project, and covered in cement. I close my eyes and see Stephen mow the lawn. I would watch him from the window sometimes, and be amazed at how he would push that mower so quickly and with one hand, iPod in place, mowing to the rhythm of whatever was playing in his ear. I can remember seeing him on those days, and realizing just how lucky I was. You never had to ask him to do things like that. He just did it.

In the bath, I read a book called, "The Shack". It is about a man whose daughter is murdered, and after a period of time, returns to the shack where her bloodied dress was found, summoned by God himself. The book was given to me before Stephen died, by Brady's mother. I had read a little about the success of the book, but actually based on the premise, I did not have any interest in reading it. I find that so ironic. I did not want to read the book because it was about a parent losing their child. Forget the rest of the story, just that premise alone made this mother run for the hills.

But, it is different now. And I must look, at this story, and my own reality. In a way, I wish I could have a sit down meeting with God, to discuss a few things. I can't explain it, but I think if God could tell me that he really needed someone special, that he had a job of greatness, and there was only one man who fit the bill, I might feel better about the whole thing. If I could imagine him up there, in heaven, given the task of bringing people together, championing an important cause for all of heaven and God himself, I could find some justification for what has happened. Because, as I look at it now, I struggle with the fact that it was his time to go when there was so much good he could have done in his lifetime here on earth. But maybe that is it. Maybe the greatness I always talked about was what he could bring to people through his death. Maybe, through his death, the people left behind will have a greater appreciation for their own life. A greater desire to do their best, with the understanding that their time is fleeting, and their choices important. I do not have delusions of grandeur with regards to my son, but with any death, doesn't it show us, with brutal honesty, about the sanctity of life, just as Jesus' death on the cross was to show the world?

If only God could come for breakfast. Strawberries and blueberries, with low fat vanilla yogurt and Kashi cereal sprinkled on the top. I'm sure he/she would like it. And green tea. For some reason, I think God drinks green tea. If only reality was like that book, and I could have a meeting like that one. But, it is a book. And, although I love the message within it, I understand I have to find peace in my own shack, or at my own cove at Jordan Lake.

And I will find peace. And I will find purpose. I believe there is something in all of this, the writing, the trying to stay positive even in the bleakest of circumstances. I think this is part of the purpose, but it is too soon to tell. So, I will continue to go with the flow of things, as I have been since the 4th of July. This control freak, Type A, everything in order girl, will just go with the flow. Because I don't know if it is Stephen, or God, or both, but I feel like I am not driving the bus. And, that works for me right now.

As I write, I am listening to Stephen's iPod, the classical Playlist. Right now, George Gershwin-Rhapsody in Blue. The classical playlist has 29 songs, all remarkable classics from the world's finest composers. Simply amazing. Walt Whitman books in the closet, classical playlist on the iPod.

So, what would be my one little thing for the day? What would it be? Would it be the music I listen to, first classical, then party music, then upbeat? Would it be the Jim Sturgess tunes from the Across the Universe Soundtrack? As they started to play, I remembered an afternoon a couple of years earlier. Stephen and I were home alone, Brendan at school, and Brady at work. And, after one of our chats, we completely blew off the afternoon, and watched this movie. It was a wild movie, blending all the Beatles music intertwined into this far out movie about a guy and a girl in the craziness of the 60's. I had forgotten we had played hooky together like that until the moment that the song started. Maybe that is my little thing for today. The memory of that afternoon with him, and our decision to make our time together more important than any list of tasks. Or our giggles as we realized we had lost track of time and Brendan would be dismissed from school in two minutes; we had to fly to pick him up. Or maybe it is bigger. Maybe it is knowing that I have hundreds, maybe thousands of those memories tucked away in the recesses of my mind, and when the time is right, Stephen will guide me to them. He will lead me to them, for comfort, to learn, to grow, to grieve.

But bigger than that, it is the knowledge that time spent with your child, however frivolous it may seem when your list is long, is worth more than anything else in the world. All of our crazy projects, watching that movie, our late night chats. They are more precious to me now than any accolades received professionally, more than any time I have given away to life's worries or annoyances. I am thankful.

August 1st: Quiet mornings, Quotes, Sun Drenched Lazy Days of Summer and Butterflies

Happiness is as a butterfly which, when pursued,
is always beyond our grasp, but which if you will
sit down quietly, may alight upon you.

-*Nathaniel Hawthorne*-

Moving on. That's what it feels like with the beginning of a new month. And, I'm not sure if I like it. I don't think I am ready to move on, to let go of July, the last month he was alive. I awoke early, 6:30 in the morning, and just lay there for a bit. I still like those early moments of wakefulness, when reality hasn't quite kicked in with me, and I still believe that all is right with my world and Stephen is still alive.

But, time marches on....that's what they say. And I have to march on with it, I suppose, but will still silently protest it.

The quiet of a Saturday morning has a name in our home, "National Sleep-in Day", and it is a beautiful thing. But, I've never enjoyed it for the extra snooze time. I rarely sleep in, and have always been an early riser. So, as they sleep, I have some time to be alone with my thoughts. This is nothing new, I've always enjoyed this time.

My writing is going well, and I have tens of thousands of words so far, I guess that is a good "one little thing" for the day. And, they keep coming.

I am also enjoying my daily practice of posting a quote on my facebook page. I take time at the beginning of the day to find the right one, a quote that fits my mood, but also may plant a seed of thought in the minds of my friends. Part of my purpose, however insignificant. It makes me happy, and reading all the quotes provides me with solace, knowing I was never alone in my pain, that others have walked this path before me. And more will come, and follow me. Maybe that is the purpose of my writing, to leave a light on for those who will follow, to help them find their way through their own dark days. As I've said before, I don't have it all figured out, but somehow know this is what I am supposed to do.

4:53: Update for the one little thing for today. And it is actually a couple of little things. First, Brady, Brendan, Rudy and I spent the entire afternoon swimming in the pool. The clouds blew off and it was a tremendous afternoon. Sunny and really warm, the perfect day to be wet. And the second thing? A butterfly flew all around us when we first went outside, flying around Brendan, then me, Brady and Rudy. It would flutter around, and then pitch, and sit quietly, peaceful. We ate lunch poolside, and it lingered, sitting on a little rock wall, and I felt him. I felt him with us, and could feel his nod of approval at our choice to have a fun filled day. For almost an hour, he stayed with us. I am glad that Brendan did not notice my tears in the pool. But, they were good tears. Tears of gratitude, for being given the gift of feeling connected to him, even if that feeling is only in my heart.

I love being in the water, it is so peaceful. I read a few things about families that stay away from the water after losing someone to a drowning. I just can't do that, not to Brendan, or me. Helen Keller said,

"Security is mostly a superstition. It does not exist in nature, nor do the children of men as a whole experience it. Avoiding danger is no safer in the long run than outright exposure. Life is either a daring adventure, or nothing."

Now, if you want to look at someone who made a conscious decision to be happy in spite of adversity and challenge in her life, Helen Keller would be your girl. And, I agree with her. There is a plan bigger than all of us; I have come to know that now. So, whether we are in or out of the water, it makes no difference. That statement is not defeatist. In fact, I say that with the most resilience I can muster at this point. We choose to live, and live we will. Even if we have to force ourselves to do so for a little while. We choose to climb trees, just as Stephen did, scrape knees, and ride our bikes into the waves. And, when I finally get called home, and see my child again, I want to be able to tell God, "I used it all, everything you gave me". And I want HIM to tell me I did good.

So, the swimming afternoon was blissful. Sun kissed and smelling of chlorine, we strolled back over to the house, a good tired. I like doing enough these days to have that good tired. It helps me sleep and it helps me dream, and I always like to dream.

August 2ⁿᵈ: Insight, Forgiveness, Harry Potter and God's Plan

To bring up a child in the way he should go,
travel that way yourself once in a while.

~JOSH BILLINGS-

THE DAY BEFORE MY BIRTHDAY. 29 again this year. Ah, no, not this year. I feel that I could be turning 100. I feel like an old woman this year. But, I am still here. I still am surrounded by love and I still have the most loving little boy.

So, as it has been a pattern, I have had more than one little thing today. First, I only cried a couple of times today, and both were when I was writing about something particularly painful. I still physically ache, and I am not being a Pollyanna, but I feel that my focus on these "one little things" has helped shine a light for me in the darkness. It has kept me focused on the fact that there is still a lot of good in the world. A lot of beauty and a lot of life left to live. Amazing. I sound like Stuart Smalley from Saturday Night Live. I'm good enough, I'm strong enough and dog- gone it, people like me.

My writing is going well, and I am getting into a rhythm. I love to write, but this is the longest I have really stayed with a project so daunting without the self doubt kicking in.

The other thing is this book I mentioned, The Shack. It is changing my perspective, and it is helping me with this internal conversation I am having with The Big Guy. I say that, having read some of the reviews about this book and its departure from religious doctrine. I wish everyone would take a deep breath. The world moves so fast these days, I find that as fast as someone puts a thought out there, someone is chasing them down to discredit it. If only the scholars of the world could only share their knowledge with ink and quill, maybe it would give some more time for people to absorb the words prior to judging. I find it all very tiring. I have actually stopped watching the news, and reading the newspaper. At least for a little while.

Prior to Stephen's death, I was not so much having a crisis in faith. I was actually reading the bible, and exploring my faith more than I ever had before. But, I always had this sort of inferiority complex about the whole thing. That has changed, and although my faith is very personal to me, the conversation is going well. As it goes in general, I can't imagine facing something like this without faith. Looking at it from my shifted perspective, I can now see clearly that my insecurity in faith had nothing to do with God. Rather, it was with the interpretations of the various religions of what God means to the world. It did not make sense, to see someone present themselves as righteous and pious, but their outward behavior and treatment did not appear to be Christian. I am including myself in this analogy. It is truly about walking the talk, and I struggled in finding peace with the version of God I was being presented with. But, I think I have it figured out now. At least for myself, as I am no religious expert. For me, I no longer feel the need to look outward towards the various religions and organized churches to tell me what God is for me. It is personal. And, because it is so personal, and between the two us, I could go to any church in the world and now feel like I belonged.

As I write this, I am surprised that my daily reflections keep going back to faith. But, truly, how else could I find gratitude in grief without faith? I think back to an email from Stephen. He was exploring his faith in the spring, and he and I had some wonderful conversations. I want to paste an excerpt in here, so I don't lose it:

During Jesus' lifetime, he did not look up to those wealthier than him, or those who spent all of their days worshiping in temples, he cared about the type of person you were. He ate with tax collectors, the most hated people of his time, and it did not matter to him. On his last days of living, a prostitute was by his side as he was approaching death and his eventual resurrection. If we are called to be good Christians, which is to essentially be more like Jesus (we can never achieve his status, all we can do is strive to be better Christians in his eyes), how do we do it? Going to church every Sunday does not make you a good Christian automatically, it is how you live your life, and whether or not you accept faith and Jesus into your heart.....That is what makes you a true believer.....Stephen P. Russell -April 2009-

I will admit, reading this makes me sad a little, and I do wonder why someone like this had to go so soon. I am humbled by his perspective, and I agree with him. This is the faith I will carry forward with me, and I am no longer confused.

Anyway, as I continue to read The Shack, I pause, and I meditate on a certain thought or concept, and try to figure out a reasonable application with what I am dealing with. Today, I was thinking about a person who played a big part in Stephen's and my life, but who treated him wrong. And there was a lot left unsaid. I am struggling with it, as I have been wondering if I should be the one to make sure the message is conveyed. The whole thing ties me in a knot to be honest. So, today, I just had a conversation with God and Stephen about it all. And, I feel like I am figuring out the answer. That is a "one little thing".

Finally, Brendan and I went to see Harry Potter and the Half Blood Prince. Great movie, even if I did not really understand some parts. But, it was a joy to just be with Brendan, and it was the first real place I had ventured outside of the house, other than to church. Up to this point, I have spent a lot of time at home. In the dark of the theatre, Brendan and I held hands, and I could sense that it made him feel good.

On the drive home, we were talking about Stephen, and the topic of God's Plan came up. And, Brendan said, that he was wondering about God's Plan and what the purpose would be in this happening. And, I was honest. I did not know. I told him I did not know if Stephen dying was part of God's plan, but I did believe that part of his purpose and his plan is to make sure that he takes care of us as we miss Stephen, and surrounds us with lots of love. And, I do believe that God must have needed him for something really special. But, all of that felt quite insufficient, and I simply don't feel I have the qualifications to speak on behalf of God.

So, I explained it in the best way I could, and then offered him an example. "Brendan, do you remember how I told you how I had Stephen when I was younger?" I asked.

"Yes", he said.

"Well Brendan, as you can imagine, I was a teenager, with all my friends, and music and school, and when I found out I was pregnant, I thought my life was absolutely over. I believed that everything had ended, and there would be no joy left in anything I did. It was the worst thing! As far as God's will and plan, I could not understand."

He nodded, listening attentively.

"But, when Stephen came, I could see it. I could feel that he was meant to be here, and was part of something special, something much bigger than me, or school dances or music lessons. Today, as your Mom looks at things, I can see that when Stephen arrived, just like you, they were the two best things that ever happened to me. And, 23 years later, I can see just how intricate and special God's plan really was. Think about all the people who have emailed us, called us, sent us cards, posted on facebook. All of those people have been touched and affected by Stephen. Think about all the people he helped, or loved, or was kind to; think about what he did for all of us. That is what I believe God's Plan was. I think God knew how Stephen would touch so many people, and how much joy his life would bring to the world."

I exhaled. I had a proud and momentous smile. I was a damn good parent. My God, we just had a moment. I was feeling pretty good about myself, and for once, not feeling like my explanation was inadequate.

And he looked at me thoughtfully and said, "Yeah, well okay....I have to pee."

I would laugh at that for days after. I thought I was worthy of a feature story in Parenting magazine and he was thinking about urination. Life does have a way of balancing the serious and the ridiculous. That is a very good little thing.

I am thankful.

August 3rd: Happy Birthday to Me....

Refuse to fall down. If you cannot refuse to fall down, refuse
to stay down, lift your heart toward heaven like a hungry
beggar, ask that it be filled and it will be filled. You may be
pushed down. You may be kept from rising. But no one can
keep you from lifting your heart toward heaven-only you. It
is in the middle of misery that so much becomes clear. The
one who says nothing good came of this is not yet listening.

-*CLARISSA PINKOLA ESTES*-

AT THE STROKE OF MIDNIGHT, Brendan jumped on my bed, and with one
whisper to Brady, they sang Happy Birthday to me. It was beautiful. The
tears fell freely from my eyes, and they were mixed, with both a sadness of
this day starting without Stephen, and happiness for the kindness that lies
within the heart of my 12 year old. He has it. It is evident and people can
see it. The goodness.

After a so-so night's sleep, I awoke as Brady was sneaking out of the
room to go to his meeting, long enough to get a kiss and drift off back to
sleep again. So thoughtful and kind and loving, Brady has been my one
little thing for many moments in the last month.

Sitting here on a quiet morning, feeling good about staying focused on
this "project", that has been a good thing. As I see the number of words I

am typing continue to grow, I am feeling more confident about what I am doing. I am still not completely sure where it will lead, but I do know that this daily focus has helped me and has allowed me to keep holding the rope.

A couple of notable things from the day.

Brady's parents are so thoughtful, and want so much to be able to comfort me. Knowing that this birthday would be strange for me, they sent me a card, and written on the back of the envelope was "This is not a Birthday card." Inside the card were beautiful words of love, and I felt so thankful to have them both in my life. And, recognizing I was hurting, they did not call purposely, keeping the day low key. She told my husband she couldn't, and did not want to upset me or remind me of my birthday. And I could not help but find that very funny. I am hurting harder than I ever have before, so not acknowledging my birthday seems like an excellent course of action. I totally understood, but my sense of humor is warped. I felt their love and their approach to my special day gave me a huge smile. I found it hilarious. Finally, I called them in the evening, and told them I'd been waiting all day for their singing….and they both sang happy birthday to me. I am thankful.

As far as birthdays go, it was pretty low key this year, and that was much by my choice. As I walked down over the stairs, Brady had a Happy 29th Birthday sign on the foot of the stairs. Breakfast in the fridge, I love you notes everywhere. Big hugs from Brendan, and his obvious desire to make sure I am happy. And, the birthday card in my planner, from last year, from Stephen and Brendan. Handmade, as I liked it. And the words he wrote,

"Thank you for being such a great mother and influence to the both of us. Every day you show us unconditional love and support, and what it's like to be part of a loving family. I hope we can make every 29th birthday as special as you do for us, every day. Love, Stephen."

The great news for me is, as I never intend to go past 29, I will always have a birthday card from Stephen, every year. That is a big thing.

August 4th: Butterflies, Beaches, Books and Brendan

*The sea does not reward those who are too anxious, too
greedy, or too impatient. One should lie empty, open,
choiceless as a beach - waiting for a gift from the sea.*

–Anne Morrow Lindbergh-

A month. Wow. It is so weird to think that a month has passed already.
In some ways, it seems as if it was only yesterday. In others, it appears I
have been on the same roller coaster ride of emotions for an eternity. I am
reflective this morning, over my coffee, thinking back to the people I have
encountered in my own past, who, had loss. I wondered if I looked at them
after a month, and thought that is was time for them to move on, to start
living again. I had an email from an acquaintance just like that. Telling
me it was time to heal. But grief is not like that is it. Grief has no agenda
or schedule. It is what it is, and it can affect you at different moments,
whether it is a week, month, year, or a decade.

There are many one little things again today, even though it seems
they were mixed in with tears. Going to the beach is always a great one
little thing. The ocean, with the rhythmic pattern of the waves, the water washing away the sand, always makes me feel closer to things, closer
to God. As the water crashes down on the sand, and cleans the palate, it

reminds me somewhat of healing. I need that. I need to wash away some of my hurt so I can figure out what my next painting will be.

Brendan's excitement is another little thing that brings me the greatest joy. To see his smiling face, is one of the things that has kept me moving in a forward direction for the past month. He is so excited to see his friend and to simply let off some steam. I know we have tried to live life as much as possible, but I am sure there have been moments where this house has felt like a tomb.

One of the most beautiful things today was the drive itself. We took back roads and drove through some wonderful communities. Old plantation houses, some run down, some renovated back to their days of glory. Amazing little places, in the middle of nowhere. I love the history of the South. It is one of the things I appreciate most about living here, next to of course the weather. The stories are fascinating, and in some ways are ones of perseverance in difficult circumstances. I can relate these days.

As we drive, Brendan made up silly songs to entertain us. But the best part was the butterflies. Oh so many butterflies. Each turn in the road another butterfly would flutter across our path. Almost as if Stephen were urging us down the road, telling us to continue towards the ocean and have a good time.

We are greeted by good friends when we arrive at the cottage. But that descriptor does not adequately describe what an important piece of our life they are. The fact is I don't know what we would do without them really. They are simply "there", not with any expectation of how we should be grieving. They stand on guard, waiting for a moment when we may need them. And when we do, they step in without fanfare, listen, provide comfort, and laugh when we need to laugh. Again, we are blessed.

We get settled in our room and I notice a small wrapped present on the night table. A sweet homemade card offers birthday wishes, again, without fanfare, just kindness. Inside the wrapping paper is a beautiful book, the 50th anniversary edition of Anne Morrow Lindbergh's "Gift from the Sea."

Grabbing the last few moments Oceanside before dusk, we had a quiet evening with Mary, Patrick, the kids and Mary's family. Her family welcomes us with open arms, and her nephew actually bakes me a cake. Kindness surrounds us.

That night, Brendan came into our room and wanted to have a little cuddle before retiring to his own bed. It is funny, as he does not say much, but his actions tell me he needs the comfort just as much as we do right now. And, my main goal is when he feels that he needs us, that he only needs to glance in one direction or another and we will be right there. Not so much physically, but emotionally. I think we are doing a good job at conveying that message to him.

With Brendan cuddled in, I began to read the introduction to my new book aloud to him. Written by the author's daughter, it told her perspective regarding this book, and of her mother. I was fascinated by her use of words, as they were so descriptive, and I could feel her mother's spirit as I read on.

The author was a world renowned aviator, given much public praises for her talents far before any other women had burst on the scene. She was truly a pioneer. But, as I read on, she was much deeper than that. Having lost her first child, she went on from that point in her life to live a deep and meaningful life. This book was a reflection on her part, about how she lived, heart open to all the things in life, good and bad.

So, obviously, this treasure of a read would be one little thing for the day. But bigger than that, the true gift was in the person who gave it to me. So, I explained it to Brendan. "Do you know what reading this introduction tells me? ", I said to Brendan.

"No, what?", as he cuddled in further, listening to the words about this woman.

"It tells me that Mary is one of the most thoughtful and caring friends, and how lucky I am to have her in my life. It tells me that she took a long time to pick out this book, and when she found it, she knew me well enough to know it would be exactly what your Mom needed at this point in her life."

"Okay..." he said. I always love these deep conversations with Brendan. I pour out my heart and soul, and he responds to say he needs to go to the bathroom, or some other one word response. Oh, to be twelve. The great thing is, I know he is hearing me. I know he is listening to my interpretation of the events of our lives over the past month, even if he is not saying so. And, I hope I am setting a good example.

I am thankful, as I hold my baby, and smile at my husband and the tide crashes in on the night sand of the beach.

August 5th: 1812 Overture, Sunshine and Jewel Kissed Waves

I read and walked for miles at night along the beach, writing bad blank verse and searching endlessly for someone wonderful who would step out of the darkness and change my life. It never crossed my mind that that person could be me.

-ANNA QUINDLAN-

I WOKE UP EARLY AFTER a good night's sleep. I lay there for a long time in the quiet. Coming out of a dream, the mornings are still the time when my soul is most peaceful. A rested mind, I am better able to put things in perspective. As the day wanes on, I find that fatigue brings out the highs and lows of my emotions, and my thoughts are more erratic and not so serene. It is good that I recognize that. I think back to when my parents died, and I was unable to recognize much of anything in my grief, because of youth, or denial, or both.

In any case, the mornings are good. It is a great morning for a walk. And, as much as my husband loves me and I love him back, I like my walks on the beach to be solitary. It is then that I am closest to my thoughts and maybe to God when it is just me with the waves and the early morning sunlight.

I set out, baseball hat on, water, and Stephen's iPod. Oh, what comfort this little gadget has given me in the past month. A window into his soul, truly, from the music itself to how he titled his playlists. From this and from his other things I have found, I continue to get to know my son, even after his death. And, I love what I am finding.

I walk the boardwalk to the beach, and the sun is glistening on the water. Feeling good about the lack of beach goers at this early hour, I know this is going to be a stroll that will bring me peace and allow me to gather my thoughts and strength for the day.

I turn on the iPod, and select his Classical playlist. For anyone who is interested in experiencing the magnificence of a walk on the beach on an entirely different level, do so while listening to classical music. Listening to the 1812 overture while watching the pelicans dive down for fish, as the sun glistens across the morning waves is simply splendid. Canon in D and Ave Maria were the closing numbers on my return to the beach house, and a fitting closing to a long dialogue I had with Stephen and God.

I find that I am having conversations more so than what some would call praying. And, as I walked, I would talk, sometimes to Stephen and sometimes to God. I would, as I listened to each different piece, marvel at the fact that this boy was my child. His appreciation for this music makes me so proud! Some of the pieces I know he heard from my father, who had a lifelong love affair with the classics. Others were instrumental versions of songs I would sing to him. As a music student, I would sing to him in Latin and French. Ave Maria, and one other in particular, with the melody of the "Pathetique Movement" by Beethoven, I can recall singing to him on many an occasion as I rocked him in my arms.

I wonder as I walk if he remembered that, and that was why he downloaded the piece from iTunes. Did it give him comfort? Did it remind him of his youth, of us? My own memories only sparked when I listened to his iPod. How funny, just as the Beatles songs reminded me of an afternoon we played hooky and watched a movie. His iPod has been a gift to me.

As I continued walking, I was kind of asking for a sign. Thinking about the butterflies that followed us down the road yesterday, and wanting yet another sign that both he and God were with me and everything would be okay. I looked out over the water, sparkling as if the rarest of jewels had been sewn into the tip of each wave. The water felt cool on my bare feet, and the warm breeze blew softly over me. And, I smiled, thinking that God was saying, "What more do you need Kelly? If you don't see this as a sign everything is okay and we are with you and love you, a butterfly is probably not going to make you feel better." How very true Big Guy. This is some pretty good evidence; I just have to want to see it.

August 6ᵗʰ: Lessons Learned from Falling off the Gratitude Wagon

If one dream should fall and break into a thousand pieces, never be afraid to pick one of those pieces up and begin again.

-FLAVIA WEEDN-

I AM WRITING ABOUT THIS day a few days later. I cannot tell a lie, I had to come back to this one. I made a huge mistake, was caught up in the activities of the beach and skipped this day of writing. I think I thought being at the beach would be enough to carry me through, to keep me in a positive mindset. I don't know if I let myself be distracted by the people or the location, but it was not the right thing to do. Looking back on this day now, I can see the reason I felt off balance was due to the fact I did not write. I did not allow myself that private moment to be balanced. I did not look for the good in the day, and focus on the gratitude. And, as I did not look for it, I did not find it. Instead, I found reasons to be sad and to be overwhelmed. I shifted my perception, and the day was consumed with questions and thoughts. Why did this happen to Stephen? Why did this happen to me? Why does God punish me? Things will never get better. My life is over.

In retrospect, I can see my "one little things" quite clearly. But at the time, that was not the case, and I felt short of breath in a way, my emotions choking the life out of me. But now, I can see, just as with the fifth of July, there were many things that helped me through.

The boys, gone fishing, left Mary and I with some time to sit and chat, which I appreciated so very much. I find it curious that Brendan loves fishing so much, as it requires sitting still and patience, and at 12, those two skills are not always strengths. But, he does. So, that is a good thing for the day, as he is doing something that is giving him great joy.

I so appreciate my quiet time with Mary. My conversations with her are always gratifying, and we share a kinship of sorts, having both lost our parents at a relatively young age. It gives us a perspective on life that is similar, having survived hurt at a time in our lives that we did not have as much wisdom as we needed to process such a life event. I value her opinion, and her gentle soul, and for that I am thankful.

The conversation is extended and long, and that is an understatement. In most cases, I am talking, and my thoughts are random, varied memories or questions asking Mary and the universe how I move forward. When the boys return to the cottage, we leave and just drive around Pawley's Island, and finally just park. And the tears flow for me, as I come to grips with the fact that Stephen is in fact gone forever. We sit in her car, as a butterfly flits around in front of us, and we come to terms with the facts. Even though he was amazing, and good, and one of a kind, he is still gone.

Heading to the beach later that day, I am touched by the kindness, and comfort from both Patrick and Brady. They kept a safe distance when they could sense Mary and I were having deep discussions, and the warm greeting I receive is appreciated.

I am thankful for good friends today.

I am grateful for my tears, and my random thoughts and words. I am happy that I am letting out what is bubbling up inside me; it is helping me come to terms with my new reality. It is helping me put myself back together.

But, the biggest little thing for this day was insight into what I need to do to ensure I survive and thrive in my grief. And that is finding the gratitude in the grief, every day, not just when it is convenient. Finding the little things that will become a bridge over the deep chasm of sadness I feel in my heart.

August 7th: The Big Dig

The wave of the future is coming and there is no fighting it.

- ANNE MORROW LINDBERGH-

THE LAST DAY ON THE beach. Even on the best of days, it leaves you feeling a little sad. I've always found it curious at the end of a week by the sea. You are starting to tire a little of the sand in every orifice, but at the same time, you can't really imagine going back to normal life where you can't look out at the endless sea, the morning horizon seeming a lifetime away. It has been a refreshing few days for me, and I am thankful for the time here, with friends, and with the ocean itself.

Lathered up with the sun screen we headed down to the beach. It is funny, how you can find all of these tasks, jobs and projects when you are at the beach. From setting up gazebos to shoveling sand, everyone seems to find something to do. And, I am one of them, but also see the value in simply sitting and staring at the waves. I always feel like once your toes hit the sand; you regress back to the age of eleven or twelve, regardless of your calendar age. There is simplicity about the beach, and it takes you back, no matter how grown up you may think you are on any other day.

I watch with pride as Brady and Brendan brave the waves and currents in the sea kayak. The waves win. They try again. Waves 2, Boys 0. One more time. Waves 3, Boys 0. But, they try and try again, and that is why I love them so. They don't sit on the shoreline and wonder if they can do it. They just go for it. Brady has been good for us in that regard. He is a doer, and is not afraid of the agony of defeat. He does not hesitate in grasping at the opportunities of life because of the risk of things not going according to plan. I have learned so much from that facet of his personality, as have my children. For that, I am thankful.

In between my observations of the two sea kayakers, I stare out over the sea. I've always been mesmerized at the repetitive motion of the ocean as the waves hit the shoreline and cleanse the palate. I sit and look at that motion for a while, and wonder what I have in my own life that cleanses my palate. Do I have something that wipes away the things of the past and allows me to create a new masterpiece? No, rather I think I get a new set of paints at certain points in my lifetime. A new palate of color that can make the existing painting deeper, and more valuable. This is quite a new set of paints I have these days. I hope God threw in some new brushes as well. One of the things I love to do at the beach is build sand castles or sand creations. There is something wonderful about regressing back to the days of childhood, to immerse yourself in a task with such seriousness, even though it will be, in a few hours, washed away with the coming tide. It is funny when you think about it, as it is the same with life and what you create day to day. Nothing is permanent, and the tide and movement of life will wash away your creations as well. The tide of life naturally removes things and experiences and people from your life. All we are left with is the memory and the mark of love it leaves in our heart.

But, as we are with the tide and the sand castles, we don't just accept the changes we are presented with as part of the cycle of life. We fight it, we complain, we grieve. We mourn what we have lost for so long, we have no ability to see what has arrived, and is sitting right under our noses. Hmm, I think I just hit on something. That is a good little thing.

I am thankful, for my own reflections on this, as well as the ones shared in the book by Anne Morrow Lindbergh.

So, I look at the mound of sand the boys have created for me, trying to decide what to do. In my initial sketches, I had thought I would do a hockey themed creation. A goalie in the net, with a hockey player right there at the tip of the crease. But, for some reason, I could not bring myself to do it. So, instead I decided to build a car. Not a simple task but one I quickly jumped into, carving the main components of the car from the mound of sand. Slowly, the wheels, the doors, the seat, all started to take form. Every year, I forget how much I enjoy the power of creating something. I am reminded of my passion for it at the beach with sand, at Halloween with pumpkins. I also forget that creation requires patience, and at the end, when you persevere, how good it feels. It is, on a smaller scale, a good reminder for me at this time in my writing.

The little kids come, from time to time, as they begin to see what the mound is becoming, and add their two cents, pick up a handful of sand and add to the body of the car. Mary's son, Thomas, is especially passionate about putting his mark on the car, and spends a great deal of time working along side of me. He is so sweet, and as he sits next to me, I am reminded of July 4th, 2008, when Thomas sat next to Stephen for the better part of the afternoon, creating in the sand. Some of the best pictures I have of Stephen were taken on that day.

With the car finished, I left the beach, needing to shower and regroup. I later found out that kids had their pictures taken in the car, and it gave me a smile. And then, I found out about The Big Dig.

About an hour after I had returned from the beach, Brady came to tell me that Brendan and the boys had dug the most amazing hole. Yes, you read that right. The pleasures from being at the beach are simplified. The need for complex video games or material things is stripped away. The ocean takes you back to your core, what makes you happy on the inside. I walked back down to the beach, to see this creation. I will admit, when Brady came barreling into the cottage to tell me I needed to see the hole, I was not initially intrigued, thinking if you've seen one, you've seen them all. But, to my surprise, this was an impressive digging project! I saw not only Brendan, but all of the men/boys from our group, shoveling and yelling at each other as they created a canal from our position on the beach all the way to the ocean. It was a grand canal that ran uphill from the shoreline. And, they were convinced that the ocean water would flow uphill to reach the pinnacle, the hole that Brendan dug. I walked towards the large gaping orifice in the sand, and looked down to see the most wonderful sight. My boy, covered in sand from head to toe, digging, telling the boys to "Keep going!"

The funny thing was the boys, in their determination, had pulled in the interest of other families on the beach. They had a bet with some young couples sitting just down from us that they would make it work. It was so funny. The young man who made the bet would periodically inspect their work, egging them on in a good natured way, telling them he did not think they could make it happen.

And, when nature helped them out and filled the canal with water, the young man complied with the terms of the bet and delivered ice cream to the boys. It was a wonderful thing to watch my boy, with his buddies, eating ice cream in the hole. It was more than one little thing. It was a big thing, as he had a sense of accomplishment and joy. That joy still existed for him; he was still able to find it, just as I was, when you looked for it.

It was as if the day did not want to end, or perhaps it was that we did not want it to conclude. The last day at the beach is like that. As the sun started to set, the last moments of the beach savored, all was good.

August 8th: Home Again, Home Again, Jiggity Jig...

Where we love is home, home that our feet
may leave, but not our hearts.

-OLIVER WENDELL HOLMES-

ALL GOOD THINGS COME TO an end. And today, it is time to go home. In one regard, I am glad to be returning. I've missed my haven a little; I've missed Rudy the Wonder Dog. But, on the other hand, I am hesitant. Reality once again waits for me. Life is very real at the home base, with his bags on my bedroom floor, his things sitting on his bed, the pictures in frames around the house.

But, it is time, so off we go back to life as we know it. The drive is pleasant, and once again, I am greeted with multitudes of butterflies on the road.

Arriving home, we exhale. It is always such a pleasure to come home when a dog is part of your family. No matter if you've been gone for two minutes or two months, they greet you with an enthusiasm that warms your heart. Dogs show us how to love unconditionally, and Rudy is particularly good at it.

Rudy has been a valued teacher for me since Stephen's death. He has been faithful, sitting next to me that morning in the cove or at my feet as I compose my daily thoughts of gratitude. He serves as confirmation of the love that is around me every day, with the wag of his tail. His eyes are old, and knowing, as if he can sense all that we feel. And, in his doggy way, I feel he hurts too. I am thankful to see him.

The rest of the evening is quiet. We are all adjusting to being back in our home surroundings. And, although we don't speak about it, it seems as if we all feel the same thing. The ache has returned.

That evening, we sit to watch a movie, and I notice we are all piled onto the same couch. It is as if we are clinging to each other for dear life. Perhaps we are. I am thankful. Because, even though I ache, I am not alone.

August 9th: Deep Chats, with my Husband and the Big Guy

Faith is the bird that feels the light and
sings when the dawn is still dark.

- RABINDRANATH TAGORE-

AH, SUNDAY MORNINGS. LOTS TO be thankful for on Sunday mornings. Waking up in my own bed, the sun shining, the quiet of the house and getting back to my writing. I always get a sense of renewal as we plan to embark on a new week. I don't know what it says about my personality, but I do enjoy the preparing. I say that knowing that as much as I plan, I cannot plan for everything, I cannot make life go in the way I want 100% of the time, that's for sure.

On this Sunday morning, Brady and I take some time to talk openly and honestly about how we feel. I appreciate how truthful we are with each other. I longed for this kind of communication in earlier relationships in my life, and our marriage is a gift. We cope with grief very differently, and it is good to have a checkpoint chat to make sure we are both moving in the same direction. I recognize my introversion and introspection may appear to others that I am shutting them out. I want to make sure he never feels that way. I also know that Brady's happy exterior does not always reveal what is going on in that head of his. I could see him laugh at a joke at the beach, but I noticed he could not bring himself to play Bocce ball, a reminder of his happier times with Stephen. So, it is good for us to lay things out on the table.

Life is imperfect and messy. But I am glad I have someone like him to work through the mess.

One of the things we talk about is taking the right steps to keep ourselves in the right frame of mind. We have not always been good at self nurturing, and we really need to take care of ourselves right now.

We talk about the crutches in our lives, and how we want to live, without Stephen here with us physically. We talk about eliminating any negative and toxic forces that are around us, as we are no longer able to deal with it anymore. We talk about faith, and our trust in God.

I am blessed. Because, I know that talking about feelings must feel like a trip to the dentist for Brady. But, he does it just the same, because he loves me.

And finally, it hit me today. I've realized that my writing has in fact been my conversation of sorts with God. Not in a prophet, or Neale Donald Walsh kind of way, but in an individual reflection on faith kind of way. I've been having this ongoing conversation with Him for over four weeks now. I've been working through this with Him, and He has not left my side. Not since I asked Him to help me. Not since I just surrendered and trusted in the fact He was listening. Because, to be honest, I did not know what else to do. And, I knew I needed help, fast. And somehow, since I made that choice, I've realized that I should have known to trust Him well before now. You see, He showed me a long time ago He knew what He was doing. He showed me with Stephen.

This grief stuff is sure making me deep. But, it is a good deep. I am thankful.

August 10th: Stephen's Computer and the Effects of Writing on my Soul

To me, the greatest pleasure of writing is not what it's about, but the inner music the words make.

~TRUMAN CAPOTE, MCCALL'S, NOVEMBER 1967-

IT IS A PRODUCTIVE DAY, in a weird kind of way. From the perspective of housework, it would not appear productive. My house is "up around my ears", and the dust bunnies have names and are starting to receive mail.

But it is an industrious day just the same. I am making emotional steps forward, and I am dusting out some rooms in my mind that have not been visited in a long, long time. I am reflecting on Stephen's life, and in the process, I am learning about my own. When I step back, and look at this for what it is, I am simply amazed and impressed. I still have no valid answers for how this started, but I am thankful I've kept it going.

So, I am thankful today for the progress. I am scared, but I am brave at the same time. I was lost, as I sat on the shoreline July 5th. I had no idea where my life would go from that moment. And, to be perfectly honest, I still don't know. But, I am figuring it out. I know I can never go back to being the same person I was and that scares me, because I know nothing else. And I have not yet figured out who this new Kelly will be. I am finding myself, and that sounds cheesy, like I am having a midlife meltdown.

This personal discovery is coming to me from the writing, and through my tears. Today, I am thankful for the very words I have typed everyday. They have saved me, from myself and from my sorrow.

Later in the day, I take some time to look at Stephen's computer. It is funny, as I tried to look at it shortly after his death, and it would not work. It was as if Stephen was not ready to share his thoughts with us. Today, I once again take some time to go through his emails, documents. There are no big surprises or shockers in what is on his hard drive. The contents serve as additional confirmation that he was authentic, and was exactly who I thought he was. It is bittersweet for me to think that and to type it, as I am both comforted by the confirmation and saddened that he was taken away.

I smile as I look at his ultimate Montreal Canadiens Roster, built from players that played on the team since its inception 100 years ago. I love that he took the time to do that, and it tells me he was quirky like his mother. He also had an excel sheet outlining all of his hockey statistics, for his entire college hockey experience. Every shot, every save, the goals against average, he recorded all of it. This speaks volumes about his personality. I am thankful for the personal look into his life, but at the same time, my heart is broken all over again. I read some of his emails, and I see the excitement he had over the life he was building. He was feeling good about the future, had great friends, and so many people who loved him. His life was a combination of boy and man, and he was getting ready to start the next chapter. I cry hard now, and cross my arms over my chest, as if I need some sort of brace to keep my heart from falling out on the floor. It hurts so much.

But, I am thankful. Not for the loss, but for what I am learning. Here's some of what I have so far:

Life is short and precious.
Good times or bad, you've got to have faith.
I am stronger than I thought I was.
God is with me.
Stephen's spirit is all around me.
There is more good in this world than bad.
The moments that crush you can transform you. .

I miss him desperately. I am learning and I am changing. I am thankful.

August 11th: "Guidance"

No man is great enough or wise enough for any of us to
surrender our destiny to. The only way in which anyone can
lead us is to restore to us the belief in our own guidance.

–HENRY MILLER-

I'VE BEEN THINKING A LOT today. The wheels are turning and the theme is guidance. I've had a lot of people offer me guidance and advice in my life. Some was good and some was bad. Some was requested and some was just given to me no matter how I protested.

Everyone needs guidance in their lives at one point or another. As the song goes, *No Man is an Island.*

As of late, I have received direction from many as I journey through grief. It has helped us so much. But, I have to be truthful, there are some tidbits of wisdom that have been offered that honestly made me tilt my head to the right and just wonder. First, let's talk about the good stuff. "The Grief Lady" has been amazing, and has helped us in so many ways. She has not pulled us in a certain direction, but rather allowed us to discover our own path in our own time. Through her gentle facilitation, we have found what worked for us as a family. The self discovery has been tremendously helpful for us, as well as her gentle reassurances that we are, in fact normal.

But, we have also received advice, opinion and so called guidance that is 100% outlandish. Let me give you some examples:

"It is never really going to get any better, and you
just need to make peace with that."
"It is good and healthy to be angry, and you shouldn't deny
your anger. You may be angry for the rest of your life."
"This is the worst thing anyone can go through in life and you will
never be the same. If I were in your shoes, I would wish for
death."
"It is August now, and it is time to move on."
"It's time to get back to work and keep moving, it will help you."
"I know you miss your child, but you can't be like my friend, who turned
their house into a shrine. I feel so uncomfortable when I visit them."

And my personal favorite from my physician, said to me during a routine visit for a renewal of a thyroid prescription. Note: I did **not** say I was depressed.

"Let's talk about Paxil and Prozac."

The list could go on and on. I know that people really did mean well, but did they think about how their messages would be received? Perhaps not, I think they struggled to find anything to say to me, and this is the only statement they could muster. In some ways, I would rather have something like this than the silence from other acquaintances, who avoid me like I have leprosy. Neither group is truly upsetting to me, it is just funny how people deal with people who are grieving, especially in a tragic and unexpected death.

Now, take a moment to reflect on all of the statements, even the physician's instant assumption that because I was sad, I was depressed. A common theme emerges. People are uncomfortable with grief. They want you to move on from it, bury it, put away the photos, and just make peace with the fact it will never get better. People don't want to look at it; society feels better if we medicate such emotions. Smooth out the rough edges of life if you will.

But we can only learn from it if we look right at it. Medicating the hurt does not make the pain go away. It numbs it. Stop taking the pills and you are back to square one.

So, in my analysis of these off the wall statements, I can't help but reflect on my past and some of the wacky things I have been told all in the name of "guidance".

Don't get me wrong. I've had wonderful teachers in my life. I would have the best, most life changing chats with my parents, with my Aunt Lorraine. And, as I have reflected on earlier in this record, some of the people who have caused me the most friction in my life have actually taught me a great deal as well.

One particular memory of guidance comes to mind today. I am back in high school, standing in the guidance counselor room, looking with interest and excitement at the brochures for the universities in Atlantic Canada. It is scary and exciting to think about going away for higher education, as I have a lot to consider. I have Stephen, and my mind is somewhat confused as I contemplate the need for university education and the effect it will have on my parenting. On the best of days, with my youth and inexperience, I feel inadequate as a mother, watching my parents or older siblings and wondering why it seems to come so naturally to them. But, in my heart, I know that becoming educated beyond this moment will be the only way for me to truly give Stephen what I know he deserves. And thankfully, I have a family that agrees with me and both encouraged and supported me through that learning so I could give Stephen a better life. So, I stand there looking at all of the information. I snuck in the room quietly, without any of my friends, feeling unsure about this and so much more in my life. I've worked to get good grades, and I know I should be able to go to the school of my choice. But I am scared.

And, as if she could read my mind and was feeding off my inner dialogue, the guidance counselor approaches. Genevieve, a small and frail woman, whose paper thin appearance did not match her abrasive and aggressive approach in communication. She had this inherent ability to get under my skin, and her very being oozed judgment. Just the individual you wanted to have in a position designed to encourage young people to reach for their dreams.

"What are you looking at Kelly?" She asked, with a hint of something in her voice I could not quite place, but knew it was not genuine curiousity or kindness.

"I'm looking at the brochures for school. My mom and dad wanted me to bring them home so we could read about the different options."

And then it happened. And although it is well over 20 years ago, I can remember it like it was yesterday.

"Kelly, you need to be realistic, university is not for someone like *you*."

Her words hit me like a sledge hammer in the chest, and I felt the lump grow instantaneously in my throat.

"You need to take care of your child, and you can't do what everyone else is doing anymore."

"But this is how I will take care of my child. By becoming educated; and I've already talked about it with my Mom and...." My words were cut off mid sentence, as she interjected with her confident judgment.

"Kelly, your life has a plan now, and you should not think you will be able to do this." she said. She was positive in her appraisal of my situation, although I do believe it was the first one on one conversation I had with the woman. She did not know me, my family support system, she did not know I was on the Honor Roll, she did not know my personal ambition. She certainly did not know my love for Stephen.

And, although I was raised to be a respectful girl, I could feel the lava bubbling up from within me, and I knew I could not stop it.

"You can't tell me what I can and can't do. You don't know me. I will see you in ten years!" I said emphatically. Typing the words makes it appear as if I had control over my emotions, but the truth is, my voice was at least two octaves higher than usual, and my neck was blotchy. My neck looks like a road map in times of conflict, with blotches showing up in an instant, and bears a resemblance to a map of Europe.

And, with that, I turned on my heel and walked out of the room, never to speak with her again. In fact, I ignored her, even when she spoke to me directly. I suppose I could have had issues with treating a teacher like that, but for some reason, she had made the smart decision not to approach it.

And, ten years later, I thought about her. I was educated, and working in a great position and giving Stephen the things I wanted, and she came to mind, one day, out of the blue.

GUIDANCE

The very word brings me back to that day. And it is a good thing to re-member. For with this trip down memory lane, I am reminded that the best guidance for your own life can only truly come from you, and the Big Guy upstairs of course.

You are the only one who understands all of the moving parts of your life, your inner strength that no one else can see, but you know exists.

You can listen to different points of view of course, but you need to find out how to tap into the kind of guidance that you can rely on 100% of the time.

That internal guidance comes from becoming quiet and still. Quiet the voices, both outside and inside your head. Become still, and release the need for constant motion. Trust your gut. Talk to God. And then wait. Sometimes, we veer off in the wrong direction because we are not patient enough to wait for the answer.

And, as I have found, the answers will come.

Now, if I could figure out how to put that in every school counseling room in every school, the future of the world would be bright indeed.

I am thankful.

August 12th: The Blubbering Driver

I find the great thing in this world is not so much where we
stand, as in what direction we are moving: To reach the port of
heaven, we must sail sometimes with the wind and sometimes
against it, but we must sail, and not drift, nor lie at anchor

-OLIVER WENDELL HOLMES-

Wow, I've been holding a lot inside. Because this morning, it appears that I have burst. Driving to hockey camp, Brendan and I were quietly chatting. And he asked, "Do you think Stephen knew what was going to happen to him?"

And I did not have an answer. For years, I have wondered that same question about my dad's heart attack. Always keeping his keys secure and belongings safe, he left his entire set of keys in the mailbox on the morning he collapsed. Days before that, he had a weird conversation with me about the family home, and his will. It kind of shocked me to think that Brendan had those same feelings, similar questions. I did not know how to answer, only to say I did not think so, but did not know. After dropping Brendan off at hockey camp, I pulled out of the Ice House parking lot, and the tears in my eyes began to flow, and then actually shot from my eyes like a dam bursting. By the time I started to drive down the road, in morning traffic, I was openly sobbing, collapsing with a grief that overwhelmed me, encompassed me, enveloped the car, and made it difficult for me to breathe.

Note to self: start carrying tissues and always have sunglasses within arm's reach. I just can't explain it, because I like to think I am a smart person. But, since this happened, I cannot, for the life of me, remember to put some tissues in my purse. I am a grown woman who has been using her sleeve for over a month now.

I did not make direct eye contact with the people next to me in morning traffic. But, I could feel their eyes on me as I sobbed, mouth open with my head kind of hung over the steering wheel, waiting for the light to turn green. Even through my tears, I could imagine that they were surmising the reason for my waterworks. Perhaps I just found out my husband was leaving, the dog ran away, or, in this culture, my Botox appointment had been cancelled. I just kept looking forward. That is what I do. I keep looking forward, whether it is to hide from onlookers, or to get through a trial in life. Because really, what is the alternative?

So, where is the good thing in this? I suppose, after some reflection, it is the fact that I am letting it out. I am letting my tears cleanse my soul, to wash away some of the hurt. Instead of looking away from all of this, I am looking at it. I am realizing that in order for me to come out on the other side, with my lessons in my pocket, I have to grieve. I have to face the reality that my precious little baby is no longer here. He is not away at school, or at work, or visiting in Canada. He is gone.

I am thankful that I hurt. Because through the hurt, I am taking from this that I need to become a more compassionate human being. I am thankful for the pain, because it is much like an emotional GPS, and is taking me on a journey through Stephen's life and my own. Through the pain of this voyage, I am writing and capturing whatever I can before the ache subsides, and things like laundry and bills and life numb the hurt, and make me forget all these lessons.

August 13th: How a Healed Heart Loves and Grieves...

*Faith is the bird that feels the light and
sings when the dawn is still dark.*

-RABINDRANATH TAGORE-

TODAY, I DID NOT CRY like a baby as I was driving. That is a good "one little thing". I did not have to avoid eye contact with drivers in the lane next to me. I did not have to wipe my nose with my sleeve. All good. All progress in my mind. I did cry. But I was home, I had a tissue, and there was no morning traffic to navigate. It is amazing to me how I am letting it out. I have always suppressed my emotions before this, thinking that it was a sign of weakness. Thinking I could not live the persona of this tough cookie if I collapsed in tears, or let people see me admit to my imperfections.

But truly, my emotions have been softening for some time now, well before Stephen's death. Truly, it has been since my husband Brady. I've found that since he became intertwined with my soul, I see the beauty and wonder of the world, things I did not even notice before him. I think I was afraid to feel things in the extreme, whether that be good or bad. I was comfortably numb. Having had some hurt from the past, I had closed my heart. I never thought I would love again. And then, he arrived in my life, bounding in like a bull in a china shop. And since that moment, I have seen the world in color, no more black and white, but vivid color.

So, today, I am thankful for a few big things. First, I am grateful for Brady showing up in our life, coming together and finding each other in the most unlikely of circumstances. If that had not happened, I would still have been that closed, hurt woman, keeping people emotionally at arm's length. If it had not been for this man, I would not have loved Stephen so freely in the last years of his life! Oh my God! This is huge. I've been thinking for 39 days about how he was the fertilizer that allowed Stephen to blossom. But truly, he was the fertilizer for all of us. He helped us and through his unconditional love, showed all of us how to have a relationship that was richer and fuller. Where would I be in my grief right now, if he had not entered our lives? To be honest, it scares me to think about it. Stephen and I had always had a beautiful relationship, but the last four years had been the most magical. Funny what being happy can do for all of your relationships. So, I am thankful for Brady, but unsure if he would appreciate me describing him as fertilizer.

And today, I am also thankful for my boy Brendan. My wonderful boy, who jumps out of bed and gets ready for hockey camp with no complaints. He is stiff and sore from the week, but he is tough stuff. After camp, we go for lunch, and then to Target for school supplies. He is a joy, and we take pleasure in a light conversation at lunch. I ask him what his favorite color is, and he says very definitively, "I have two, red and blue. I don't think you need to limit yourself to just one. "

We talk about silly things. We act normal. Every now and again, we catch a glimpse of each other, and we know the pain still sits behind our smiles, but we push on. We check off all the items on the school supply list. We have a long and detailed conversation about erasable pens versus pencils, and Brendan expresses his concern over the quality in erasable pens on the market today. I smile as he lists out all the reasons.

I am thankful because he is stronger and more resilient than I. He keeps me going, he makes me brave enough to leave the house and shop for school supplies and go for lunch. He is helping me move forward, because I see him doing it, and I know he deserves a childhood, happiness, and so much more. If he was not here, I don't know if I would bother, and it scares me to contemplate that truth. So, I am thankful for him.

We arrive home, to Rudy the Wonder Dog, waiting patiently for us, nibbling at the garbage as he killed time.

We have work to do this evening. Stephen's friends have called, and are coming to spend the weekend with us. Imagine that. These boys, in their prime, with many other things on their agenda I am sure, choosing to come and spend a weekend with a grieving family. That is another little thing that speaks volumes about those boys, and about Stephen. Brendan is excited, as they have told him to be prepared with his "A" game for Frisbee golf. So, we go upstairs to prepare the rooms for them. The guest room and Stephen's room. There is an unspoken discomfort as we change the sheets and dust off the night table. Finally Brendan breaks the silence and asks, "Do you think they should sleep in here?"

I say, "Well, I am not sure. What do you think? It is up to you. If that is what you want to do, and what you feel comfortable with, let's do that. I want you to be comfortable. So, let's do whatever makes you feel good."

"I'm just not sure *they* would want to sleep in here. Maybe I should." he said.

"Good point", I said. "You think on it, and I will trust your judgment on this."

It is funny to work through this with Brendan. I am learning from him. He is expressing things I too am feeling, but I dismiss them at times because I feel I need to be grown up. To be honest, when I heard the boys were coming, I felt exactly like Brendan did, but only worse. I was not ready for any guests to stay in his bedroom, it was his. His things were in there. Let's both think about it.

As we finish our preparations, Brendan and I laugh over some silly things, and pull Brady into our jokes as well. His smile is like an elixir for my soul. To see that he can still smile and laugh that rich full belly laugh gives me hope that someday, I may find my own laughter again. I am thankful.

August 14th: Seeing the Boys

I am beginning to learn that it is the sweet, simple
things of life which are the real ones after all.

–LAURA INGALLS WILDER-

I AM NERVOUS. AND, I don't know why. The boys are coming to see us
this weekend. Two of Stephen's closest friends, Ross and Nathan. They
are wonderful men, and I like them both very much. They have stayed
in touch with us since the 4th, and Brady and I continue to marvel at the
character of the individuals our son associated with. But, I am edgy.

I have not seen them since the memorial. The last month has been a
flurry of activity with travel and milestones, and this will be the first time
we will be face to face. I am apprehensive, although I don't know why. I
suppose it stems from the fact that I have some questions about "the day",
things I did not ask when we were in the midst of the crisis. Perhaps it is
not seeing the boys that make me nervous. Rather, maybe it is what the
answers to my questions could potentially be.

When you lose someone you love more than life itself, it is tough. You
think about the times you will no longer have with them, occasions like
graduation from college, weddings, and grandchildren.

But when you lose someone tragically and suddenly, you think about more than the lost moments of the future. You think, over and over, about the final moments of that person's life. You wonder what they felt, if they hurt, suffered, felt hopeless or alone. I've found myself, thinking these thoughts, having the same recurring questions cycling in my mind. And, when I knew they would not fade away, I knew I had to ask the boys, the people who were with him in his last moments on earth. So, I suppose my apprehension lay in my fear of the answers, and in my discomfort in knowing I HAD to ask the questions they probably did not want to revisit.

Was it fair for me to do that to them? They had stood with me at the lake, maybe they had been through enough? But, good or bad, I knew I had to talk to them, to be able to move forward from these inconclusive thoughts circling my mind.

Thinking about all those things, I cleaned the house, preparing for their arrival. I find that I have let go of a lot of the trivial things in my life since Stephen's passing. Unfortunately, housework has been one of those things. I could use a Hazmat crew to assist me.

Later that night, the boys arrive, and Brendan is so excited. They are a direct connection with his older brother, and he needs this. This is important to him, and I can see his joy as he greets them.

So, in terms of gratitude, what can I find today? First, the boys themselves. They had choices when this happened, and I am so thankful they decided to stand by us. It would have been easier and less uncomfortable for them to bolt. And, I think I would have understood. But truly, their presence in our lives has helped us like no therapy or sympathy card ever could. They have helped us connect the dots, and tell the story of Stephen. They have helped us more than they will ever know.

And, I am thankful for my questions, no matter how I lament over saying them aloud to the boys. It is confirmation that I am working through it. My questions are normal, and I need to ask them to help me understand and accept this very big change in our lives. The answers will help me in navigating this journey not only for me, but for Brendan.

Grateful for my courage, I will ask these questions and that is new for me. In the past, I have hesitated in asking questions or expressing feelings that would help me heal, so this is a big step.

But, alas, no matter how much this gratitude stuff is working wonders for this grieving mother, I am still not thankful for housework.

August 15th: It's a Beautiful Day in the Neighborhood.

Let us be grateful to people who make us happy-they are
the charming gardeners who make our souls blossom.

–Marcel Proust-

I AWAKE IN THE MORNING, with a smile, and that is one little thing to be thankful for indeed. That has not happened in what seems to be an eternity. I can hear the rumblings downstairs, and it seems the boys have risen earlier than me. They are on a mission and have big plans for Disc Golf with Brendan. I hear the three of them leave the house, and I lay there and listen to the car start and drive away. I know how much this means to Brendan, and I am so, so thankful that Stephen had the kind of friends who would understand this. The noise downstairs on a Saturday morning initially sends one of those electric shocks through my heart, reminding me of the mornings when Stephen and Brendan would be up early on a weekend, off for some adventure. Those electric shocks are starting to lessen, but I still find they hit me hard at the oddest moments, when I am reminded of something related to my sweet boy.

Brady and I take advantage of the time alone and have a peaceful breakfast together, reflecting on the visit, and how blessed we are. With yard work on the agenda, he quickly gets to work. I marvel at how hard he labors, and how he takes pride in a job well done. I look outside, but don't join him. I have not really stepped back into the neighborhood as of yet, and I am not sure if I am ready to talk to people. Not that I don't appreciate their kindness, because this tragedy has shown us we have amazing neighbors. I am just afraid I will collapse or crumble in front of their very eyes. From a distance, I can look like I am doing okay. Up close, you can see all the cracks. And lately, I am like a piece of fine china that was dropped on the floor, and then stepped on by an elephant. I could crumble to dust at any moment.

I work quietly inside for a while, and then see Brady talking to our neighbor Mike in the driveway. Mike is a wonderful neighbor. He and his wife, Andrea, have been so kind to us. They came to us immediately when they heard the news, and they've been checking in ever since. Mike is a minister, and he gave me two books before we left for Newfoundland, and they helped me tremendously. So, when I saw him there, I wanted to say hello. I felt brave.

And, as I walked out the driveway, I was brave, and I was okay. Until I opened my mouth. And I found the most amazing thing. Anything I tried to say made me cry.

So, I went with it. I accepted this was where I was and I talked to him through the tears. It felt good to tell him about the outpouring of love we had experienced, to tell him about Stephen. It felt good to speak to him about our faith and our "conversation with God" since Stephen's death. And here I was, this private girl who always walked her path alone when it came to emotional hardship, standing in her driveway bawling her eyes out, waving to the neighbors as they drove by, tears running down my face. Either I really have finally figured it out, or I've finally lost it.

It felt really good. I was proud of myself, as it was a huge step on my healing. And, when we talked about faith, Mike made the greatest suggestion. He said he sometimes suggests that people write letters to themselves from God. To answer the question, "What would God say to me?" He explained that if we believe that the Holy Spirit is in all of our hearts, we are qualified to write that letter. And sometimes it can really help.

What an interesting idea! I appreciated the suggestion, and said I would try it. Inwardly, I knew I was not ready for that. We'll see.

Later that day, the boys returned, having had a great morning, minus some wasp stings. Bounding into the house, I saw the look on Brendan's face, and knew this weekend would be a turning point for him. His hat on backwards, smiling and joking, I knew he would be okay. I was thankful.

They both show us their tattoos as well. In memory of Stephen, they both proudly display "One Lifetime". They explain that others on the team have also been "inked" in his memory. I am thankful.

I had a chance to have some quiet time with just Ross and Nate, as Brendan had a hockey practice. He and Brady took off and I sat with the boys, and had my list of questions. They were gracious, and quiet, and I did wonder if they thought I was a loon when I walked in the living room with a bulleted list of questions about the day Stephen died. Even typing it, I think I am a little wacky. But I had to do it this way. It was so emotionally charged. If I did not write it down, I would have missed something, forgot to ask one thing because I was upset. And I promised myself and them that I only wanted to have this conversation once. I did not want them to feel that every time they saw me, I would have more questions about July 4th.

And the second purpose of the conversation was to talk about our theory about what happened to Stephen. With the hard hit at hockey, the coughing up of blood and the severe pain earlier that day in his chest, we thought it may have been a clot. Sadly, this medical emergency presented itself when he was swimming. I really wanted to talk to the boys about this, especially Ross. He tried valiantly to save Stephen, and I wanted to lessen the burden, and let him know that even if his efforts had been successful, it may not have changed the outcome. It has been something I had to tell him, and in some ways, I feel Stephen wanted him to know that. And finally, I wanted them to know that everyone has a time. And, there is a plan. I believe it, even though I don't have a copy of the manual.

The conversation goes well, although it is uncomfortable. I can't lie about that. The topic is heavy, and we all have been forever changed by the loss of Stephen. I have questions that they don't have answers for, topics I will not understand until I see Stephen again. But I am glad we took the time to talk together. Later that evening, the chats are lighter, and filled with laughter. We talk with Nathan about being an identical twin, and how surprised we were to see his brother at the memorial. He is intrigued about how Stephen gravitated towards twins in his lifetime, and tells us stories of his own experience. And Ross shows us the pictures of a bench he is building in Stephen's memory. In the shape/design of a Canadian Flag, it will be beautiful, and he plans to place it at a course on campus where Stephen and he played many a game.

We plan for the morning, as we are driving to Raleigh to get Stephen's belongings. They have been in storage, and Phil, his roommate is back in town.

I am thankful. For these two boys, who blocked off the entire weekend to simply be with us. I am thankful for what their visit and presence in Brendan's life has done with regards to his grief. I am thankful for my sobs in the driveway and my chat with Mike. I am anxious and thankful about tomorrow. I want to touch his things, but I am so scared, as tomorrow will serve as another confirmation that he is not away at school, he is gone.

August 16th: Well Packed Storage Unit, My Own Phoenix Process, the Love of College Boys, and Brendan's Need for Answers.

Only when we are no longer afraid do we begin to live in every experience, painful or joyous, to live in gratitude for every moment, to live abundantly.

-*DOROTHY THOMPSON*-

WE AWAKE EARLY ON THIS Sunday morning. I sit on the edge of the bed, again. I stare at the bags, again. Good morning bags. How are you? The same? That's terrific. Oh, and me? Slightly short of breath and anxious. Why, you say? Well, my husband and I are driving up to collect my dead son's things from a storage unit, and I'm not really in the mood. You know, not feeling like I want to have my heart broken all over again. Tears wash the sleep from my eyes. And, for the record, my conversation with the knapsack was my lame attempt at sarcasm, I really am okay.

I stare at the bag for another little while, thinking that later today, there will be other bags and boxes I will have difficulty moving or unpacking, as if they have been nailed to the floor. But, time keeps moving, and we can't just leave the stuff up there. Nor would I want to.

My husband, who would do anything to protect me, asks me one more time if I really want to do this. He has said for some time that he could go without me, but I want to be there. It is much like the knapsack on the floor; I need to see this storage unit. I remember talking to him that day as he and Phil were moving their things in there for the summer. He and I laughed together as he described them piling their belongings into the unit. I had to see it for myself, as he touched these things. He piled all of his stuff in there, in anticipation of his senior year at college. He talked to me about this being the last time he would have to move this stuff and we joked as we knew the majority of the things he had moved from place to place in his college years would be ready for the trash by graduation. He was, after all a boy living with boys.

So, although I appreciated Brady's valiant efforts to protect me from the pain, I knew that experiencing the pain was part of it. And I also knew if I did not go, I would have regretted it. No regrets.

Brendan left for Raleigh earlier, wanting to go to church with Ross and Nathan before meeting us at the storage facility. That makes me smile, as he was curious about their church, and was pumped about the possibility of spending more time with college age boys. So, they were up earlier than us on the second day in a row, and off they went.

Through all of "this", I have noticed some changes in myself. Prior to July 4th, I would have been stressed or pressured about being up at the crack of dawn, or lamenting over Brendan going with the boys, or having everything just perfect. But lately, I've just let a lot of that stuff go. I don't have time to be that way anymore. I know that does not mean I still won't exhibit that neuroses from time to time, but it has been freeing to not worry so much about the small stuff. And, what has surprised me even further, is, even when I wasn't worrying about it, the small stuff still had a way of working itself out. In exactly the way I wanted it to work out! My gosh, how many hours have I wasted on that alone?

So, with Brendan off with the boys, Brady and I had a quiet drive to Raleigh, where we chatted, about Stephen, the days, memories. It was tough, and our conversation was a little tentative at best. It was as if we could not completely exhale in anticipation of the day. I had many thoughts about what we would find in the storage unit. I hoped for many things, although I could not articulate exactly what. I suppose in a perfect world, I would love to find a letter, laying out his entire life and feelings, written to me to explain it all in the case of his untimely death. "In case of emergency, break glass and read letter." Not quite realistic.

We arrived at the storage unit with two sets of keys, hoping that one of those sets had the key to the lock on the door. Phil had told us that Stephen had the only key. And, as if he was with us, and I think he was, the first key worked and the lock clicked open with ease.

We stood there for a moment, pausing for an instant, knowing when the metal door clicked open; we would receive another wallop in the face from reality. I wish reality would stop smacking me. My cheeks are flushed and burning these days from the sting of life.

And then it opened. And we looked at this most amazing packing job that could only have been completed so creatively by two twenty something boys who just wanted to get the stuff in there so the summer could begin. Stephen was always a great person for packing things. I suppose it came from the numerous moves we made, or the numerous hockey trips. Goalie gear is not small, and sometimes, we were hard pressed to find a cubic centimeter of free space in the vehicle. He was brilliant at consolidating a large amount of "stuff", organizing it in a way that only he could. And disassembling the masterpiece when you arrived at your destination was no simple undertaking. In many cases, he would have to take the lead, as the process of unpacking was as precarious as cutting the wires on a bomb or playing a life sized version of Jenga. One wrong move and you would be found under a mound of smelly hockey gear and dirty laundry after a long weekend of travel.

The storage unit was no different, and I could not help but smile at the sheer amount of personal effects that had been crammed into the very small space. Boxes and furniture were balanced at angles that any master mathematician would want to study. It was Stephen.

Phil and Ben arrived shortly after we opened the unit, and we hugged. But we also shuffled our feet, looked to the ground periodically, and made small talk. It was great to see them, as I had not since the memorial, since

Ben had sent the beautiful letter. But there was an unspoken hurt that hovered over all of us, as the person we really wanted to unpack this stuff was not here. Speaking briefly, they quickly got to work, removing items with care, and separating out Stephen's belongings from the pile.

We knew it would take several trips to get it all out and delivered, so Brady offered to make the trips with the boys, and I decided to stay at the storage unit, and continue to go through some things.

Being alone there at the storage unit, it was as if he was sitting with me, awaiting the return of Brady and the boys. I quietly went from box to box, looking inside, assessing the contents. But, I could not do that for long. I sat in his desk chair, with the pink flowered seat cushion, letting the late morning sun shine down on me. I looked around at the boxes and the furniture and I cried a little. Then I cried a little more. It was so hard. I wished I could close my eyes and wish for this all to be erased, to go back to July 3rd, and to change the course of history. I would not be here in the hot sun waiting to pack up his belongings. Perhaps we would be helping him move into his new apartment with Ross, laughing and joking and feeding off his excitement as he entered into his senior year. We would help them, as we did last year, and we would take him to lunch, and hug him lots, and slip him some money, and then let him get back to his life. But, not this year. This year, we were here, but only to pick up the remaining pieces of his life and bring them home. There was no level of anticipation in that task, just plain old sadness.

And, as I look through some of the boxes, I can feel him. I can feel his spirit and his love all around me. I look around, and expect for some reason to see a butterfly, but it is not there. But, he is. I don't need the confirmation of the butterfly, as he is with me. And his presence is not much different than when he was alive. It is quiet, as we never really needed a lot of words. And the moment is filled with love. So much love.

I decided to read a little of my book to pass the time. I thought it would be a better option, rather than to continue to touch his things, and have the boys return and find me collapsed with grief, clutching onto a pair of his socks and crying outside a storage unit. I am reading some great books, and this one has been tremendously helpful. *"Broken Open-How Difficult Times Can Help Us Grow", by Elizabeth Lesser.* The book covers something that I have been fascinated with for most of my life, resilience. Elizabeth describes moments in life as the "Phoenix Process," or positive life change that can emerge from very difficult life events. Examples that are used relate to divorce, loss of a child, or suffering a terminal illness.

The topics resonate with me, and I do really feel as if I've been broken open. In fact, it is a term I've used to describe how I feel, before I even found this book.

And, as I read about the stories of others, and how they came through their own Phoenix process, I realize that this has not been the first one for me. I have, in fact, had a sequence of these life changing events that have affected how I live, parent, and relate to others. And, as bad as they were at the time, I cannot deny the obvious truth. I am a better person because of them.

So, the most logical conclusion would be that I will become a better person because of this too. That is a hard pill to swallow, but I somehow know this is accurate. I wish I could have had this transformation in my thinking, in my very soul, without the loss, without the pain.

My thoughts of personal analysis are interrupted as the boys arrive back. The morning progresses, and Brendan arrives with Ross and Nathan, and everyone helps us to pack up the truck. And, with everything piled in, it takes me back to the day we moved Stephen to Raleigh, to begin his adventure at North Carolina State University. With all of his belongings piled in the truck, we looked like the Clampetts from The Beverly Hillbillies. It seemed fitting that we would bring him home in that same way.

Before we leave, Ross wants to take us to a special spot. The Disc Golf course on campus, he wants to show us where his bench will be placed. We drive to the course, and walk a ways until we reach a particular hole. He points to a shaded area, where brush has recently been cut, and explains that this is where it will be placed. It means so much to us to know that he is doing this. He has designed the bench, and with shape and stain, it will look like a Canadian Flag, in honor of "Canadian Steve". We stand for a moment, taking it all in, knowing that only a few short months ago, Stephen was bounding up this trail, laughing and living. But, if that can no longer be, at least he had touched people who loved him enough to show such respect for his memory. As we walk away from the spot to return to the car, Nathan points to a lone butterfly following us out the trail.

We hug the boys, and tell them they are loved, and we head home. It has been a long and emotional day, and we still have a few hours to drive. As we merge onto the main interstate, we are all quiet, with the reality of the situation sinking in. This was the last piece of him we had to collect. Now, the only job left is for us to figure how to live this new life of ours. We notice other vehicles heading towards to Raleigh, loaded down with "stuff". Parents bringing their excited children to university, anxious to start their new adventure. I can imagine the electric feeling in those vehicles. The child, excited about the new beginning, and the parents' bittersweet emotions as their babies take their next steps in life. I watch as one after the other, they drive towards the city, taking their kids to school. As we drive away from the city to take the last pieces of Stephen home.

It was rough, I cannot lie.

Finally, we reached home. We quickly unload everything from the truck, and survey the now full garage. And we head inside the house. I am drained.

And then Brendan starts. He asks quietly at first, and then more emphatically if he can go and look at the stuff. I explain that we are tired, and let's wait. He nods, but fifteen minutes later is back, asking the question from a different angle. Okay, I get it. And, no matter how tired I am, I know he needs to do this.

So, out we go. Brendan approaches his exploration with wild abandon, pulling open boxes and ripping out the contents. It makes me a little short of breath, as my approach with Stephen's things has been a little different. I open things slowly, inspect not only the contents, but how they were packed, drinking up every detail. Brendan, however, appears to be on his own personal mission. He is looking for something, something specific. And, although I am uncomfortable as he rips open the boxes, I let him go. He needs this, to find a connection, just as much as I do, but in a different way. After a few boxes, he finds it. An ESPN magazine that he and Stephen had talked about, with a cover story on Carey Price, the Montreal Canadiens goalie, and a T-Shirt. And, as if this was enough to hold on to for now, he smiled, and said that was good. He went off into the house, and I lingered, peeking inside the open boxes at the contents. And, beneath a stack of school papers, here it was. Leather bound journal. His godmother, Tracey, had given it to him for Christmas in 2003. At that time in Stephen's life, he was going through changes. Normal changes as a part of his growth, but also changes because the dynamic of our family was changing. A journal, although unbeknownst to Tracey was a perfect gift, an outlet to express his feelings much the same way as I am right now.

I remember seeing this journal from time to time over the course of the next few years. In Canada, when I was so worried about him. Life events had left him with feelings he was struggling with, and I now know he let some of those feelings out in that journal. I tucked it away in the basket of laundry and took it upstairs. I did not want to read this in front of Brendan or Brady, but have it to myself at first.

The entries were erratic, and beautiful, and emotional, and painted a picture of a boy growing into a man. In his notes, he was working through some important issues. Things like love, his parent's divorce, the relation-ship with his dad, and girls. And, then I found the final entry. April 19, 2009. He had not written in the book for some time, and you could see the difference. His first entry was filled with youth filled angst. This final entry was made by a man, a wonderful and centered man who was excited about the opportunities that lay before him.

He began by joking about his previous entries and their relationship to his raging hormones. I smiled, and had to agree. He went on to give a sum-mary of where things were going in his life. He mentioned Brady and I, his wonderful relationship with Brendan, his love life and his future. And, what no iPod, or piece of clothing or chat with a friend could tell me, he told me all on his own. He told me he was happy.

I buried my head in my pillow and just let it all out. I was so thankful to be able to read his own words and understand he was really happy. But, at the same time, I could not help but feel an overwhelming sadness that he was taken away so soon. His final written words said he was excited to see what life had in store for him, and would write more at the end of the summer.

So, what am I grateful for on this tough day? His friends, who love in a way I did not expect from college boys. My husband, who is my rock and Brendan, who is my anchor.

And Stephen. As I have written, I wonder if people know, have some unconscious understanding about their end of days. But, whatever the motivation, your words comfort me. They confirm your happiness, and that somehow makes me feel like I did my job as your mother. They confirm your love, for life and for others. They confirm you were exactly who I knew you to be, and knowing that we really were that close does comfort me.

So, now we have all your things with us. I am thankful, not for the things. Rather I am most thankful for the new found knowledge. It was not the things. We've had Stephen right with us in our hearts all along.

August 17th: There is No Ceiling in Our House.

If I had my child to raise all over again,
I'd build self-esteem first,
and the house later.
I'd finger-paint more, and point the finger less.
I would do less correcting and more
connecting. I'd take my eyes off
my watch, and watch with my eyes.
I'd take more hikes and fly more kites.
I'd stop playing serious, and
seriously play.
I would run through more fields and gaze at more stars.
I'd do more hugging and less tugging.

~DIANE LOOMANS, FROM
"IF I HAD MY CHILD TO RAISE OVER AGAIN"

TODAY IS ANOTHER BEGINNING FOR US. The start of another week, and the week that Brendan returns to school after a very eventful summer break. We've been talking about this week for some time now, and I think we are both apprehensive. Up to this point, we have truly not had any other agenda, other than grieving at our own pace, and once school and hockey are going at full force again, that will change. It will be time for us to emerge from the cocoon we have built, and enter back into the world. Brendan has been brave, and excited and anxious at the same time. It is difficult for him, and he is concerned that everyone will know about Stephen. A natural response, he just wants to be normal like everyone else.

I take the time to communicate with the principal to let him know what has happened, and to ensure that the support network is in place for him at school should he need it. And we talk a lot today, about different scenarios. The great news is we have openly discussed things, and I feel good about the tools we have given to Brendan for coping with the varied reactions.

One example of how we readied Brendan was the meeting he had with Father Cahill. They talked and worked through some scenarios of what people could say to him. They role played, and Brendan practiced how he would handle things, if people knew about what happened, and if they did not. I was so proud of him for being open to having that conversation with Father. He is so, so brave. And, he is navigating through the same things I am, just in a middle school environment. I am not sure if I could be as strong as he is.

In our conversations, I tell him that he is going to be okay. I tell him how brave and smart and capable he is. I tell him he can do anything he sets his mind to, if he understands that the fulfillment of dreams means not only dreaming but working to get it. We have these conversations often, not only today in preparation for the beginning of a school year.

I had those exchanges with Stephen as well. The email exchange I have written about was an example. I am proud of that. I have always felt imperfect and inadequate as I try my best to parent, but this is one area I feel I have it right.

I've always seen parenting as a job that relates to cheerleading or Mystic Guidance. It is my job to build him up, because let's face it; the world will beat you down at times. You have to train yourself and practice building up that shield, and your home should always be your haven, where you know, without a doubt, that everyone loves you without condition. Imagine if every home and parent tried that for a year. How would the world change? How would the world be different if all of the children walked out their front doors in the morning feeling loved and confident in their gifts, and knowing at the end of the day, they had a safe place to return?

I know that some would say you should paint a realistic picture for your child, to help shield them from disappointment. But you know what? You can't shelter your child from disappointment, no matter how hard you try. It is there, and it is part of life just like death is. If you could, I would have been able to shield Brendan from July 4, 2009. But I could not. It comes, we deal with it, and we figure out how we use it to make us stronger and more compassionate people.

So, rather than shield children from disappointment, why not teach them how to deal with it? Why not give them a strong sense of self by telling them you think they are the best thing since sliced bread, and here are the 182 reasons why? Then, when disappointment comes, they will see it is a disappointment for one thing, one part of their life, not *all* of their life. What about the value of raising resilient children?

Maybe I am completely off target, but I think we only get to do this once, so why not dream big? Why not believe that you can do anything you set your mind to, and then see what happens? Why not build a strong foundation for your child's house instead of building the ceiling first?

Thinking about this brings up a memory of Stephen, not accepting limitations, and going after what you want.

He had applied to NC State. Having spent his first year at a community college in Charlotte, he was now ready to get going. He attended the college to prepare, take the SAT's and get used to this new country. In our first year here, I was thankful he was home with me, and not away. Now, looking back, I am blessed that he was slow to start with his university education. I had two extra years with him at home that I now know were a gift.

He was on the Dean's list at the college. So, when we applied to NC State, we simply assumed it was just a matter of time before we received his letter of acceptance. And, when the letter arrived, Stephen was smiling as he opened it. But it was not a letter of admission. It was a letter indicating he did not meet the criteria for a transfer student, and would need an additional 6 credits. Please try again next time.

The look on his face broke my heart. He had worked so hard, and was so diligent in his planning. He had already been in touch with the Hockey coach at NC State. But now, it appeared it was over. He showed me the letter, and I read it carefully.

After some reflection, I looked up and said, "Stephen, we don't accept this. This is not saying they don't want you. This is saying you need some extra courses to come. There is a difference. I will call them and ask them what we can do."

He looked anxious but slightly relieved. We had always found solutions in the past for whatever came up, and I think he was glad to see this circumstance would be no different.

I called the school and spoke with the most wonderful person in the admissions office. She explained that yes he did need the courses to qualify as a transfer student, but if he could get those courses, he would be admitted because his grades were terrific. I asked her to put a hold on his application and assured her he would have the grades by her deadline of mid July.

I hung up the phone feeling encouraged, but knew this would mean Stephen would have to take an insane number of courses in the compressed Spring Semester in order to make this happen. I talked to him about it, explaining that it would mean he would have to study for the next three months if he wanted this. But, if he did want it, he could have it.

He wanted it, and he worked non stop for that semester, getting all A's and B's. And, as promised, the Admissions department processed the application, and he was ready to go for the fall. At the end of the process, I actually sent the Admissions counselor flowers. She was so professional and so good at her job, and she went above and beyond for us. Do you know why? Because we asked her to, because we did not take no for an answer.

I think back on that now, and all that he did to make it happen in his life, and I am amazed. At the time, it just seemed like it was the thing to do.

That's my one little thing for the day. Realizing that my job as a parent is to be "the keeper of the dream". Sounds like I should be part of some sort of Trilogy of stories about fairies and monsters, but not quite so dramatic. Rather, it is simple. I am thankful because I now know, by reflections on my life with Stephen, how important it is to encourage your children to dream big, and not accept no for an answer in life. And, coupled with that, when things don't work out, and sometimes that will happen, you show them how to bounce back. I am thankful that even though we feel a little beaten up, I am continuing to parent Brendan with that same sense of resilience.

August 18th: The Fork in the Road and the Sense of Renewal

*To get through the hardest journey we need take only
one step at a time, but we must keep on stepping*

-CHINESE PROVERB-

THE RETURN TO SCHOOL IN the fall of the year has always been a time of renewal for me. As a child, I loved packing my school bag, sharpening my pencils, getting new uniforms, and shoes. Back to school time was getting new shoes time, one pair of school shoes and one pair of sneakers. It was a glorious time. The air was beginning to get crisp, the leaves changing, and it was a time for a fresh start. Leave the last year behind, and move forward into the exciting unknown.

Even when I had long finished school, I would still have this feeling of renewal in the fall. Perhaps a restoration of my eating habits, as I had enjoyed the freedom of summer eating way too much. Or the renewal of getting back into a schedule of sorts. But, for whatever the reason, it has always been a wonderful time, and fall is my favorite season.

This year, that feeling of renewal is still there, but it is a little different. It is bittersweet. And actually, it feels a little early for me, as school starts in August down here in the South.

In any case, the sense of renewal I feel comes for a couple of reasons. First, Brendan begins school tomorrow, and we are getting ready. It is another step towards living life again. And second, I am finding as each day passes, I am feeling a personal sense of emotional rejuvenation. It only comes to me in glimpses, but it is coming. Brief moments in time throughout the day where I don't feel the ache as deeply in my chest. It both comforts and scares me.

These moments remind me of a conversation I had with my brother about these very moments of healing. Following the death of Gerard's first wife Kay, he felt much the same as I, and it did not seem like it would get better. And one evening, he was in the car with his two small boys in their seats in the back. A shooting star shot across the night sky, and they were going to make a wish. Nick, his eldest, said to his brother, "we should wish for Mom to come back from heaven." As Gerard described it, when he heard those words, they had the initial sting of pain. But, for a brief moment after, he felt okay, and he smiled at the innocence of his children. Explaining that although their Mom would love to be able to come back, she could not, the boys accepted the answer and moved on with their chatter as kids do.

But, it was a turning point for Gerard, and he described it as a moment where he finally felt he was going to be able to go on, that he would be okay. As I cried on the phone, he explained to me that those moments will come for me too. Slowly at first, and then more frequently. And then, one morning, you will wake up and find that you feel happy again. You will always miss them, but you will be happy again.

I have to make a note to tell Gerard how important that story has been to me in my grieving. I have valued his honesty and his support so very much. He has given me hope. I look at him now, with his wonderful wife Karla, five year old Blake, and his two fantastic grown boys who have pieces of their Mom shining through them both. They did it, and they give me hope that I can too.

It is with that sense of renewal I think about Stephen through the day. Because, through his death, my feelings about life have been renewed, changed, improved. I always said to people that he was my fork in the road. A young girl, a new baby, he truly set a new path for my life, and I will always be grateful to him for that roadmap. He was an amazing miracle, changing not only the direction of my dreams, but also transforming how I looked at life.

"Fork in the Road" has truly been one of the descriptors I have in my mind when I think of him. So, with renewal in mind, how can I let this become the end of the road?

He was my fork in the road, and his death does not mean the end. That would take away from the miracle that he was. In fact, I think in a different way, it is a beginning of sorts. A beginning of a new way of life for me, and for all the others that Stephen touched in his short time here on earth.

Deep I know, but I am thankful for my analysis. I am thankful I am taking the time to dissect this and come out with an understanding that I can apply to this new life of mine.

The rest of the day is busy with back to school activities. I do take some time later in the day to look through the art supplies found in Stephen's belongings. He did complete a visual arts class last semester, and loved it. He was always so artistic, though never felt confident in his abilities. As I flip through the amazing sketches in his book, I cannot help but be humbled at his talent and also be reminded of my own father, who also had so much talent that he did not see. These sketches are a gift from Stephen to us. I am thankful, as they are pictures from his very soul.

So, today, on my parent's wedding anniversary, I give thanks for renewal. Even though it is a little scary, I give thanks for it just like I did when it meant new shoes and freshly sharpened lead pencils.

I give thanks for my brother, who has been a candle in the darkness of my grief.

I give thanks for my fork in the road, and for continuing the journey.

August 19th: I-I-I-I-I-I-I A-A-A-A-
M-M-M-M Astro Boy!!!!!

Up, Up and Away!

-SUPERMAN-

I AM THINKING ABOUT SUPERHEROES today. With Brendan back at school, I took some time this morning to quietly look through Stephen's things. While removing boxes from his bedroom closet, I came across a board game and a figurine that made me laugh out loud, and then cry. Astro Boy. A few years back, Brady and I found these treasures on a back shelf at some store, and I knew we had to have them. And, on Christmas morning, Stephen laughed with a full and rich guffaw as these two simple and goofy presents gave him a trip down memory lane.

You see, Stephen was obsessed with Astro Boy. No, obsession is an incorrect description. He wanted to BE Astro Boy. For a period of time between three and four, I believe he thought he WAS Astro Boy. One of his favorite cartoons, he would watch and then imitate the boy hero with rockets for feet and a heart of gold. He really thought he could do it, become this super hero and save the world.

It was beautiful to watch him, his innocence, and his unwavering belief that he could do it, being young enough to not yet be told that some things were not possible.

Aunt Lorraine in particular would get such a kick out of him. Dressed for the day with pants, and a shirt and socks, he would disappear. Minutes later, he would saunter out the hall, with nothing but his briefs and his blue rubber boots on. This was his super hero outfit, and closely resembled the uniform of his hero, Astro Boy. He would run into the room and then jump into the air. And when his feet hit the ground, he would have his hands on his hips as any super hero should, and would announce in a loud and authoritative voice,

"I AM ASTRO BOY!!"

His enthusiasm for the role was hilarious. So was the fact that for a period of time, it was difficult for me and my family to keep him dressed.

As he grew, he moved to different superheroes. He loved the Ninja Turtles, and Batman. Superman played a huge role in his life. When I was away at school, he would send me mail, and draw the ninja turtles on the package or the envelope. I still have those stick figure turtles. One Halloween, he and Aunt Lorraine dressed as Ninjas Turtles together. Now, if anyone has any question about why my family sees life for the miracle it is, just look to my Aunt Lorraine. She made it magic, for me and for my son, and for anyone else who crossed her path.

Anyway, regardless of the time that passed, Astro Boy held a special place in his heart. It was a fond and happy memory for him. In the spring, he explained Astro Boy to Brendan, and we all agreed we would need to go and see the upcoming film release.

I decided to Google Astro Boy to see what I could find out, to share with Brendan. And, I came across the opening and closing songs. And, for some reason, I feel the need to paste an excerpt here. Here goes:

Soaring high in the sky,
He may be small but only in size.
AstroBoy, AstroBoy,
He is brave and gentle and wise!

OSAMU TEZUKA

How very fitting as I read the words. And, although he did not have rockets in his feet, or a laser in his behind, I think Stephen was a superhero, just like Astro Boy. He was kind, and looked out for others, and had people's best interests at heart. He had all of the characteristics of a comic book hero, without the cape or super powers. At least that is how I see it.

Perhaps that is what we should all be doing with our children. Nurturing the super hero within. Cultivate those characteristics that make them stand out in a crowd and stand up for what is right. Superheroes may bend, but they don't break. They may not win every battle, but they persevere and never lose sight of what is important, good and just. With superheroes, they show us there is always a next time, another time to get up and dust ourselves off, and try again.

Ah, the randomness of my thoughts. I don't need a plane ticket to travel.

Later that day I wait for the bus with nervous anticipation. And, as I looked at his face, walking towards me in the parking lot, Brendan smiled the biggest grin I've seen in weeks. He did it! He came back happy. Thank you for that.

So, today I am thankful for successful first days. I am thankful for happy memories and how many of them I have stored away.

And I am thankful for superheroes.

August 20ᵗʰ: The Face of Adversity, the Roots Knapsack, and the Education of Kelly

Pain is inevitable. Suffering is optional.

~M. KATHLEEN CASEY~

PEOPLE USE STANDARD PHASES IN times of trouble, strife and challenge. These are things that can inspire or commiserate, comfort and irritate.

One of the things I can recall reading and hearing more than once since July 4ᵗʰ is this phrase.

"In the face of adversity"

In the written word, you hear this phrase in the description of someone who faced insurmountable odds. Faced with adversity, they…..and so the story goes. In the spoken word, I have had well-meaning people tell me that you learn about yourself in the face of adversity. I believe that to be true.

But, that is not what I wanted to explore. In finding my little thing for the day, I have been thinking about "the face of adversity". In my little play on words, I have been imagining just what the face of adversity would in fact look like. So, humor me as I play with my analogy. Let's imagine for a moment it is an actual face of a person.

In my youth, I would probably say the face of adversity looked like the people who hurt me, the people who were mean to me, made fun of me. But, as I have aged, like a good red wine, I have more character, more depth, and yes, I have a fuller body. I understand that the people who hurt me are only a normal part of life.

I also probably would have said that the face of adversity was me, my reflection in the mirror. As I looked upon the changing landscape of my face, I could say that adversity was mapped across my cheeks, in the darkness beneath my eyes, the crows' feet or frown lines. But again, I see that as a youthful interpretation. Things happen in life, but they do not define you or anyone else for that matter, unless you let them.

Today, after having time in this reflective state of grief, I can tell you exactly what the face of adversity looks like. I can tell you, based on the recent loss of my child, and every other difficult time I have had along the way. All of those events, with their pain, have given me wisdom.

And, as I see it, the face of adversity is one of a gentle teacher. She is quiet, and she looks towards you, feeling empathetic for the hurt that is in your life. I think we should look gently into the eyes of adversity and see that there is love and compassion. She has old and knowing eyes, and she has seen pain like yours before, many times. She understands. She has cried with me, tears for the loss of an extraordinary human being.

In her eyes, her laugh lines, and frown lines, there is wisdom. There is knowing, and an understanding of what your life event can teach you. In her face, if you are brave enough to look at her, you can see what is truly important, and you can become a better person, no matter what has happened to you.

I think we should understand that even if adversity is looking upon us right now, she will turn her head and looks towards others as well. We are not alone, and she looks upon everyone from time to time in life. No one lives without a visit from her.

I have been reading ferociously since July 4th. I have been writing with a passion that I have never had before. It is as if I have been given a secret message from my teacher Adversity, and I am trying to get it all down before I forget. And, in my reading, I have learned from so many others, who faced insurmountable odds, and came out better because of how they dealt with it. One book that tells such stories is *"A Blessing in Disguise"*, by *Andrea Joy Cohen, M.D.*

I think we should stop looking at the "face of adversity" in much the same way we look at a cartoon Halloween image of the Grim reaper or a scary monster. I believe we need to look at her as a friend, who brings with her a bag of wisdom. She loves us, and she is with us to comfort us.

She is beautiful, and within her eyes, you can see the real story of what you have lost, and you can learn all that you need to know to move forward; if you are brave enough to look at it, be honest with yourself, and accepting of your new reality.

We must learn that visits from adversity are much like life and death itself. It is part of our existence and is not something to fight, or resist. We are not in control of the calendar or the agenda; it is set by something larger than ourselves.

Seeing "her" for the beautiful teacher she is has changed me forever. It has allowed me to take good from this situation rather than shut my heart down and become bitter. It has allowed me to understand and see that there is so much love surrounding me. It has allowed me to become a better parent, to take all the lessons and work at becoming more of who I was designed to be. It has allowed me to understand what the phrase, "God's Grace" means. Looking at her, and taking her hand gave me strength and grace I never knew existed.

She is not someone you want to visit often. But, when she does, and she will, we all need to stop, and make ourselves still, and know she loves us, she feels our pain, and has something to teach us. Something that will help us go on and live again. Better than we were before.

So, I am thankful for that silly thought. It makes me feel good to put a face to it.

And, moving on from the deep stuff, I am thankful for another big thing today.

Ta-ta-ta dah! (Trumpets sounds of announcement)

I removed the bags from the floor of my bedroom.

It was time. I knew that. So, this morning, I looked down at them, and gently explained.

"I love you. And you've really been there for me, taught me so much. But, it's time we move on and go our separate ways. I will always hold you in my heart, maybe take you on some hockey trips, but we can't go on this way any longer. But, let's still be friends."

I joke as I write this, but honestly, it was tough. I picked the bags up off the floor, and put them on my bed. I looked at them for a long time;

I took out some of the things and put them back. I smelled his t-shirts. I held my breath, which really did not do me any good.

And then I carried them out of the room, as I cried. I took them down the hall, opened the door to Stephen's room, and laid the bags on his bed. I did not unpack them. I just dropped them off and closed the door.

I returned to my room and exhaled. It was time. It was time to take the next step. It was time to remove the 49 days worth of dust from that spot on the floor. Okay, from the rest of the floor too. It was time to open the blinds, and let the sun in, and clean the room.

So, today I am thankful for my two teachers. Adversity and the Roots Knapsack. Through them, I have been presented with both memories and lessons. I have been given opportunities to understand the mysteries and glories of life. Even through pain.

I am thankful.

August 21st: Don't Worry, He Can Take It, and My Personal Grief Soapbox

People are like stained-glass windows. They sparkle and shine when the sun is out, but when the darkness sets in their true beauty is revealed only if there is light from within.

–*Elizabeth Kubler-Ross*-

It is interesting for me to hear how others perceive my grief. One of the phrases I use to describe my writing is "I am having a wonderful conversation with God". I think it sums it up really, as this whole experience has been so personal; it is, in some ways, like a long fireside chat with Him. I just feel it is better to explain it that way, rather than tell them that I knew hours after Stephen was gone that all of this was inside of me, and I started to write feverishly to get it out. I am thankful for it; this needed to happen, well before the loss of Stephen. I truly feel blessed I opened my heart.

But, for some reason, people don't understand my description of how I am dealing with my grief. When I say I am having a wonderful conversation with God, mostly everyone replies with some variation of the statement, "Well, that is okay, He can take it." Even with the use of the word wonderful, people still make the instant assumption that I am angry at God, and going through one of the classic stages in grief.

I know their intention with this statement is one of support and love. They want to make sure I know anger is a natural response to grief. They want to let me know I am normal, and God will still love me even if I am angry right now over losing Stephen. We have all been prepared by the ground-breaking work of Elizabeth Kubler Ross, and the Five Stages of Grief. I can still recall the stages, having studied them in a psychology class, and then by working with patients during my time as an oncology nurse.

Denial
Anger
Bargaining
Depression
Acceptance

I am not denying these findings in any way. I recall she did say that not everyone would experience all stages, but everyone would experience at least two in their own grieving process. I agree with that, though my written approval of her theory seems hilarious as I type it.

But, here, in this daily journal of my own grief, I want to make my own hypothesis. With a focus on gratitude in grief, a shift in your personal mindset on life and loss, you can change the grieving process, and reach the point of acceptance earlier in your journey. That is a big statement I know. Sounds like something someone would say who really felt they knew what the heck they were talking about.

I think I do. That is not to say that it will take away the hurt. It will not. The hurt will stay with you, and you will wear it like a heavy pair of boots you slip your feet into each morning. And grief can be cyclical. So, you may feel these stages all over again months later. Life is not black and white. It is all the shades of grey. It is imperfect, and as such, no theory will ever completely describe the reality you will experience.

But, no matter the cycle, you can change the journey, as well as make it more bearable with gratitude.

So, I find that curious, that the immediate assumption would be I am calling the Big Guy out for what has happened in my life. People immediately assume that I am working through the bitterness and the anger, and I honestly am not.

I believe that they assume this standpoint because we, as human beings, rarely approach times of hardship with an open heart of gratitude. We become angry, and upset, and feel once again the world has done us wrong. We stamp our feet and cry out, we feel entitled to feel that way for what we have lost. We are focused on the misconception that our life is supposed to be all sunshine and roses. That is an illusion that we have created. We bought into as we watch the weekly shows displaying reality as something that is perfection, in situation, in body size, in looks, in attainment of material possessions. All of it. We have numbed ourselves from what is real. And real life sometimes hurts. And hurt can be our greatest teacher, if we decide to sit ourselves down and absorb the lesson. If I focused on the loss in this situation, I would be so angry, "Going Irish" all over God right about now. But, through the shift in my thinking from consciously focusing on gratitude, I have been able to remove the anger and the bitterness from the process of my grief.

Do I have moments where, for an instant I feel like I picked the short straw in life? Yes, I am only human. But, for the other 98% of the time, I am able to focus on what is good in my life, what good we can take from Stephen's life instead of what we have lost.

So, my little thing for today? My outlook on life. I am proud of myself, and I think Stephen would be proud of me as well. It is my decision to grieve in this way that allows me to keep breathing, to keep going, to keep parenting Brendan, and being a partner to Brady. It is allowing me to record this entire journey. And, it is changing my life without a doubt. Sounds like a big thing to me.

August 22nd: Two Goalies in the Crease

When life takes the wind out of your
sails, it is to test you at the oars.

~ROBERT BRAULT~

TODAY, BRENDAN HAS HIS BIG kick off weekend for hockey, so the house is filled with nervous anticipation. For Brendan, this is a big step, to get back out on the ice and start with a team that he worked so hard to become a part of and Brady and I are so proud of him and how hard he has worked to get here. As the tryouts were approaching in the spring, he worked out every day. He went to camps and he would do dry land training with Stephen.

Those are happy memories for Brendan, leading up to this moment, but I also know it is bittersweet as he knows Stephen's not here, physically at least, to watch him play. On the weekend of the tryouts, Ross and Nathan were at our house visiting. And although those three twenty something boys went out for some fun the night before, they were all up at the crack of dawn to come and cheer Brendan and encourage him for the tryout. I could see how confident he felt, walking into the Ice House that morning with three college boys as his personal fan club following behind.

But, today, he is walking in there alone, and we have had quiet conversations about it. Brendan's questions and comments about Stephen and grief are random, and spurt out of his mouth when you least expect it. Last week, he posed a question to me about Stephen's remains as we were standing in the checkout line at Target. I actually love that about him, and I feel truly blessed that we are talking; we are working it out, even if it is not pretty as we do so.

So, this morning, as he prepares, he is laying out his equipment, making sure his skates and stick are ready to go, getting the right socks. And, as I type this, I know it does not sound like this is a big deal. But to truly understand the ritualistic tendencies involved in the preparation process, you would need to be here, to be the mother of a goalie. It is all about doing the same things, in the same way, wearing the same socks, drinking the same beverage, listening to the same music as we drive to the arena.

They say that if you want to be a really great goalie, you have to be a little "off", a little crazy. I don't know about that, but you do have to march to your own drummer. Anyone who willingly stands in the cold waiting and wanting to be hit by a frozen hard black disc has to be a truly unique individual. So, what does it say about me, that I produced two goalies? Don't answer that.

And, in between the prep work, he stops here and there, and asks a question. His words tell me he has been thinking about Stephen all morning.

"Do you think he would be proud of me?" he asked.

I of course, know he was proud of Brendan before he made this team, and he was so excited when Brendan heard that he had in fact been selected back in June. I tell him so, but my words always seem to fall short, because I am the wrong person telling him. I am not Stephen.

"Do you think he is with me?" Big question for a little boy. Big question for a Mom. One I have been contemplating myself.

"Yes, I think he is with you. I think he is with all of us, in our hearts, and watching over us." I type this, having no idea what the experts would say about presenting the information to my child in this way. Nor do I care. I feel flawed in how I am helping him sometimes, but I am trying my best. When I don't know an answer, I tell him. And I do believe Stephen is with us every day. I believe he is with others he loved as well.

And then, Brendan gives me confirmation that I said what he needed to hear. He smiled the biggest smile and we joke about how an extra blocker and glove in the net is going to be helpful.

I am thankful.

The day goes great for Brendan. He plays well, and we receive confirmation that he will be able to have Stephen's #20 for his jersey. He wanted this from the beginning, and we were hoping that it would happen. Thankfully, it did, because of the kindness of others; Mike and Moe, fellow parents on the team, and the owners of Extreme Ice. They sprang into action when they heard the story and simply made it happen. He is smiling and proud and feels so good about it and I am thankful.

And the day goes well for us too. It is truly my big trip outside, back in the world, for the entire day and not just a few minutes at a time. I was apprehensive about it. I still find myself at a loss for words, and when I do have the words, I also have the lump in my throat when I begin to speak. I wonder if I can do this, be around people, who are happy and cheerful, who have lives that are still normal. I am also apprehensive about the safety of Brendan on the ice. I think about the hit to the chest Stephen took, and I cannot deny I worry about my remaining son. But, Stephen was hit thousands of times before, and it was just something that happened. It was his time, and God needed him. I cannot put Brendan in a bubble. He has to live, and live large, because we know how short and fleeting our time here can be. But, just as I told Brendan that Stephen is with us, maybe I need to tell myself that very same thing. Perhaps I can ask him to use his blocker and glove to save me from some things as well, even if those things are just fearful thoughts.

I am thankful. For the bravery of Brendan, walking back into that ice house, good friends, awesome husband, and knowing that we always have someone in our crease.

August 23rd: You've Got Mail

I know God will not give me anything I can't handle.
I just wish that He didn't trust me so much.

~Mother Teresa~

Today is a good day. More hockey, but that is only one of the reasons. Today, I am finishing my *Letter from God*. As suggested to me last week by our neighbor and friend, I have been quietly working on this for some days now. And today is the day I complete it.

The process of writing this has been remarkable and life changing. I have not only shed tears through the writing, I have howled with sadness. I have made sure to only work on this when Brendan was out of the house. Although I am open and honest about my sadness and show him my tears, I don't think he would be prepared for the display.

Every so often, Brady peaks around the corner of the office door, and smiles. "Is everything okay in here?" He is so gentle and kind to me and his support is unwavering. I usually respond through tears, to tell him it is all good. Because through and despite the tears, this exercise is healing me.

I've written for some time about my relationship with God and my faith since July 4th. I am thankful for it, grateful for the path I did choose. Not that I can take credit for it. I felt I was being guided, and I also felt like there was no alternative but to surrender to God. I type that with humility, because I know I would not have admitted that I had surrendered to God and His will before all of this happened. My faith was real back then, but was a faith of convenience, one based on tradition and family history and school doctrine, and Irish Catholic female guilt. I will admit it. Guilt played a part in my relationship with God.

But now, it is different. My relationship with Him has progressed. And, as I walk through the valley, He is walking with me, and as that famous poem says, in some places He is carrying me.

As I write, I am reflective on my journey, but also on the journey of others. I have read so much about people who have suffered unspeakable hurts and persevered. I am humbled as I learn more, and understand that hurt and loss is an inevitable part of life. And, as I have read, there is a choice. You can't choose not to hurt, but you can choose not to suffer. I feel I am making that choice. I am choosing to embrace the hurt, but not the suffering. You can also choose to see God as a loving and healing God or a punishing God.

One example in particular came from the book, "When Bad Things Happen to Good People." I know this is a classic, and I purchased it for that very reason. But, as I have read it, I found that not all parts resonated with me as I thought they would. However, the one piece that struck me was an excerpt inserted from another book:

> *"It never occurred to me to question God's doings or lack of doings while I was an inmate of Auschwitz, although of course I understood others did….It never occurred to me to associate the calamity we were experiencing with God, to blame Him, or to believe in Him less or cease believing in Him at all because He didn't come to our aid. God doesn't owe us that, or anything. We owe our lives to Him.*

> -Brenner, The Faith and Doubt of Holocaust Survivors-

This man, facing so much hate and anger, hanging on to life with almost no hope never entertained turning away or against God. Even when it seemed that no one would come, and that the world and God had abandoned him in his time of need, his faith remained. He never once thought to blame God for his hardship.

I find that both amazing and validating for me. Because, although the two events are so very different, his statement is exactly how I feel about my pain. I finally found someone who viewed hardship and God in the same way I did.

There is something divine and miraculous that comes from looking within. As I write this letter, I honestly feel the weight of my hurt lifting. I also feel that what I have written is what God would say to me, or *is* saying to me. It slows a racing mind and quiets the dark thoughts. I will be thankful for this letter for many years to come, because it was a turning point for me.

At first, I thought I would not share it here, but I've decided it is part of my journey. Here goes…

Dear Kelly,

I wanted to send you a little note, as I know you've been having a tough time lately. I thought a letter would be better than parting the clouds, as I know you've spent a lot of time with your own words since Stephen died. I've watched you try and work through this, and I have cried tears right along with you. Losing a child is the hardest thing. I know that, as I lost my only son. The pain is unbearable, and it feels like a heavy robe that is weighing you down each and every day.

You need to take comfort in some things. I know you are working very hard on keeping the faith and I am proud of you for that. Stephen is proud of you too. He is watching over you every single day and sees how hard you try.

Here's what I need you to know:

❋ *Stephen is safe, and he is happy here in heaven with me. He is finally with his brother Matthew, and what a reunion that was! You always said that you thought he was searching for something, and I want you to know that he finally found it. Matthew was with him that night, and so was I. I need you to know he was okay, and he wasn't alone. He was never alone.*

❋ *Stephen said to tell you he loves you dearly. He had a great life and you were a wonderful Mom. He wants you to hold on to those amazing memories. He said to remind you of how happy you all were as a family. That is rare these days Kelly. Hold on to that, as some people live to a ripe old age and never figure out the secret of life is love. He wants you to give Brady a big hug and tell him he was so thankful for the last four years. What they had together was rare and the love they shared helped him fully blossom on earth. He wants Brendan to know that he is the best brother ever and that he is always with him. They have a special bond and that bond cannot be broken by death or anything else. Tell Brendan that Stephen is right there in the crease with him for every game, and right beside him in life.*

❋ *Stephen is here with his brother, your parents and your aunts and uncles and a whole bunch of others! They welcomed him with open arms and your mother had one of her special hugs just for him. Your Dad was so happy to see him. We've all been so excited to watch him play hockey, it's quite a popular sport up here you know. And you were right when you joked with Brendan about that Thunder and Lightning storm. It was Me banging on the boards after an amazing save by your boy. Stephen was so honored to see how his NC State teammates decided to remember him. From tattoos to retiring his jersey to the memorial tournament. I, of course, was not surprised. Tell them Stephen will be watching, and to show up for every game and to skate like it was the Stanley Cup final.*

❋ *I have some special work for him to do. I know you said you always thought he was destined for greatness and you were right. And that greatness will be achieved by serving Me. There is a lot happening right now, and I know you can feel it. Stephen will be terrific for what I have in mind for him. And you will see him in things in your life and others as they unfold. You will smile and know he played a part. I know it is hard for you to understand now, but one day, I will explain everything. One day, this will all make sense. You know, God's Plan and all that stuff. I liked the way you explained God's plan to Brendan. Stephen was a surprise wasn't he? I love surprise parties. I am proud of you for being able to see the good in difficulty. You are allowing yourself to learn from these things, and that is what I need you to do to be the person I was thinking of when I created you. Even this situation. You will find it, I will help you. Have faith; trust in My love for you.*

❋ *Your grief, it says a lot about the depth of your love for him. You are hurting pretty hard. But keep reminding yourself, it is not from regret. When you reviewed over your relationship, I think you know you loved him as hard as you could. He knows that too.*

❋ *I am so glad you listened to Me and made the changes in your life that needed to happen. I know that right now, you are so thankful you did. You gave Stephen a once in a lifetime relationship with Brady, and a happy home, and an opportunity to grow into an amazing man, be happier than he has ever been, have an amazing college experience and feel the thrill of the crowd cheering for him in net. You did that because you listened to the whisper in your ear. That was Me by the way. Continue to listen and talk to Me, I will show you the way through this too.*

❋ *The Butterflies. Yes, it's him. There was so many at the memorial because he and all of your family up here wanted to envelope you with our love. We knew how hard you were hurting, and how it was hard for you to breathe with your heart broken open as it was. And, we wanted to be there and celebrate Stephen right along with you. And all the butterflies since then, that was*

Stephen too. For you and for those who loved him. The one that followed you on your walk, all the butterflies on the road to the beach, the one that stayed and stayed at the pool with you, Brady and Brendan. And the one that sat on the trunk of the oak tree as you cried on Saturday. That was Stephen saying he loved you, and saying thank you for having Ross and Nate come and stay. He was really happy that you told Ross your thoughts about what happened that day. I know Ross did not say much, but it gave him a lot of comfort and will help him move on. He has carried a heavy load since then and we need to help lift that for him so he can have a happy life.

* *You are doing well with your writing. I know it is foreign to you, to just let go, but it is a good thing sometimes, to simply submit to something bigger than yourself. If you can't do it now, when can you right? I also know you sometimes doubt yourself, and wonder why the heck you are doing this, but please know I am guiding you. I believe that you can help yourself and maybe others by sharing your story, by sharing your lessons. I know deep down, you know that too. Have faith in that, and trust that I have this all figured out. Keep focused on doing it for the right reasons, and I promise it will give you happiness in your heart.*

* *I've been watching you wrestle with two issues. Don't you love my curve balls? Just kidding. I want you to know that Stephen and I are on the case with both, so keeping sending love, and everything will fall into place as it should. You know, just like it did 23 years ago.*

Now, on to the next thing, doing one last thing for Stephen by airing out his concerns; I know you struggle with this, and you feel uncertainty as to how you should proceed.

First, Stephen was a smart cookie. And, in the situation you struggle with, you are right. All it would have taken was two words to make it better, **I'm sorry**.

Life is like that you know. People build walls up against each other, when two words could start the healing and fix everything. So, you need to stop carrying the burden of this unfinished business. Back in the spring, you talked about forgiveness, and that was big. It took a long time for you to forgive, and I knew it was difficult to talk to Stephen about giving people another chance when you were just learning yourself. And Kelly, he did forgive, he had moved on, he just needed to get it out.

So, where does that leave you? What should you do? I know you hoped to find it all neat and tidy in a word document on Stephen's computer, or to receive some vision of the solution. But as you now know, life is not neat and tidy. And I also know you are not strong enough for all of this just yet. I want to tell you, I am proud of you for thinking this through instead of lashing out in anger, however justified. I know how much you've thought about it, and how you want to do the right thing, for you, for Brendan, and most of all for your precious Stephen.

I am so proud of you for wanting to do the right thing here, especially when it seems it would be much easier to drop the bomb and walk away. That is strength.

I am right beside you as you weigh out all the options. And you are on the right path. The path is love Kelly. Anger never achieved anything, it never helped people learn lessons, or helped people communicate more effectively, or changed how a person will treat people, adults and children. Anger closes doors and love opens them. You know that. I know what your favorite quote is,

"Forgiveness is the fragrance that the violet sheds on the heel that crushed it".

−MARK TWAIN−

That's a good one Kelly, and it's true. I may have given good old Mark some help with that one.

255

So, continue to think with Me on this one. But know, all that hurt that Stephen felt over things from his past is gone now. He understands it now. I've spent some time with him, and I've explained everything.

I believe you can figure out a way to make this into a lesson Kelly. I think you can turn this around with love, and make this into something that will show you and those around you how to be better people.

I hope my words give you some comfort. I know it is hard to breathe some days, but I promise it will get better. Love the people around you, and let them love you back. Keep looking for the good in life, and I promise, I will lead you to it.

I love you, and I will take care of you. Stephen loves you too and will be with you to watch over and guide you. Have faith in that, and watch for the glimpses of his love in the days to come. Watch for my blessings too, because you are My child and I love you, in the same way that you love Stephen.

And finally, have faith that the love that you both had cannot be diminished by the passage from life to death. You will one day see he was just in another room in My house of love, waiting to give you one of his famous hugs.

Love and Peace,
God

August 24th: Our Family is Made From Special Stuff....

Families are like fudge - mostly sweet with a few nuts.

-AUTHOR UNKNOWN-

WITH BRENDAN BACK IN THE swing of things at school, I have taken some private time in the garage, to begin to unpack and sort Stephen's belongings. It is a surreal experience, funny at times and heart wrenching at others. I am given more confirmation that he had grown into a man of character, one who was human, and having a terrific time in his youth, but someone who cared about the needs of others.

He was also an eclectic soul. As I peruse the boxes, I can see he had varied interests, he kept things that had memories and moments attached, and he was sentimental. He was quirky, he had a lot of cleaning supplies, more than the average college kid should or would be expected to own.

I open a Rubbermaid container full of clothes, but I am confused. It does not look like clothes he would wear, and for an instant, I think we have taken some of Phil's belongings in error. But, as I pull them from the container everything becomes clear. This is the costume container. As a child in Canada, Stephen watched a wonderful and classic children's show called Mr. Dressup. In fact, I watched it as a child as well. Mr. Dressup had a trunk full of magnificent costumes that was called the "Tickle Trunk". With each show, he would plan to tell a story, and magically, just the right outfit would appear inside the truck. From ballerina tutus to giraffe costumes, it was a magic you believed in, and you wished you had your very own Tickle Trunk at home.

Well, from the looks of things, Stephen did. I had heard the stories of the hockey team Christmas parties, with outrageous outfits. And I pull one of them out. A red turtle neck sweater, with a Kelly Green suit jacket, ivory paints with a green pin stripe, scarf, pipe, and white patent leather shoes, it was something out of a bad Christmas movie.

I remember a call I had with Stephen as he readied for this party. Going to the Goodwill to find these treasures, he was excited for not only the outfits but for a Secret Santa exchange with a great friend of his. It was so funny for these hockey players, but each year, they would show up wearing Christmas sweaters and exchange presents. The presents were gag gifts of course, and from the high level details I had been told, most were somewhat rude, obnoxious or slightly inappropriate. Kind of like the average college kid at moments. Add beer and I am sure you can see it would have been a fun night to say the least.

One particular year, Stephen gave a friend of his a membership to match.com. His buddy had recent girl troubles, and was newly single. Stephen also received some outrageous gifts. I am not sure if he knew it, or if those boys know it now, but these are the moments they will remember for their lifetime. When they are middle aged, chasing after their kids, and paying their mortgage, they will think back to those crazy nights, and know they were the best days of their lives.

So, I am thankful for those crazy nights and the fact that Stephen was able to experience them during his time on earth. And, looking further into the depths of Stephen's Tickle trunk, I am thankful that he inherited the eclectic gene from the Russell family. I came from a family that dressed up, had crazy St. Patrick's Day parties, and made every occasion magnificent. Halloween was of course an amazing time, and Aunt Lorraine in full costume, could have been an event planner. I can remember hat parties, mopping up parties, and parties for no reason at all. On Boxing Day, a holiday celebrated in Canada on the day after Christmas, our house would be full, music billowing out into the cold night air. And truly, if I break it down, the central theme of that party was leftovers. Christmas Hash, as we call it, where everything that wasn't eaten the day before is thrown into the roaster and slowly baked throughout the day. I know it doesn't sound like much, but I am salivating as I type this, it is really that good.

Our family knew how to celebrate and appreciate the good times in life. There was an understanding that the days were in fact special, and something to live to the fullest, not just to endure or get through. And now, as I review over Stephen's short life, I see that lust for life was passed onto him. I can see that he understood the power within a good party, a funny costume, in making a regular day special. Making it unique and memorable by how you approach it.

I am thankful. It makes me happy to see his happiness. I feel that happiness all around me right now. And I am grateful for the reminder of those times, and how I got here, how I learned how to parent. I will make more of an effort for the remainder of my days to make each day count. To be silly, to dance more, to laugh more, to have more parties, for whatever reason I can find.

Later in the afternoon, with Brendan home from school, he tells me an important thing that happened in his day. In a discussion about superheroes with a classroom friend, Brendan mentioned Stephen in conversation. And, when his friend asked about Stephen, Brendan explained what had happened over the summer. The friend said he was so sorry. It played out exactly as we told him it would, how he and Father Cahill had practiced. And he did it. What a huge step for him!

I am thankful, because with each moment like that, he is beginning to understand his own inner strength. He is beginning to understand, like I am, that he is going to be okay.

And finally, I am thankful for bedtime cuddles. First, with Brendan. It is our quiet time, and I appreciate how honest our discussions are when the room is quiet and dark, the glow of light coming from the hallway. Brendan is thoughtful at this time of day. He is coming up with questions that will help him to understand things that perplex him. At other times, it appears he is grasping for any subject matter so he can stay up a little longer.

It is our quiet time, and we chat about this and that. I notice that he doesn't seem as raw. Like me, the darkness is starting to dissipate somewhat. He is beginning to see the good again. He asks me questions about Stephen and I answer them as honestly as I can. This is such unchartered territory for me, and I wish I knew for sure I was handling this in the right way. He listens to my answers, and then begins to talk about how he wants to step up and be a leader. He explained to me that he wants to be like his brother. I tell him in many, many ways, he is like his brother. He smiles when I say that, and I hug and kiss him. And, like the change of a breeze, he begins to talk about hockey. He explains he works at his hockey drills like they are games. And when I ask him why, he says, "Mom, what you do in practice becomes a habit, and you bring those habits to your games."

Ladies and gentleman, I present to you the next world leader, because if we all looked at our life like that, the world would be a better place.

I am thankful.

August 25th: Moving On? No. Moving Forward? No. Moving In...

Our deepest fear is not that we are inadequate. Our deepest fear is that we are powerful beyond measure. It is our light, not our darkness that frightens us most. We ask ourselves, 'Who am I to be brilliant, gorgeous, talented, and famous?' Actually, who are you not to be? You are a child of God. Your playing small does not serve the world. There is nothing enlightened about shrinking so that people won't feel insecure around you. We were born to make manifest the glory of God that is within us. It's not just in some of us; it's in all of us. And when we let our own light shine, we unconsciously give other people permission to do the same. As we are liberated from our own fear, our presence automatically liberates others.

-MARIANNE WILLIAMSON-USED BY NELSON MANDELA
IN HIS 1994 INAUGURAL SPEECH

I HAVE BEEN WORKING A little on myself. Okay, not a little. The scaffolding is up, and the crew is working overtime. I've been thinking about all of the times in my life I've put off self exploration because of fear, and I am thankful I decided to take this leap. But, I can't take much credit, as I honestly don't feel I had a choice in the matter. In any case, this writing, and what is coming from it is changing the way I think, look at the world, and look at myself.

The focus on gratitude is shifting me and I am seeing the world in a different light. I am beginning to understand what it means to live a life that is on purpose, to be doing what you are supposed to be doing. I have discovered that by looking into my own soul, gazing into the depths of my being to see if I was, in fact still in there after all this pain.

I am still learning, and some days, this leap of faith, changing the way I live and work is scary. But again, just as I did not feel there was another option for me but to grieve with gratitude, I don't believe I can stop this train of change.

MOVING ON

Those words keep coming up, in my mind and out of the mouths of others who mean well when they phrase the passage of time in that way. Those two words are said with firmness, a suggestive tone, as if giving a verbal nudge to the receiver. We've had enough of this now, we need to move on. You need to move on.

I've heard those words before. When I buried one baby and took another home. When I had sleepless nights, worried about returning to school and the looks and snickers after giving birth to Stephen. When I had to be away from Stephen for school, no matter how right it was, it felt so wrong. When my parents died, way too soon, without seeing me fully blossom into the woman I knew I was on the inside. When I was married, and embarking on a new journey. When I had to move far, far away from my home and family, with doubts and an uncertain future. When I was hurt by someone I loved, so bad, I could not see myself anymore, and lost myself for years. When I found myself and divorced. When I quit my really, really good job, and skipped out of the office, knowing I was listening to my soul. When I moved to another country, and drove across the

United States with my children on our "most excellent adventure." When I started fresh, and gave myself another chance. When the stars and the moon aligned, and God brought me to an amazing man and I fell in love. When I married that man and knew in my heart I was meant to be with him for the rest of my days. When I looked around my life and it was all so, so good, and I had to pinch myself. When I lost my son, my pride and joy, and I had to figure out how to put myself back together.

Whew! I've heard those words more than I thought. Don't tell the Lifetime channel about me, they will want to do a movie of the week, or a miniseries.

But, for as much as I've heard and said those words, I don't think they are correct. Because moving on is not what I am doing. I can't simply move on from this, and the assumption that I could is ridiculous.

Moving forward? Yes, to a point, but it does not adequately describe the change that has happened in my life. We move forward every day, whether we like it or not.

I feel it is more like a moving in. Moving into my own soul, my own being, finally letting go of everything and just being me, hurt and all. Imagine, I had to be completely broken in order to do it. Life had to pummel me in order for me to let go of some of my old thought patterns, fears and anger. Much like the quote for the day, I have held myself back in a way, for fear of what I may find behind curtain number three. But I am not afraid anymore.

Yes, moving in sounds more accurate. And now that I am finally here, I think I'll stay a while.

I am thankful today for the progress I've made, and for the journey to come.

August 26th: Sharing the Letter from God, the Priest and the Butterfly

*The weak never forgive. Forgiveness is
the attribute of the strong.*

-Mahatma Gandhi-

With Brendan off to school, I print off the letter from God to bring with me to my appointment with Father Cahill. I've requested a meeting with him to review over some things I have been thinking about. I've been struggling with some things, things that hurt Stephen, and wondering if there is a reason to bring them up to the offender now that he is gone.

So, I head out, bright morning sunshine beating down on my face as I walk across the parking lot to the church offices. As I walk, I am thinking back to a few years ago, where I did not feel like a part of this building. That has changed. That is a good thing.

I am also thinking tentatively about the letter from God. Is it inappropriate to march into a Catholic priest's office toting a letter that you wrote, assuming what you think God would say to you? I don't have a Catholic etiquette book to refer to, but kind of wish I did. But, I have a feeling if it was really inappropriate, my parents would have somehow shown me a sign, flattened my tires or something. In any case, it is too late for that now. I emailed him a copy before the meeting.

The letter from God, as a suggestion from my neighbor Mike, has been a major source of my healing. Since writing it last week, I feel I have turned a corner of sorts. Thinking about and penning what I think God would say to me has been a cleansing experience. And I honestly feel that I am not far off when it comes to content.

Arriving in his office, Father Cahill meets me at the door with a hug. I still smile when I think that he is not much older than Stephen.

And we begin. It is funny, the last time I was here with him, was the day after we returned from the funeral. Now, an entire month has passed. Where did that time go? What have I been doing with my life in that time? My Gosh, I've been focused on trying to live, trying to get all of this out of me and on to the paper.

We talk about my letter from God, and he does not seem too shocked about it, so I assume I have not been judged in the eyes of the church as blasphemous. Not that I think he would, he is pretty relaxed when it comes to me talking to him about my faith.

I talk to him a lot about one of the nagging questions I have had since Stephen's death, and how I have tried to work through them within the lines of this letter. It is complicated, and there are no easy answers in something like this. As we talk, I realize that I may have assumed that father would say, "This is the solution, this is what He wants you to do."

But that is not how it works is it? It is up to me. Father can add perspective, but ultimately, this really is something that is between me and God. Free will and all that stuff. I have to choose how I will respond to this, how I will handle it.

And here's the kicker. Before Stephen's death, I would have responded, reacted, said my peace and moved on with my day. I would have let that lava bubble inside of me until I erupted. I would have let myself feel justified for saying it too.

But now, I am painfully weighing out the pros and the cons. For days, I have thought about this, wondered, weighed out what could come from it. I am asking myself what a good person should do, what would God do? And I think I have the answer. It is written in the letter. The answer is love. So, I will love this issue for a while longer, and let the solution savor, age like a fine wine, until it is something I can be proud of. Because, as I wrote in my letter, this is not something that hurts Stephen any longer. Stephen understands now. And, as much as I would appreciate an email or fax from heaven laying it all out for me, I know I have to figure this out in my own way.

Father and I have the best conversation, and I feel I am working through some mental mindsets I have held on to for most of my life. I enjoy his perspective. As we finish up, he hands me a poem he has printed for me. He has been so thoughtful and has helped me work through some tough issues.

As I walk out into the bright sunshine, I feel the warmth of the Carolina summer. I do like living here. There is something very extravagant about the warmth. As I make my way to the car, a beautiful yellow butterfly fluttered in front of my face, as if to flap approval for my approach.

I am thankful for the letter; I have grown since writing it. Thank you for the priest, who has guided, not pushed me towards the answers. And thanks for the butterfly, which makes me feel connected, with Stephen.

I am thankful.

August 27th: The Grief Lady, Comfort in Words, and Perspective from Listening to the Shouting Lady

Perhaps they are not stars, but openings in the Heaven,
Where the love of our lost ones pours through and shines
down upon us, To let us know they are happy.

- AUTHOR UNKNOWN-

TODAY WE RETURNED TO VISIT the "grief lady". That is Brendan's title for her, or the one he anointed her with before he first met her, emphatically telling me "I don't need to see the grief lady!"

Dr. Clarisse is a gentle and old soul, skilled at helping the individual work through the emotions that you are faced with in great times of change. It has truly been healing for me to accept help to get through this tragedy in my life. And, through that acceptance, I have awakened a part of me that has been much like Rip van Winkle, asleep for many years.

The plan we have with our grief counseling is I attend in the morning and Brendan meets with Dr. Clarisse in the afternoons.

This morning's appointment is a wonderful release, and I explain where I am with things, where I am with my grief. And, as strong as I feel as I walk into the office, I am reduced to tears by verbalizing the words, "I am starting to feel better…"

Because truthfully, I am not. For a moment, a blink, a heartbeat, I think that I can, but one song on the radio, once glance at a picture or memory, and I am right back to that shoreline on the lake begging for some sort of negotiation with God.

But, despite the tears, and the moments of weakness, I do feel strong; I do feel I am doing this (whatever this is) in a way that is best for our family. Talking through this helps. This is a lesson I have learned late in life. Sometimes, it is not about finding answers or solutions; sometimes there are no immediate answers to be found to the difficult situations or questions of life. But, simply, letting it out is the answer.

With my appointment successfully complete, I head off to try and write some more before picking up Brendan. I am finding that I can keep myself together more these days, but still carry my sunglasses wherever I go so I can cover my eyes when need be. I am sure the employees at the grocery store think to themselves, "Here comes that crazy sunglasses lady again."

In the afternoon, before Brendan's appointment started, he needed to have a bathroom break, so I sat quietly in the office waiting for his return. I looked on the wall, and in a beautiful calligraphy, was a gorgeous poem. I had not heard of it, but it was called the **Desiderata**. Looking it up later, I would find out that the name translated to Latin means *Desired Things*. Written in the 1920's, by Max Elrmann, there has been swirling confusion about the actual authorship of this poem. As it was read in a church in Maryland, some years later, the recording of the event implied it was found in the church in the 1600's. Funny how things get twisted up sometimes. It was so beautiful, and I was surprised that I had not come across this before. Perhaps I had, but was too busy, enveloped by my own ego, or plans, or agenda, or how others were hurting me, I did not see it. But, boy, I saw it today. Here is an excerpt:

> Go placidly amid the noise and the haste,
> and remember what peace there may be in silence.
> As far as possible, without surrender,

be on good terms with all persons.
Speak your truth quietly and clearly;
and listen to others,
even to the dull and the ignorant;
they too have their story.
Avoid loud and aggressive persons;
they are vexatious to the spirit.

-- MAX EHRMAN --

That pretty much sums it up doesn't it? It is funny, as what I am attempting to describe in this book of mine has been told and retold throughout the ages. But, for some reason, we humans simply choose not to be enlightened; we have to have our hand forced through hardship.

Smiling at Brendan, I left him in the capable hands of Dr. Clarisse, and made my way to the waiting area. I am happy about that. I think he needs to be able to let it out, without worrying about me and my feelings.

I sit outside, tune the radio to some classical music, and open my planner. I like gathering my thoughts, righting the ship at certain points in the day. I write a little, and then remember I forgot to read a prayer that father Cahill had given me the day before.

Sitting quietly, with canon in D playing in the background, I read:

I Have My Mission
God was all-complete, all blessed in
Himself, but it was His Will to
create a world for his glory. He is Almighty,
and might have done all
things Himself, but it has been His will
to bring about His purposes
by the beings he has created. We are all created to His glory-we
are created to do His will. I am created to do something for which
no one else is created; I have a place in God's counsels, in God's

*world, which no one else has; whether I be rich or poor, despised
or esteemed by man, God knows me and calls me by my name.
God has created me to do Him some definite service; He has
committed some work to me which he
has not committed to another.
I have my mission-I never may know it in this life, but I shall be
told it in the next. Somehow I am necessary for His Purposes, as
necessary in my place as an Archangel
in his-if indeed I fail; He can
raise another, as he could make the stones
the children of Abraham.
Yet, I have a part in this great work; I
am a link in a chain, a bond
of connection between persons. He has not created me for naught.
I shall do good, I shall do His work; I shall be an angel of peace,
a preacher of truth in my own place, while not intending it, if I
do but keep His commandments and serve Him in my calling.
Therefore I will trust Him. Whatever,
wherever I am, I can never
be thrown away. If I am in sickness, my sickness may serve Him;
in perplexity, my perplexity may serve
Him; if I am in sorrow, my
sorrow may serve Him. My sickness, or
perplexity, or sorry may be*

*necessary causes of some great end, which is quite beyond us. He
does nothing in vain; he may prolong
my life, He may shorten it; He
knows what He is about. He may take
my friends, He may throw me
among strangers, He may make me
feel desolate, make my spirits
sink, hide the future from me-still He knows what he is about.*

Oh my God, I give myself to Thee. I trust Thee Wholly. Thou art wiser than I-more loving to me than I myself. Deign to fulfill Thy high purposes in me whatever they be; work in and through me. I am born to serve Thee, to be Thine, to be Thy instrument. Let me be Thy blind instrument. I ask not to see, I ask not to know-I ask simply to be used.

-FROM JOHN HENRY NEWMAN'S *MEDITATIONS AND DEVOTIONS*

Wow. I am saying that a lot lately. Surprise has become a regular occurrence for me as I explore my spiritual side. Father Cahill shows me, not so much in words, but by passages and readings that he is listening to me very carefully. I am very thankful once again to have reached out instead of turning away from my faith and God during this time.

So, I am feeling pretty good, all things considered. Seems to me that I have received a lot of comfort from simple words today.

And then, through the thick hardwood of the office door next to Dr. Clarisse, I hear it. It is loud, and abrasive, like fingernails on a chalk board. It is obnoxious and rude and just plain angry. It is the voice of discontent.

The classical music, although soothing, cannot drown out the complaints that echo throughout the hallway. Apparently, this woman feels that raising her voice during this session will express her opinion more emphatically. I sympathetically take a moment of silence for the counselor sitting across from her and wonder what she does to decompress after listening to a client like this one for an hour. Maybe she has a special negativity chamber that she immerses her body in for hours after a session like this one.

"Have I not done enough? I tell you, I am the one to take him to soccer, and to basketball!! And what does he do? Nothing! Absolutely nothing! He sits there and says nothing. And when he gets into trouble, he does not discipline him. He lets him get away with everything. "

On and on it went. There was no pause, and I wondered how this woman was breathing. And in this twenty minute litany of complaint, there was not one thing said that could be remotely considered positive. Not one thing good about the man she married or her child. I was desperately trying not to hear it, but I could not help it, it was so loud.

The kicker for me was when she said "have I not taught him how to pray and be Christian?" See, this is where I don't get it. Is this being Christian?

This woman had a list of all the things she did right, a long list of all the things she did for her family every day. And, no doubt, it was a lot of tasks and action items. But she could not, in an entire hour find one thing that they did for her, and was unable to verbalize one good thing about them. She could only see what they did wrong, and how she was a victim.

For an instant, a surge rushed through my body. I shifted in my chair, prepared to pounce. What a scene I could create, bursting in the room, and telling her a thing or two about what she was missing. I could say something like "At least your child is still alive, you selfish pile of crap".

And then I exhaled. No, that is not who I am. I still felt like bursting in, if for nothing else, to save the therapist from a death due to over exposure to negative energy. But, this is what I would say.

Let me reframe this for you. Your family is not content because you are not looking for things to be content about. You are looking for all the wrong things in your life and in them and you are finding them. You are missing the point as your happiness can be found by simply flicking a switch in your brain.
Be grateful.
Love solves it all.
Your husband probably feels like a failure in your eyes, and wants to feel like he is loved and respected by you. Show him some of that, and you may be able to meet in the middle instead of feeling like he is out to

undermine you. Your child wants the same, he wants to feel like you are proud of him, and that you see his goodness. Your recognition of his goodness
is like sunshine to a flower, and it will allow his goodness to grow.

And, let's be honest here. You want love too. Because if you felt loved, you would not be screaming so loud, announcing all of the things you do for everyone, looking for recognition. It seems like there has been a running tally in your house for way too long, so no one can show genuine gratitude anymore.
If you want some of it, give some of it back honey. Tell your family what they give to you each day. One day soon, your child will climb into a car and drive off, to create a life of his own. And, if you never appreciated the one he had under your roof, why would he invite you to be part of one that is independent of your rules? You only get one chance at this sugar cakes, wake the heck up!

I realize I don't know the entire story, and I have only been privy to a few moments of this woman's ranting. I am jarred from my thoughts as the doorbell to the office rings. The outside doors are kept locked for security reasons. I jump up to answer, so the counselors can continue their sessions, and this kind and gentle looking man is standing in the doorway smiling at me. No way, I think. You cannot be the Ogre that the shouting lady is talking about. There's just no way. As I hold the door and let him walk beside me towards the office, I check his head for horns. Nope.

He quietly knocks on the door, and, although I cannot see her, I picture her springing off the chair to the door. As he was walking in, his wife continued with the list of wrongs, but the sound of her voice abruptly stopped when the quiet knock was heard from behind the door.

The door swings open and she sticks her head outside. "You're early."

She barks at him, and points to the chairs, as if telling Fido to sit in his place during mealtime. As she does so, she looks up and notices I am sitting there quietly. To be honest, my mother told me never to stare, but I can't help myself. To make it worse, I think my mouth is gaping open. She and I make eye contact for a split second, but I know she does not see me. And that is okay. She is too involved in her own story, so even if she had been sitting with me for the past forty minutes, I doubt she would have seen me then either. I feel bad for her, and look away, feeling sympathy because she is missing the point. I say a little prayer that she is never brought to her knees by life in the way I have been.

The husband sits quietly in the chair that she directed him to, waiting to be called into the room. I look down to my planner, and fumble around, wondering if I should try to make conversation. I look up and ask him if it has started to rain outside. The dark foreboding clouds told me on my way into the office that it was a sure thing, so I think this is an easy question to spark conversation.

"A few drops here and there", he says, "but nothing too much yet." His voice is soft, his smile is genuine. I am confused.

The wife pops her head out of the now quiet room. "Come on, we're ready for you now."

He gets up and walks towards the door, slowly, head down. He seems a little beaten up by life to be honest. With my sick sense of humor, I can hear the "Funeral March" in my head. Better you than me guy….

So, my little things for the day? It would have to be The Grief Lady, with her kind and understanding heart, helping us through this. Brendan likes her, and that is a gift, as I so want him to be okay through all of this.

Next would be the words, from prayers and poems, reaffirming the direction I am moving with my life. My daily quotes, my writing and these gifts are guides to me, old scribes holding candles on the pathway as I make my way through a deep gorge in my life.

And, last but not least, the screaming lady. She showed me how far I've come in my own life. I can recall a time where I was wound tight, and caught in my own story. I could not see the good in the situation, and it took me a long time, a divorce and a move to a different country to find it.

So, thank you screaming lady. You've reminded me of a lot today. The fact that I am at a place of peace, at this time in my life, is a big, not little thing. I hope someday you can find that peace as well, but I suspect that will not happen without a painful journey of your own.

August 28th: You Gotta Have Faith...

*Faith is the art of holding on to things your reason has
once accepted in spite of your changing moods*

-C.S. LEWIS-

IT'S BEEN A HARD DAY. I've been emotional and I've felt the tears and sorrow bubbling up within me since I awoke this morning. I feel weakened, and slightly frustrated by the feeling. You see, I find that I am tiring of the roller coaster ride of emotions. I feel that descriptor is lacking, for at least a roller coaster gives you a hint of what's to come with the click, click sound as your car climbs the steep incline in preparation for the terrifying drop. You have an idea that something is about to happen. But with this, I find I am feeling strong, and all of a sudden, without any click or other warning sign, I fall. Today is a day like that.

A person called me regarding an appointment this morning. And, when I answered the telephone, the first words she said breathlessly were, "I have some really bad news."

My reaction was instinctive, and I could feel the acid beginning to burn in the pit of my stomach. My muscles were tightening around my bones and I was physically bracing myself. For an instant, I thought, "Not again God. Please, Please, I cannot be hurt like this anymore."

"I have to cancel your appointment." she said.

She was generally sorry for the inconvenience she had caused, and quickly talked about a rescheduling option. I muffled my way through the conversation, saying yes to whatever she was saying. And I hung up the phone and I sobbed loudly. My chest was beating fast, my throat was tight, and my gut just ached. I am sure there are more adequate descriptive words, but ache seems to be the most accurate. It is a dull and burning pain I feel, worse than any injury or illness I have ever experienced.

Really bad news. It's all relative isn't it? When I heard those words, I immediately thought of what was most important in my life, and it had nothing to do with things, appointments, or life in general. It was all about love, the special people who could, even in my grief, make my heart sing. And her words, though quickly explained, struck me in a way that completely derailed me for most of the day. Because they reminded me of something. These kinds of things happen all the time. People who have lost and hurt don't move to the back of the line, not to be hurt again until it is their cosmic turn. Things happen, that we cannot understand, and when we least expect it. That scares me.

I push through the day, thinking about this concept at length. I've been working through some of this fear based thinking for weeks to be honest. I had quite a bit to work through when Brendan started back at hockey, or when we went for a swim. One particular day at the beach, I watched Brendan and Brady take quite a spill from the sea Kayak, and I held my breath until I could see the both of them pop up from beneath the water. And then, there's the general stuff. Brendan leaving for school, Brady going out to work in the yard. And me, left to work through my doomsday mentality.

With motherhood, came a deep sense of worry for me. I would worry about the potential consequences of child's play, what could happen, who could get hurt. I worried about the most inconsequential things. I would come home from a particularly tough Emergency room shift, and announce to Stephen he must never ride a motorcycle, or snowmobile, or horse, let alone try any substance given to him by a stranger, drink from someone else's water bottle, or run with scissors. For a while there, I was the Queen of Contemplation when it came to the worst case scenario.

But then, I let some of it go. I was still super protective over my children, but I lightened up a bit. I would still tell Stephen not to walk home alone at night as he finished his junior year at college, and he would laugh with me; but I understood that he was going to be okay. Perhaps it was due to the fact I was no longer working in health care. I was not seeing those consequences each day, and it gave me a chance to exhale. Or, perhaps it was my choice in partners, with a husband who loved adventure, and everything just seemed to work out. But, for some reason, I had a more balanced look on the potential outcomes of situations.

And then Stephen died. I still hate using those two words together.

When that happened, I was groundless. Everything I had contemplated had in fact come to pass. I was right all along, and wrong to let my guard down. Groundless. I've listened to some of what Pema Chodron says about that feeling, and it comforts me to know I am not alone, and it is a normal part of being human. I enjoy listening to her audio books. As a Buddhist teacher, she has offered me yet another perspective as I think about my personal spiritual journey.

It has been quite the trip. In some ways, I feel like it has been a crash course in spirituality. I have been raised Roman Catholic, and our church has been a big part of our healing. But I have read and listened to other religious leaders, wanting to hear more and find out more about the differences and similarities. I'm not sure why I have been on this quest of sorts. I suppose it stems from the fact that my faith was the only thing I felt I had left when I lost Stephen. It was the only thing I felt was sitting with me on the shoreline, other than Rudy the Wonder Dog.

With that being the case, I guess I am searching so I can be well informed, and I can refine my spirituality skills. And what I've found is through all of the teachings, and readings and denominations, one thing keeps coming back to me. The answer is love. It is the only answer, the only thing to fix a broken heart, a broken relationship, and a broken world.

I like that. But I find I have to work very hard about loving *all* that surrounds me in life. Whether it is a challenging individual or a stress filled situation, I find it difficult sometimes to give love to the harder elements of life. Sure, it is easy to love those who love me back. It is easy to love the butterflies, the beach, puppies, or chocolate. But what about someone you know has hurt you in the past and looks to be hurting you again? What about giving love to a situation like this one, losing your son and no longer recognizing yourself in the mirror?

This is what occupies my mind as I work through what to believe, how to act, how to go on with my life. How do I let go of the fear, and embrace all the beautiful moving parts of complete faith in something? How can I completely embrace the love?

I can't spend my life worrying about the worst case scenario, or the next horrendous phone call. Fear is not real. It is all in your head. Nor can I spend my life saying the spiritual answer is love, and then in the next breath tell you who qualifies as loveable.

Because, when I do attach conditions to my faith, I don't feel the connection. And I don't like not feeling connected with the power bigger than me, and with Stephen's spirit.

It is hard, relinquishing what control you thought you had over your life.

So, today, I am thankful for my faith. For what it is now and what it is growing into each day.

And I am thankful for the cancelled appointment. It reminds me that I still have some work to do on letting go of the fear and anxiety. It reminds me of the simple truth. I could get another call, or another hurt, or another disaster in my life. It is part of life, and is not to be feared but accepted as part of your path if it should come.

I am thankful.

August 29th: Living….

He is a wise man who does not grieve for
the things which he has not,
but rejoices for those which he has.

- Epictetus -

Early Saturdays, a blessing for which I have always been thankful. I think pretty clearly in the mornings. I find fatigue clouds the clarity of my thinking these days, and it is harder to see through my emotions when I am tired. The evenings have been difficult for me, so I am very thankful for the mornings when I awake refreshed, knowing that I really can make it.

Last night was one of those nights, and as I typed, yesterday was one of those days. I completely collapsed with grief in bed last night, sobbing and crying for my baby. My typed words cannot adequately describe the depth of the emotion or the breakdown. My husband held me as I cried and he cried some tears of his own. We just miss him so much.

Awareness in the early morning is what I give thanks for. With that, I have come to understand that if I am going to survive; my approach needs to be healthy. I need to take care of myself, mind and body. So, this morning is about making commitments to myself about how to grieve in a healthy way, through reflection, eating the right things, exercising, getting enough sleep. It sounds simplistic, but truly making the commitments makes a difference to me. In a time where everything feels so out of control, it gives me a sense of personal responsibility.

And, with that renewed sense of purpose and peace after a good night's sleep, I set out for the day.

Today, I am thankful for many things. For the sunshine of the morning, and the bright red cardinals sitting on the bell we have outside. For the warmth of the Carolina sunshine and the blue of the sky. In all the places I have lived, this one feels the closest to home for me. Perhaps it has something to do with the house being filled with love.

And today, I feel as if I want to enjoy that sunshine, that day. I don't feel I need to sit and reflect today, to write and remind myself it is good to be alive. Today, I just want to be alive. So, I am off to live. And for that, I am thankful.

I will close the entry with a poem I thought was beautiful and powerful and so, so true.

May you listen to your longing to be free.
May the frames of your belonging be large
enough for the dreams of your soul.
May you arise each day with a voice of blessing whispering in your heart
...something good is going to happen to you.
May you find harmony between your soul and your life.
May the mansion of your soul never become a haunted place.
May you know the eternal longing that lies at the heart of time.
May there be kindness in your gaze when you look within.
May you never place walls between the light and yourself.
May you be set free from the prisons of guilt,
fear, disappointment and despair.
May you allow the wild beauty of the invisible world to gather you,
mind you, and embrace you in belonging.

- JOHN O'DONAHOE

August 30th: Dignified Resilience

*The world is a looking glass, and gives back to every
man the reflection of his own face. Frown at it, and it
will look sourly upon; laugh at it and with it,
and it is a jolly, kind companion.*

-WILLIAM THACKERAY-

I'VE BEEN LOOKING AT SUPPORT. Looking around, outside of my own coping, to see what other people are saying about grief. In particular, I've been looking at how people have coped with losing a child. I have been surprised by what I've found. There are some wonderful sites out there, and I am going to endorse them in my daily gratitude because they deserve it.

Sites like Compassionate Friends and Grief Share. I find them to be focused on things that are aligned with my thinking.

But, there are some sites that are bewildering to me. I am not judging them, because everyone grieves differently. But I do not feel comfortable with the "My life is over" approach. I know it is part of it. I know there have been moments I have felt that way. But through my gratitude, I have only had moments of those feelings, not months.

In my loss, I went looking for the right group, the right website, people who knew where I've been and who could help. And what I found is as individual as one person's grief is to another.

The sites have helped me tremendously. Even the ones I did not particularly connect with helped put some things in perspective for my own personal journey. It is important to get out of your own head, and explore what the rest of the world is saying.

This whole reflection leads me to think once again about resilience. This past weekend, I took some time to watch the TV coverage on the funeral of Senator Ted Kennedy. Having always had a fascination with the Kennedys growing up in Canada watching American television, I was riveted as I watched a documentary about the lives of the brothers in this famous American family. Growing up in Newfoundland, I would watch the American TV stations with intrigue, never realizing I would one day live here. The Kennedy family in particular personified everything that fascinated me about the country.

But there was more to them than just the political roots and their commitment to service to a country that they loved. There was more than the look of celebrity they all had, sun kissed faces, and adventuresome spirits grabbing at all that life had to offer.

It was the resilience. I watched in it the faces of the family in the footage of the loss of JFK and then of his brother Robert. I saw it again in the subsequent losses of other family members throughout the years, like the tragic ending of JFK Jr., and his beautiful bride, taken far too soon.

I think the real reason I have loved watching this family is because they have something that I work at possessing every day with the struggles I face in my own life.

I call it a *"Dignified Resilience"*.

I believe a big part of how they as a family have been able to move on from those heart wrenching events in their life is because of choice. Choice of how to react to the reality of their lives, and a bigger choice as well. To be in service to those less fortunate than themselves. That is the ultimate form of gratitude don't you think? To, on a larger level, realize the benefit of your position in the world, and use that position to help others who do not have a voice. They make a choice to do that, and understand that this is not simply something you do every now and again; it is a part of your life. Woven into the fabric of your family, into the shirts of each of your children, it is a garment you wear every day, a garment of service.

I think I am on to something here. I am humbled as I feel in the face of my own tragedy, I have only typed and hugged and cried.

You know what I believe? We used to have it figured out. Before gratitude journals, people served. People understood that they were responsible to help out, in church and school. My parents were prime examples of that. They did not need to remind themselves to be thankful each day by writing it in a book purchased at Barnes and Noble. They were thankful each day because in their service of others, their own blessings were illuminated. And, in the service of others, they came to understand that the act of helping others was the biggest act of gratitude for their own lives.

Boy, am I learning. I feel I am so humbled by this personal revelation that I can barely make eye contact with the screen as I type. I vow it will be different from here on in.

So, in my own gratitude, how can I show that dignified resilience? How can I look outward and show my gratitude? How can I share with others who need me, find a new way for me to channel the love I gave to Stephen all of these years? It's a pretty big share of love. I've got a lot to give. In fact, there's much more. As I've always told my children, your heart is an amazing thing. There is always room to love one more person.

So, today I am thankful for the wonderful examples others have shown me and the world about how to conduct yourself in times of difficulty. Whether it is the Kennedy family showing resilience in both the live coverage and daily service to the country, or the father who decided to create an informative website to remember his child who had passed, you are all my teachers.

It is all starting to come together for me. I've got to get to work.

August 31st: How Much is Postage to Heaven?

Life is God's novel. Let him write it.

-Isaac Bashevis Singer-

THE LETTER FROM GOD REALLY made a difference in my life. I never thought that would happen. I am thankful for that today. And, it has started the wheels turning for other letters I need to write.

I have started to write letters to my family that will be here when it is my time to go. For the people who mean something to me, I want to make sure they have something that reflects my feelings after I am gone. But more importantly, I've decided I will be writing some of those messages and sending them right now. The lessons I've learned from all of this have helped me understand the importance of telling people you love them. Here and now. I have postponed those moments in life in my past, prioritizing an important presentation, or housework, or some other triviality. I will work in my life to not make those choices going forward.

I am thankful, because to be honest, Stephen and I really did communicate our feelings openly and often. I am blessed with that comfort, and I know that.

But, I wanted to write him one more letter. Here it is.

Dear Stephen,

I miss you. Those three words do not describe my feelings of absolute anguish sufficiently. In the past weeks, I have poured words from my soul in the hopes of letting out all of this pain. Sometimes, I feel I need to invent my own words, some new ones in the dictionary that will adequately describe what it feels like to lose someone as special as you. But, I know in my heart there are no words for sorrow as deep as this. I also know it needs no explanation to anyone else.

I've been thinking about writing you this letter since I heard from God. His words really helped me, and I thought it may also help to articulate my feelings to you. To tell you all of the things I've thought about since you went to heaven.

First, I love you so much. The past weeks have been a time of reflection for me, and I can see clearly the depth of the love we had. I always knew we had something very special, and looking back has not only confirmed that bond, it has strengthened it. It is a bittersweet feeling for me, to look and realize it was as special as I thought, and to know it has now changed.

When my phone rang on the evening of July 4th, I smiled as I looked at the caller ID. I thought it was you. Oh Stephen, I feel so sad when I think about that moment. That instant, my life changed. I need you to know that I would have changed places with you if God had let me. I would have done anything to keep you safe. I do not understand God's entire Plan, but I hope you can see that I've decided to put my faith in it. I know that you understand all of it now, so I hope you are looking down on me and are proud of the decisions I am making as I work through this.

I've thought about it a lot, and I know you felt my love up to the moment of your death. I want you to know that Brady and I knew how much you loved us. We felt it and you showed it every single day. Sometimes I wish you could confirm you knew, call me up on the telephone, or come home and we could have one of our famous late night chats. I loved those chats, where we would stay up half the night and talk about everything under the sun. I cherished those times with you, when it was quiet and just the two of us, and you would tell me about your life, good and bad. I miss those times, but I know you communicate in your own way, helping me find emails and text messages and journal entries.

The thing is, I know that I did not really have anything unsaid. I know what we had, and how much we loved. I wish I could shake this feeling of unfinished business. Perhaps it was the quickness of it all. Brady and I were talking and laughing about you in one minute, happy that you were with your friends and having a good time, and the next, it was over. Since that time, I've racked my brains about what we last talked about, and realized it was simple things, the mundane. I don't know why that bothers me so. I don't know why I feel we should have had some earth shattering discussion. I mean, it's not like you could see this coming.

I think this is why I am writing every day Stephen. I look at this as my last conversation with you, for a while anyway. I look at this book as one of my late night chats with the most amazing boy.

In case I didn't tell you enough, I wanted to put down a few thoughts. In a bulleted list of course:

* *You have been the greatest gift, and I feel blessed and honored that God allowed me to be your mother, even for a short period of time. It is all so clear to me now, what your life meant to the big picture of things. You have affected so many, and touched so many lives with your quiet and unassuming nature. Your capacity for love and kindness, your tolerance, and your ability to know what people needed to feel safe in their lives, and then give it to them. I was so proud of you when you were alive, but that pride grows since your passing if you can believe that. I've heard so many stories about you, and they have all reaffirmed what I knew about my baby boy. I always felt you were special, the best part of myself. You made me want to be a better mother, and human being, and I learned more from you than you will ever know. Thank you for being such a gift, such a precious and wonderful son.*

❧ *Your brother aches for you, quietly. He and I talk at bedtime, and I wish I could offer him more comfort. But there are no answers for this hurt. I remember all the private moments the two of you would have, and I know he longs for those right now. We continue to love him as hard as we can, but there is a void in his life. I feel you with him. Through his pain, he has been so strong. Please continue to watch over him and love him, to protect him and guide him.*

❧ *Our life was filled with adventure, some good and some not so good. But we always made it through. As I have reflected on that journey, I've thought a lot about the last four years. I watched you blossom and I could feel your happiness. Brady and I actually talked about it on our drive to the lake. Your friends actually told us that at the lake, you kept saying, "Isn't this the most perfect day?" Stephen, I hope it was for you. I hope your heart was filled with happiness, all that you deserved in your last moments of life. I hope we loved you hard enough, told you enough how great and awesome you were, hugged you enough, believed in you enough. I hope that it all was enough, and you felt complete and happy. I pray everyday that was the case.*

❧ *God told me that you were never alone and that Matthew came to guide you home. Wow. I wish I could have seen that one. I always knew there was an unspoken longing for him throughout your life, and knowing you are together is one of the biggest things that gives me solace and peace in my heart. Was it wild to see him, to hug and to finally feel together? Promise me, when it is my time that you will both come for me. If seeing you both together was the only part of heaven I could witness, it would be enough.*

I feel you when I am writing and some of what is coming out onto the paper feels like you to be honest. I hope you can see me, and I hope you are proud of the choices I am making as I mourn. I'm not sure I understand it, but I've felt I've known what I needed to do to honor you from that moment at the lake.

Say hello to Nanny and Poppy, Matthew, Aunt Kay, Uncle Denny, Aunt Barb, Aunt Joan and all the rest of our family. I know you are engulfed with love.

Stephen we miss you so much. But we believe that you are doing something special in heaven. And we know, your death has sparked something special here on earth. Watch over us, and guide us, help us keep the faith on those dark days when we can't imagine going on without you.

I love you my sweet baby boy.

Mom

xoxo

Today, as I prepare to enter yet another new month, check off another milestone of time passing, I am thankful. I am thankful because I know whatever I wrote in this letter, he already knew. He already knew.

September 1st: My Personal Quest, and Sharing My Words

Never take a person's dignity: it is worth
everything to them, and nothing to you.

-*Frank Barron*-

THE WORLD IS A GOOD place you know. There is more kindness than not, no matter what the evening news tries to tell you. I've stopped watching the evening news. I decided, why bother listening to a group of people sensationalize someone else's pain for ratings and the top of the hour news flash. So, now, when I do come across something, I look innocently at my husband, and say, "When did that happen?" It has been a freeing and up-lifting experience for me.

I made the decision to do so when I saw how they distorted the life of my son in a few simple words. In the stories immediately following his death, they painted a picture of a boy from the snippets of information they could get. They had not had an opportunity to speak with anyone who loved him and knew him. So, instead of a story that should have read,

"A beautiful, talented, loving boy died today. He was a rising senior at NC State, a goalie, a brother, a son, a good person. He was an amazing human being that could have given so much to the world and now he is gone...."

Instead it read like this...

"Alcohol was found at the scene but no one could confirm if this was a factor in the accident."

In one sentence, the media had painted a picture of my child that had nothing to do with his time on earth. It truly was irrelevant. I know I have written about this before. But, it really bothered me. As my friend Tracey said, they did not say "there were hot dogs and chips at the scene, but no one could confirm if he ate any and if that contributed to his death." So, combine that sensationalized reporting with the anonymous hate speak on the new site discussion boards, and you've got yourself a whole big ball of negativity swirling around a family whose world has just imploded.

I read one student discussion board, where one guy questioned the try-outs and athleticism requirements for university sports, because obviously, Stephen was not a great athlete if he could not even make it across the cove.

I don't know why I could not let it go. But it has started a personal crusade for me. I am only one voice, but I vow to speak out against this from now until the day I die. Give hurting families the dignity they deserve. Make people have to list their phone number and full name publicly before they can post something on any online discussion board.

We've created this world where everyone feels entitled to comment on someone else's misfortune. We've created a world where it is expected that you will be judged if you are put in the public eye. In fact, if you read a news story online, it is the last thing they ask of you. Click here to comment on this story. They encourage it.

Why are we having a hard time finding good leaders in this world? Why do you hear people say you would have to be "nuts to get into politics"?

The answer is simple. People see what happens to others in the public eye. And they quietly look at themselves and see they have imperfections too. They may be a great leader, but they did have that DUI in college.

Our judgments are not only preventing us from evolving as individuals. We are, by virtue of our own need to feel empowered, preventing our world from being the best it can be. It's a big statement I know, but think about it. And all of this came to me by watching how people treated the death of my son. Even in the death of a truly innocent and beautiful human being, people found a way to talk about the dark side of life, assuming there had to be a negative back story.

So, for all of you anonymous posters out there, I give you notice. If I read your comments, I will be calling you out. Please understand, one day, you will have a hard time in your life, and want some compassion, privacy and mercy. And for you reporters, I want you to remember one important thing as you head out with your news van and notebook. There is a grieving mother reading your story. She held that boy in her arms and did her best to raise him to be a fine boy. All she has left of him are memories and words. Do not, with one sentence, paint a picture of him that only serves you and your headline.

So, after my rant, what am I thankful for? I am thankful for the rant, as it shows me I still have the spark within me. I am thankful that I found something to champion, however small.

This morning, I called out one of the anonymous posters and emailed the paper to express my displeasure with their policy. I am thankful for that.

I am thankful that all of the news sites I contacted took down the comments that offended me. I am also thankful that one of the news sites in particular, now posts that they have disabled the comments section for stories like this one, out of respect for the grieving family.

Let's get back to being kind to each other. I challenge anyone who reads this not to let these little things go. Step up and fight for a return to kindness and respect.

And finally, I am thankful for sharing my first twenty pages of writing with Brady. Big step! He takes the papers from me as if they are treasures. I do love him so. Because I know, even if he begins to read and sees I have typed the same word over and over for twenty pages, he would still love me. Let's hope he finds it a little more interesting than that.

Thank you.

September 2nd: My Twelve Year Old Teacher and Rudy the Wonder Dog

You think dogs will not be in heaven? I tell you,
they will be there long before any of us.

-ROBERT LOUIS STEVENSON-

BRENDAN HAS BEEN A TALKER since birth. I mean it, even in the first months of his time on earth, the baby babble was loud, and purposeful, and there was lots of it. It seems he has always had something to say. He started to talk early, and from that moment, his speech was clear, and funny and dramatic.

In Kindergarten, during our interview with his teacher, she informed us that she and Brendan would, at some point, every day have a one on one conversation at her desk, usually when the other kids were having play time. She said it was almost as if he needed some more adult conversation. He has always been verbally advanced, and has had an ability to describe his feelings or events with clarity and detail beyond his years.

That talent has not changed as he has grown, but in fact has sharpened. With the attention to the details, he has now developed a sharp sense of humor, with a touch of sarcasm, which may or may not be hereditary.

In any case, Brendan's conversations are a source of gratitude for me. To see life through his eyes is such a pleasure, such an escape. He talks more than Stephen did, although I still believe he is just as introspective.

So, today I am thankful for the hour after Brendan gets home from school. For today, Brendan spoke for 17 minutes straight, with barely a breath in between. He had so much to say, about school and friends, Malcolm in the Middle, and about hockey.

On and on he went, there was simply so much to tell me. And I was touched by his enthusiasm for life. I was humbled, yet again by the courage of another. You see, I watched my son, who had as much loss as I did this summer, and he was talking about all the good in his life. He could barely catch a breath as he tried to get it all out.

The wonder of a child will teach us. I believe that. I believe that we grown ups lose something when we decide to leave the trivial and the simple joys behind for more grown up things. We exchange play clothes for business suits, and begin to layer things on top of our lives that dulled our senses. Not only our senses of joy and happiness, but also the joy found within loss, the joy of resilience.

So, today, I have gratitude for my teacher Brendan. He is a model for how we should all conduct ourselves in pain.

I am also thankful for my other teacher, Rudy the Wonder Dog. I know that sounds like my higher education has gone to the dogs. Insert groan here for the bad joke. But Rudy has been a constant source of comfort and a valued teacher through all of this. That morning, almost two months ago now, Rudy stood by me in one of the most difficult moments of my life. He did so with a quiet, unconditional love. I can recall one moment that morning at the lake, where I cried out in despair. And he looked up at me with his eyes, as deep as the ocean, and licked my hand. We stared at each other for a long time, having an unspoken conversation of comfort. If we are all lucky enough to have either a person or animal show us the meaning of unconditional love, we have already reached a heaven of sorts. I am blessed, because I have a houseful of people who love each other without expectation.

Rudy is not an Alpha dog. He does not run around trying to exert power. Any child could jump on his back, and he would play with them, but never force them away, or hurt them. He simply surrenders to his reality. And, because he is easy with the world and with his life, life returns the favor. He does not have the struggles of other dogs that fight for control or power in their house. Because he does not exert his strength, he has been anointed as a Wonder Dog. He acts almost human, lying on the couch as if he used his Visa to pay for it. He is at complete peace with his circumstances.

I have learned much from this Chocolate Lab, who, as I type is lying at my feet. I have learned that a life of struggle is only a reality if you choose to make it a struggle. I have learned about surrendering to the now of my life. And I have learned that the truly rich in this world are those who can love unconditionally.

September 3rd: Technical difficulties, Pictures and Insights on Parenting

He who teaches children learns more than they do.

−*German Proverb*-

HAVE YOU EVER HAD A moment in your life where you feel so frustrated that you feel your head may actually just pop off, flying through the air, never to be seen again? The decapitation releasing the steam within you from whatever irritant has caused you to completely lose your cool.

Well, there is one thing that can do that to me. Computer issues, technical difficulties, or anything related to a problem with household technology. I can usually keep my cool and sense of humor in the worst of situations. I have learned that lately. But give me a corrupted file, a faulty cord, the computer "blue screen of death", and I melt down like a badly built nuclear plant.

It is one of many flaws, but it is very noticeable. I really feel for my husband, as he is usually on the receiving end of some of the lava spewing from my mouth when I cannot get the computer to do as I wish. You see, the computer does not talk back, and I need some validation. Poor guy.

Today was one of those days, where technology and I face off, like the McCoy's and the Hatfields. And, as much as I have never been a person to give up, I have to admit to you I never win. I modify, I accept. I go through the five stages of grief over my loss of control. I'm not sure if Elizabeth Kubler Ross envisioned her theory applied in this area of life.

I am trying to access a document. It is important, and I need it today. I have saved it in an obscure location, and the computer does not want to share it with me. Try after try, I search, but it is not working.

I smile as I remember the look of horror on Stephen's face when he would look over my shoulder as I was working, and exclaim, "Mom, you cannot have that many windows open at the same time! You need to close some!" Okay, well, I need to be honest. I never took his advice on all things computer, and I am now paying the price.

And then, the most amazing thing happens. Because as I am simmering in my desk chair, I open an electronic folder that turns out to be the best gift of my day, my week for that matter. My mind shifts, back from my frustration and my old responses, and back into gratitude.

Inside this unlabeled folder sits pictures, the most fantastic records of happy times. For a moment, I hold my breath. I had long since forgotten about those pictures, and because of it, the details of those occasions.

It was funny, because it was as if I created this folder to assemble a timeline of sorts, as the pictures were from all stages of my life with Stephen. The little boy, so cute, and pleasant, with an endless amount of energy. The eleven year old, baseball uniform, with a catcher's glove and pure ambition. He always wanted to win. The teenager, the smile a little more guarded, but still there. So many stories, so many journeys in these few precious photos. The teenage smile, holding back, from the usual angst of adolescence, but also from hurt. And then the shift. I still can't figure out why I clumped these all together. But, sitting next to that smile, is a picture of Stephen at the beach with Brady. July 4, 2008, exactly one year before his death. They are playing Bocce ball, and as usual, they are laughing about some random piece of information. I was sitting under the gazebo, sheltered from the hot July sun, just watching them. Content, that would be the word I would use to describe the mood of the day. Surrounded by friends and family, just the way I like it. I clicked away with my camera. And I captured this sequence of pictures that are now like precious gems to us. There is a look on Stephen's face as he laughs with Brady, and well, it just says all that needs to be said. If God were able to articulate what he wanted for each of us during our time on earth, it would be a moment like this one. Not the houses, the cars, the perfect children or two vacations a year. No, I believe God would tell us that we would be fulfilled if we could learn how to accept the simple moments of joy. And I am thankful, because my son, with the love of my husband, had so much joy on that day.

Taking photographs is something I am very thankful for. It is fantastic, to capture those memories, to click at just the right moment. I loved it before, and now, well I am just so blessed to have taken so many pictures.

This folder read like a good novel, and told a story. As I studied each photo, I could see Stephen grow. In size, and in maturity. But, the most striking thing I noticed was the "growth of happiness". You could see the light within him grow as if someone had thrown kerosene on the fire that burned inside him.

I am thankful. I am thankful for that light, and how bright it was shining at the time of his death. Oh, if only I can be so lucky. If only we can all be so lucky to shine brightly from within at any point in our lifetimes.

And, I guess by the sheer connection of it all, I have to say I am thankful for the technical difficulties. Without them, I would not have found this hidden treasure.

September 4th: With a Deep Breath, a Broken Beating Heart, and Hope in My Pocket...

*Everyone has baggage. Some people really let it
weigh them down, carrying the heavy load through
every part of their life. I use mine for travel.*

-KSB-

WELL, TWO MONTHS HAVE PASSED. I can hardly believe it in some ways, and in others, I feel as if I have been wandering the earth for years with this heavy wagon pulling behind me. The wagon of grief, filled with rocks; rocks of anguish, ache, pain, loss, sadness, confusion. I know, I label things. I give life events titles and descriptors, and they are quirky. I am thankful for that facet of my personality. You see, it brings levity to the situation, no matter how grim.

I've passed that trait along to my children. Stephen spoke of a particularly tough semester, and described it as the *T-Rex of Doom semester.* It was a running joke. We drove to the Carolinas when we moved, back in 2005, and we called it *Mom, Stephen and Brendan's Most Excellent Adventure.* And of course, who can forget Brendan's title for our wonderful counselor. *The Grief Lady.*

It seems that those labels have helped us put things in perspective. I am glad that is one of the things I passed along. Of all the fumbles and follies of parenting, I feel blessed that they got that from me.

On this day, I am thoughtful. I have decided this will be the end of the record for this book, but I will continue on for my own emotional health. This morning, before I started to write, I felt kind of melancholy. I find with each transition in my life, each milestone of time passing since he was alive and hugging me, sadness seeps in to my day. It is a delicate balance of recognition of this normal emotion, and also keeping myself in the emotional space I need to be in to continue to breathe. Don't get me wrong, I let it out. I am sure our neighbors have started to wonder if there is an Irish Banshee living next door.

In any case, this feeling of melancholy led my actions this morning. I started to look back over my writing. And this is one little thing for me. Because, I am shocked. It feels like I am reading this for the first time, I can hardly remember some of things I wrote on those days. It is remarkable to me, almost like I am reading someone else's story. Well, okay, not quite.

But bigger than the recording of events, I am amazed at what I was able to pull from those days in terms of gratitude. As I read them, my melancholy, my deep sadness lifts, and I am quiet. For you see, as I read what I felt gratitude for on the morning of July 5th, I came to an important conclusion. If I could feel thankfulness on that day, I would survive and find happiness in any day that would follow. Sure, I am going to still have sadness, but I now understand that I will continue to be thankful. I will continue to see the good in life, and I will learn from the sadness. It is only because of the gratitude I will be able to do this.

So, on the day of transition, I am thankful for:

* Bulleted lists. They are neat and tidy and orderly and seem fitting for the summation of my two months of grief.

* I have continued to breathe, even when that breath caught in my tightened throat, constricted with the sudden flashes of reality; he is gone. I have continued to breathe, even when I just thought it would be easier and less painful if I did not. I've continued to breathe, even when I begged God to take my breath away and give it to Stephen.

* My heart has continued to beat, despite the fact it is broken open and in a million pieces. And more than just beat, it has continued to fill with love each day. And in the wreckage, there is a special room where Stephen sits with me, each day, urging me on to live, to be happy, and to know he is with me always.

* I am thankful for the memories that have surfaced because of this terrible event. I have visited places in my past I had long forgotten, and it has been a wonderful trip. This journey has been so much more than grieving for Stephen. It has been a reflection on my lifetime since that glorious and imperfect night in 1986. I have grieved for Stephen on that journey, but also others I have lost. My mother, father, and Matthew. Much like life, the journey had some bumps in the road, but I would not have changed a thing.

* I am thankful for the glimpses of happiness in the past two months. The cuddles with Brendan, the swims, the beach, the friends, the family. In the first moments, I thought my life was destined for perpetual darkness. I now know that is not true. The glimpses have given me hope, much like someone worn out from a week-long weather system of rain and cloud, only to be treated with twenty minutes of bright and beautiful sunshine. The warmth and light radiate over your face, and you remember the glory of the blue sky. And, at minute twenty-one, the clouds reform and the warmth will dissipate, but you know the sunshine is still there behind a cloud. It will come back. So, thank you for the glimpses of my life of sunshine. I have hope, and I know the skies will be blue again.

 ♦ I am thankful for the love that resides in my heart and in my house. I am at peace knowing that Stephen's last days were filled with love. That deep and unconditional love that never judges, never expects anything in return, it simply endures. I am thankful for that, and I intend to pay that love forward. I feel I have a big portion here in my heart, his share if you will. I am excited for what I am about to embark on, sharing that love with those who need it.

 ♦ I am thankful for Stephen. An unconventional start, middle and ending, but a wonderful life just the same. I am so, so thankful for him, and for the twenty-three years I did have with him. I cannot imagine where I would be in life without his influence. He changed me, from the moment I looked into those eyes of his, those old and knowing eyes. He changed me with his life and with his death. I am thankful for him and for all that he gave me, and continues to give me through my reflection. I am thankful that so many others were touched by his life as well. I am humbled, silenced, and speechless, by the people who have and continue to reach out, simply to say he changed them, he affected them, and he loved them and took care of them just how they needed. Every mother should be so lucky to hear the words I have about their child.

 ♦ Thank you for bringing me to my knees. I make this statement, and feel it needs explanation. I am not thankful I lost my son, of course not. I continue to wish and pray every night that perhaps, I could wake up, and this would be a nightmare of epic proportion, and life would be back to normal. I also wish that if that is not possible, then at least let me see him in my dreams. Let me see him smile, hear his laugh, see him run and play.

But, as I know that is not possible, I say thank you for bringing me to my knees. It has allowed me to find myself, who I was beneath the day to day stresses, the bills, the material stuff, and the responsibilities, the opinions of others, the gossip, and the baggage. This has stripped my life bare, and I am now rebuilding it according to my terms, knowing what is truly important this time around. I have a renewed sense of wonder at the magic of the world, and now have the strength to live a life of purpose. A life that honors who he was and honors who I finally know I am.

Brought to my knees, I never thought I would stand again. I never thought it would be possible. Some days, I still have fleeting moments of that same feeling. Right now, I only stand part of the time. But the clarity is there. I can appreciate the view when I stand much more, having spent this time on the ground.

So, the next chapter will begin. Not only in this simplistic book of mine, but in my complex life. I don't know what lies ahead, around the corner, no one does. But I do know that whatever comes, I will give thanks. I wish you the same magic for your own life.

My Chronicle of Gratitude in Grief

Come to the edge, he said. They said: We are afraid. Come to the edge, he said. They came. He pushed them, And they flew...

— GUILLAUME APOLLINAIRE—

So, THE FORTY DAYS PASSED. And then I decided to write on, to the two month mark. You see, I knew I had to, because with each day, I could see the progression I was making, moving forward in my grief, in my conversation with Stephen and God, and with my growth as a human being. Forty days was not enough time. If I was to truly think about it, I could write for the remainder of my lifetime and I probably still would not have completely captured the journey or the insight.

And, as I sit here and reflect on it, I am stronger. I have come to the conclusion that I can in fact go on with life. I have agreed that I will live on purpose for the rest of my days, being thankful. I have written daily, quietly. I have hinted to my family and close friends that this is what I have been doing, but I don't believe they truly understand it. I believe they are somewhat concerned about my silence. I guess I would be too.

I am looking forward to sharing this. I am hoping that some of them pick up this torch and find their own gratitude in their grief of Stephen. I hope they can find gratitude in all of their days. For the days that appear to shine as the ones you will remember, as if you know you are making a memory right in the middle of it. And for the days that appear insignificant and not special. Because they are *all* special.

I also hope that sharing my story, my "method"; will shine that light for someone else. Truly, that is the biggest hope for me. That this story, the gratitude, and the story of his life, will provide some nourishment to the soul of others who need it.

I will continue on with my daily thankfulness, and will continue my conversation about gratitude for the rest of my life. I understand that some days, I will struggle to find my little things for the day. I think on those days, if I can't find anything else, I will be thankful for the strength I have found within me, for knowing I had to look for the good in life in order to survive. Looking back to before the loss of Stephen, I struggled at times with my gratitude journal. I had one. If you have ever watched Oprah, then you know of Sarah Ban Breathnach, and her book *Simple Abundance*. She began by sitting down and listing out 100 things she was grateful for in her life. I was pretty impressed with the whole thing, and gave it a whirl. I had hopes that it would help me recognize my purpose.

With this earlier version of gratitude, "pre-loss", I would list out things, stuff, lists of accomplishments on a "grander" but shallower scale. In reviewing them now, there was a limited focus, as if gratitude was dependent on appearance, situation, achievement or possessions. I did seem to have it figured out when it came to things like my kids and husband. But now, those other versions of happiness have fallen away from my definition of gratitude. I get it now.

For anyone who is out there, looking for purpose, begin with gratitude. If you are looking for a reason to still survive in this world, begin with appreciation. If you are looking for a reason to breathe, begin with saying thank you for your breath. Shift your focus on what you have been given instead of all that you lack. No matter what the situation. If you are like me, and in deep sadness, grieving the loss of the center of your universe, use gratitude as your "oxygen". It will help you breathe, I promise you.

> *Gratitude is the one miracle in this world*
> *that you can make happen at will.*

Part Three

For Those Who Weep and Those Who Will Comfort Them. Shared Thoughts From My Grief Experience

I WAS UNSURE IF I wanted to include this section in the book. I was not certain if I was qualified enough to write this segment and give people my point of view, or tips for better grieving.

But I pushed on, feeling I have completed some Master level courses as of late from the University of Life. The following are my thoughts for people who are grieving and for those who will comfort them in their time of sorrow. These are only from my perspective and are observations from my own journey, but perhaps they may spark something for someone walking their own path.

FOR THOSE WHO WEEP IN SORROW
BE KIND TO YOURSELF

Self-love is a scarcity these days. I find that curious, as there is certainly no shortage of egos. Yet, even in the best of times, we humans have lost the ability to smile in the mirror and exclaim, "Well, aren't you fabulous!" On the contrary, we spend many of our days unconsciously having a quiet conversation with ourselves about what is not up to par. Too many wrinkles, bad hair, not smart enough, too fat, too thin, too tall, too short, I've made mistakes and that makes me a bad person, I'm a failure, this is not where I thought I'd be at this point in my life. The list goes on and on.

That self-talk happens on the best of days. Imagine taking all of this baggage with you as you journey through your grief. It will not work. Now is not the time for you to continue to be caught up in those negative emotions. Now it is time for you to be gentle with your soul as it heals.

Sleep more. Take naps if you can, and let yourself be quiet. Sometimes, the best thing you can do is cry yourself to sleep. Let it all out and then drift off, knowing you are on the right path of this very important journey.

Treat your body with respect. Make some time to move each day, even for short spurts of time. It makes you feel good physically, but also elevates your mood through the release of endorphins produced with exercise. I am working on this in my own life and it has truly made a difference.

Find your faith. In my journey, finding my faith has been a huge part of being kind to myself. In fact, it is one of the good things that I can say came out of this incredibly tragic event. It is not that I did not have faith in God before July 4th, but it was a different, shallower relationship with God. I have called my exchanges with Him conversations or letters through this journal, but the reality is I have finally learned how to pray. Having something to believe in has nourished my soul, and I can't imagine making peace with loss without it. For each person, faith is personal and different. But for each person, it is essential.

Let Nature Love You. I've been learning about the magic of nature for a few years now, and I can't tell you how much it has helped me in my grief. As part of being kind to yourself, spend some time in your garden, or walking in the park. I find it to be a meditation of sorts, as you get down on the level of the dirt and the flowers and the bugs. It takes your mind back to simpler things, and when your heart is aching, that is a good thing.

Get rid of the Negative things in your life. This is not just a nice to do; it is a need to do. Negative people, energies, habits all have the ability to derail you in the best of times. But what you may be able to tolerate in normal times, will seriously hurt you in your times of grief. So, look around and let it go. I am not saying this is a time for major changes. In fact, it is the exact opposite. What I am suggesting is you distance yourself from things that are giving you pain, at least temporarily, until you feel strong enough to deal with them.

Prepare for Triggers. The "firsts" will be coming. Halloween, Christmas, New years, Birthdays, Anniversaries. Part of this is preparing yourself for those times. Think about them, and how you want those days to play out. Perhaps it is a special candle lit by a picture of your loved one to remember and honor them that day. Perhaps it is choosing to do something special for you, like a manicure or a trip to the spa. Again, it is personal. But preparing for those triggers gives you an opportunity to focus on the good things as you work through the pain of the day without the one you love. You will not be able to prepare for all the triggers, some will surprise you. But take the time to look at what you may find difficult, and find a way to make it easier.

I'm here to tell you if you want to survive you need to be kind to yourself. Let go of all your hang ups and negative self-talk. When you look in the mirror, smile and tell yourself you are a strong and courageous person. Because if you are up and out of bed and looking in the mirror, you are. Take the small victories in your life and in your journey of grief. Don't expect that you should be the rock for your family, the sensible one. Sensible is for shoes, not for your grief. Be kind to yourself. You are like an open wound right now. Handle yourself with care.

Set No "Schedule" for This to Be Over

Patience is a virtue, or at least that is what my mother always said. Take time and be patient with yourself. The world is not used to that anymore. We have to move quickly, we expect instant gratification. If we do not feel well soon enough, we medicate or numb ourselves. If we don't lose weight fast enough, we nip, tuck and suck the fat away. If we don't have the money, we charge it. At all costs, we feel we need to show constant progress. But grief cannot be rushed.

Take a deep breath and understand sometimes the best thing we can do for ourselves when we hurt in our experience of loss and change, is to just take a deep breath and become still.

There is no schedule for your grief. It is an individual journey and is dependent on how you loved the one you lost. You may grieve and feel you are past it, and then suddenly, an event will take you back. Don't be afraid of that. Don't bury it. It will only resurface at another time or in other ways.

I've started the habit of becoming an observer to my emotions. Sure, I feel them, but I also look at why I am feeling a certain way at this particular moment in time. It helps me to put things in perspective. There is no calendar that has a date circled, with a note exclaiming, "Grief and mourning now complete!" I found this to be a tough one to apply to myself in past losses in my life. But this time, I've listened to my soul and what I need, and it has made all the difference. I've decided to ignore the societal three day mourning period and let this journey map its own course.

So, give yourself time. Even when you get the vibe that others think it is time to move on. And you will. Even when you feel the discomfort from others when you are still talking about your loved one and you know they don't want to be part of the conversation. Even when you are frustrated some days and feel you should be further along.

Take a big breath, and understand that grief is not measured on a calendar. It is measured within you, as you take the time to feel sad about what you have lost, and figure out how you will go forward with your life. Taking the time now, choosing to feel it instead of being a grown up and pushing it deep within you is the best thing you can do for yourself, even if it takes longer than society deems acceptable. It will be the best thing for you and your loved ones, and will honor the person you loved and lost.

FIND YOUR ONE LITTLE THING

This has saved me. If you choose to do only one thing on my list, do this. Because, if you get into the habit of finding one little thing, everything else will fall into place.

I knew, that morning at the lake, I would need to find the good in order to survive. Because as I sat there, on that small bump in the sand, I wanted it to all be over. I wanted to die. The fact that I walked away from that lake knowing I would do this, that I would find the good and the gratitude in the coming days still bewilders me. Honestly, I think it may have been God who told me to do it. I have no other explanation for the insight, and it is not how I handled life changing events in the past.

It developed slowly for me, small things, something to focus on so I could continue to breathe. Honestly, those first days, I had no choice. The pain in my chest was so intense; I had to look for some good in the world.

But as the hours, days and then weeks passed, I realized this shift was what was saving me from despair, anger and bitterness. In my chronicle of grief, I have explained some of the statements that well meaning people would say to me. Things like "Don't worry, God can take it."

But with my focus on gratitude, I did not have that anger or bitterness that is so typical in loss. There was no bitterness in my heart. I did feel shell shocked, intensely hurt. I did wonder why this happened, and wished and prayed I could go to sleep and wake the next morning to find my precious sweet Stephen in the kitchen. But, I can honestly say it was all hurt and never anger.

Gratitude caused me to challenge the traditional approach to grief. By focusing on what I could appreciate right now, I have been blessed with a clearer vision of what was left behind and what continues to surround me, even in the sad loss of Stephen.

My daily practice also allowed me to see my connection with others, and on a larger scale, the world. In moments where I would have assumed I would feel lost and alone, I felt more connected to life than ever before. Gratitude allowed that life force to enter into my heart, even though that heart was broken open with grief.

Going back to being kind to yourself, gratitude is also thought to be a wonderful boost to your immunity and overall wellbeing. Scientific research is learning more about the value of positive emotions in helping to not only fight disease, but in the release of our body's natural pain killers, endorphins. Endorphins also stimulate the dilation of blood vessels leading to a "relaxed" heart.

Whatever your motivation, gratitude is better than any pharmaceutical to help you through your journey of grief, and the side effects are all positive. Gratitude is non-denominational; I give my thanks to God for all that is good in my life. For others, your thanks may be to the Universe, or a Higher Power. It makes no difference as long as you give thanks.

On a daily basis, spend a few minutes to find at least one little thing to give thanks for in your life. People have said, "I can't believe you would be able to find things, even now."

The way I see it, it was more important for me to find gratitude now than when things were sailing along smoothly in life. I don't see it as an "even now" situation, but rather an "especially now."

Here are some tips for finding and focusing on the one little thing for your day:

Write them down. Putting them on paper or in a word document is a powerful exercise. There is something validating about reading your words back to yourself. The process becomes more purposeful.

Look to nature. Butterflies, birds, falling leaves, sunshine and rain. They are easy to love, and easy to be grateful for. When the day is tough, it is an easy place to start your reflection. See the magic of the world that surrounds you and feel thankful that every part of it is working to give you comfort.

Notice the love that surrounds you. Sometimes, finding your one little thing means shifting the angle from which you view your life. For me, looking at all that was lost can be balanced by looking at the love that still remains. My husband, my son, Rudy the Wonder Dog, and the spirit of Stephen. It can never take away the pain. But it can allow you to feel gratitude for what is left.

Explore your memories. This is a double-edged sword in some respects. Early in grief, exploring memories can be painful. It hurts to review even the happiest moments and realize that you will not be able to make new ones with the one you have lost. But memories, even through tears, can be a source of gratitude for weeks and years to come. Truly, if we look to days gone by, happy memories shape our vision for life going forward.

Look in the mirror. Be thankful for yourself. With each passing day, notice the good in yourself. Celebrate the milestones you reach, however simple.

Look outside your window. Connecting with your community can be helpful for a number of reasons. Talking to others offers perspective in your healing journey. You realize you are not as alone as you thought, and that is something to be grateful for indeed. But looking outside your window can also connect you with people you can help. I think for your gratitude to come full circle, giving back needs to be a part of it. That is putting your gratitude into action, which I believe may be the point of our existence. You need to be ready for this, it will not happen overnight. But once it does, the feeling you get from helping another will give you a lifetime of "one little things."

Hang out with the Smart People. My parents always told me to stick with the smart ones in life, and I took that advice in my search for gratitude in grief. Each morning, I looked for an inspiring quote to start my day. From Mother Teresa to George Eliot, I was able to find and draw strength from the great thinkers of our time. There is so much goodness in this world. Take some time to find some at the beginning of your day. This can be especially comforting on the hard days, where you struggle to find any little thing.

Find the Humor in Life. I know this is a difficult time, and it is hard to find any joy. But life gives you things sometimes that are so absurd, so bizarre, you have to laugh. And sometimes, a good laugh is better than a cry. Don't be afraid to find the good in those laughable moments. Let it out.

Understand that Death is a Part of Life

It doesn't seem right. It doesn't feel natural, it shouldn't have happened yet. I was not ready to lose him. If you have lost someone, you probably have had similar thoughts.

But, we must all understand that this is a part of life. I know it is hard to believe, I know it is difficult to accept. It seems unfair and wrong and unnatural. Our fast-moving world has conditioned us to move quickly, skimming over the surface of our life experience. If you look around, things move so swiftly these days, it is as if we want to prevent ourselves from experiencing what we are here for, the good and the bad. And, the truth is we are here to experience joy *and* pain, happiness and sorrow.

Death may have come too soon. In the case of Stephen, it was way too soon. He was on the cusp of an adult life that would have left a mark on the world I can now only dream about. But regardless of the fairness of the timing, death is inevitable. And when it comes, we have a choice. We can fight it, argue with it, beg for it not to be so, be angry, have a tantrum, have a breakdown; or we can simply surrender to it and accept it, and let it teach us.

It sounds like such an easy thing when you read it on a typed page. But it is not. It is not easy to surrender to something that hurts so deeply, so intensely.

It is not easy, but the way I see it, neither is fighting it. I once read about the struggle with the flow of life like swimming against a current in a stream. That analogy is perfect for the stages that we all feel during a time of loss. But the fact is, I don't believe we were meant to swim against the current of our lives or our grief. I think we were simply meant to "go with the flow".

This scared me at first. To let the current flow, I had to let go of my own illusion of my power and admit I really had no control. We all struggle so with the letting go, not realizing the freedom we have sought throughout our lives can only truly be attained by doing so. Letting go of our assumptions, our control, our prejudices, and our need for certainty. We long for things to be in order, but the reality is when life becomes disorderly, that is when we really learn. When our lives crumble, and the pieces feel like sand slipping through our fingers that is when we begin to understand what really matters. Those moments of surrender teach us to be more compassionate people.

There was so much I could have consumed myself with following Stephen's death. The why, the how, the anger, or the unfairness of it all. But, it just did not seem like the right path to honoring him in the way he deserved. And it would not change the reality. Matthew, Stephen's twin died too soon, my parents died way too soon. All over the world, there is not one person who could not tell you of someone who was taken too soon. But the truth is, some live short lives, and some live long. And when death comes, it is like birth, a part of the bigger picture, and not something to fight against.

I know it hurts. But through the pain, something good and wondrous will come. We are all dying, every one of us. Don't make it all about the expiration date. Rather, make it about the delicious life that was, and look forward to the time when you are together again.

Find Someone to Talk to

As you have read within the pages of this book, "The Grief Lady" has played an integral role in our healing process and will continue to do so as the days and months continue. I feel blessed, that I knew instantly that this was a traumatic life event, and we were going to need some help.

Finding a good counselor who understands both grief and family dynamics can be so helpful and I would recommend it for anyone experiencing a loss of a child, or any loved one in your life. Everything is different, and it is okay to look to others for help in figuring out how to live in your new reality.

If a professional person is not something you are interested in, at least find a confidante, a person who will listen to you as you work through your feelings. You need to let it out. I have described my feelings as a volcano, a tea kettle getting ready to boil, and numerous other descriptors. Letting your feeling out is a part of grieving, so surround yourself with the right people who will help you walk your path.

There are also a number of wonderful groups that can also be helpful. The Compassionate Friends or Bereavement groups at your local churches or community center. Grief Share is another example of a faith based support for grieving persons. Know you are not alone, and others have walked a similar path and can be a source of comfort and knowledge to help you through.

Not everyone is equipped to handle this situation with you. Some will know exactly what to say, or not to say. They will hug you, comfort you, and ease some of the pain. But not everyone will understand how to do this. Some will say things that cause your eyebrows to rise. Others will avoid you, to spare you and themselves from the difficult moments of conversation. Don't be offended, take a deep cleansing breath and understand that this is part of it.

Finally, as family, keep talking to each other. Continue to check in with those you love. Let them know how you feel and give them an opportunity to tell you the same. I've been working really hard on doing that with my son Brendan and Brady. And it really helps. Have peace with the fact there are no immediate answers needed or solutions to be found. Sometimes, you simply need to listen, let it out, and cry. Make your home a safe place for you and your family to do that.

FOR THOSE WHO WILL COMFORT

It is so difficult to watch someone you care about mourn the loss of someone they love. In my chronicle of gratitude, I have highlighted some amazing individuals who comforted us with such compassion. I have also written about some of the experiences I've had with people who struggle with finding the right words.

From our journey, I wanted to put down some simple thoughts for anyone who finds themselves comforting someone who has lost a precious loved one.

YOU SHOULD:

Acknowledge the Loss. Say you are sad, or sorry for the loss. Express love and support, and try to provide comfort. I know this seems like a given, but there are many people who find it difficult to navigate this situation. But acknowledge the loss, even if it is uncomfortable for you to bring it up. People need to hear that others are there, and praying for them when they hurt so deeply and feel so alone. Your words don't need to be fancy. In fact, you don't even have to say many words at all. I'm so sorry, combined with a sincere hug would be enough.

Attend the Memorial and Extend Gestures of Concern. For Stephen, we were blessed to have two memorials in his honor. One in North Carolina and the other in Newfoundland. Because of that, my family was able to meet and talk to so many people who loved Stephen. It meant so much to us to be able to see how many people he touched in his short but sweet life. In addition to their presence, so many people sent cards, personal notes, and donations to the hockey team. It was so touching for us, and it truly made the difference. People showed us they were sad for us, they showed us human compassion. Show those who are mourning that the life of the person who passed mattered to you, and be present for them as they say good bye.

Don't Just Suggest, Make it Happen. It is difficult to move in those early moments of painful grief. So, when comforting someone, don't simply suggest you can help. Just jump in and do something. Bring a meal, purchase a book on grief, babysit, run errands. Sometimes, if you simply suggest, it won't happen because the griever won't want to be a burden. But trust me, help is needed.

Make it Personal. I have written extensively about how touching it has been for me to read the words of Stephen's friends and family. Simple, heartwarming stories about him, his life, and the fun he had and how he touched others. I can't tell you how important this is to someone who has lost a child, or anyone else for that matter. The words of others will comfort me for years to come. Don't hesitate to take a moment and pen a personal note about the person, and how they touched your life.

Remember That it Continues After the Funeral. Grief can be an ongoing journey. Remember anniversaries, special days, occasions. Understand that these days will be tough, especially in the first year. Help the griever through these days, by acknowledging the pain and offering remembrance for their loved one. Perhaps a card, a candle, or a simple coffee. Also, in conversations, use the child's or loved one's name. I found it so interesting in my first months of grief to see that people immediately stopped speaking his name. It was almost as if the uttering of the word would invoke too much pain. But in reality, I needed to hear it. I needed to hear that other people were thinking of him, remembering stories and moments that meant something. Memories of Stephen are what remain. So, keep it personal and don't stop remembering.

Just Be There. Simply being there when needed is all that is required of you. Give hugs freely, and be a good listener. Don't feel you need to have answers, as there are no answers that will erase the pain. Cry with the griever, and know that tears are healthy.

Remember the Forgotten Mourners. The Children left behind; I read something that labeled the children who have lost siblings as the *forgotten mourners* and it stuck with me. Take time to recognize the grief that mourning siblings feel for their brother or sister. For our family, the relationship between Brendan and Stephen was deep, and close, and in some ways parental. With an eleven-year span between the two, Stephen had provided him with guidance throughout his life, whether for hockey, friendships or life in general. The two leaned on each other through divorce, and navigated waters together as a team. As both were goalies, they had a special bond with the sport of hockey. This loss is profound for Brendan.

So, if you are comforting the siblings of a lost child, remember that although quiet, they hurt. There are some wonderful resources available for assisting children through grief, and I recommend a good "Grief Lady" to help steer the ship. Ensure your comforts are age appropriate, and consistent. Love, Love and more love.

FINDING UNCONVENTIONAL COMFORTS

I have been surprised at what has given me some peace, some joy in the midst of pain. Unconventional comforts were pleasant surprises for me in my loss. At first, I thought that simply recording them in my journal of daily gratitude would be enough. But, in thinking about how they helped me in my own passage, I thought it would be beneficial to devote some more time to each of them. I hope in some way, it may help others find their own unconventional comforts.

These few things lifted me and carried me through some dark days.

FACEBOOK

Who would have thought that a social media application could comfort the bereaved, and act as an online Irish Wake of sorts?

I was one of those people who resisted the charms of Facebook, grumbling about its lack of necessity in the same way my father did about the remote control. (He soon recovered) So many of my friends were on facebook, but yet still I resisted, even though my curiosity was peaked as to how Mary or Jane were doing since high school. And then, my high school graduating class had their reunion. Having already planned my travel for a family wedding, I could not swing it, and felt so left out. I was blessed where I grew up, a small town, with small classes, taught by the Christians brothers, a good place to grow up, probably the best place to grow up when I think on it. Leaving home after graduation, I was idealist and naive, and even now, even today, I can still see the wonder in the world. I am thankful for that.

Anyway, this high school reunion was amazing. Friends called and told me that it was simply a mind blowing weekend, with everyone in attendance just glad to see one another. No more social cliques, no more jocks and brains, and any other high school analogies for hierarchy that exist at that age. But, in order to see the pictures of this life changing event, I had to join Facebook.

I am a private person. Setting up a user profile on Facebook was stepping way out of the box. But, hey, I wanted to see those darn pictures. After some trepidation, I did finally give out my information, and set up a profile. And yes, the pictures were worth it. But, what was better was the reconnection with so many friends I had lost touch with along the way. I never knew what I was missing. Little did I know at the time, that less than a year later, this Social media application would be such a source of comfort.

When the news broke about Stephen's untimely death, I immediately started to receive messages, so many messages, from both my own friends, and from friends of Stephen. And, as private as I am, it was wonderful. It was a cyber hug from people on every corner of the planet, it was personal and loving, and it was exactly what we needed. Who would have thunk it?

In talking about this phenomenon, my best friend set up a memorial group, so people could join, and pass along comments, share stories, etc. And the numbers, they just kept growing. I would watch, with wonder as people joined. I would laugh and cry, as people I had long forgotten, would post the most heartfelt memories of my precious boy.

Comfort can come in many different packages. I am thankful that I let down my walls of privacy, as I would never have felt the outpouring of love. How absolutely amazing for this private girl to be able to sit in my office, laptop in front of me, and cry, being able to read the most personal of stories from people I would not have otherwise had the opportunity to speak with. And, given the generational age of his friends, I was able to hear from people who probably would not have sent a hand written sympathy card. And that is not a negative thing. This is their medium for communication. Here are some messages that without facebook, I would not have had the privilege of receiving:

"Quantity of life gives way for quality of life" - Father Hearn.
This was said at Stephen's funeral and it best
describes his life. I' ll miss ya buddy.

As I read these tributes to this beautiful boy, I know them all to be true. "Even more beautiful in his heart, a gentle soul, kind to everyone, true friend, com-passionate, his smile brightened everyone's day, we laughed till we cried, a true gentleman." He was a Russell.

You are a family of love, of grace and giving. Madge and Don Russell made such beautiful children. If every person in this world could be blessed to have a "Russell" as a friend or just to have been touched by one of them, the world would be a happier and better place.

Stephen was a gift to the world for 23 years. As all the Russell's are "gifts" to each other and us in this passage called life. Our Lord must collect Russell's as examples, to show new coming Angels what he expects of them. I think Madge and Don are CEO'S in Heaven. It's a loving home, with hugs and music and laughter and tears. Hold on tight to one another.

I was not the only one who was touched and affected by the messages from Stephen's friends. Brendan was truly comforted by all the kind words and it made him feel connected to everyone. The following is what Brendan added to the memorial page.

Hi this is Brendan I am Stephen's brother I would just like to say thank you to everyone who shared there memories about Stephen when I was sad I looked at this and it made me smile that my big brother made such an impact on everyone's lives some don't know me and some know me from trash talking at

N.C. state hockey games and some remember me from Peace River and but one of the things I remember is hanging out with Katrin and Matt at the park and at our houses. And matt I think my magnifying glass from kindergarten is still in your truck thanks for the thoughts goodbye BRENDAN

Stephen was so sweet smart and funny he was one of my first friends when I moved in grade nine. He made me laugh until I cried and I (like every other girl in school) had a huge crush on him.... I'm so angry such a beautiful human being got taken right in his prime. My heart and prayers go out to his family and friends. What a terrible tragedy.

Love you Stephen you will be forever missed and never forgotten

It is hard to find the right words to say, but when I think of Steve I have so many memories from junior high and high school. Our trip to Nova Scotia for the Heritage Fair is a memory I will never forget, being the nerds we were in grade 8, taking any opportunity to travel. I remember laughing with him on the tiny rickety plane. I had such a huge crush on Steve from that trip. He was the only one who could pull off the yellow fisherman's hat on the Harbor Hopper, and I have always held a place for him in my heart. Watching him play hockey with the rest of the boys, I'm so glad he could continue playing the sport he loved. He was without a doubt the nicest,

gentlest, kindest, compassionate person you could know. And I am so glad that I got to call him a good friend. My thoughts and prayers are with you.

Steve was my first " boyfriend", I still remember the first day I met him like it was yesterday. I have to stay he set the bar pretty high for others to come. So much of my junior and senior high school memories include Steve like the many hours spent cheering him on in the hockey arena. A while ago I read through some old dairies and there was one constant theme STEVE. When Steve moved away, I felt like he took a little piece of my heart with him. Now I have that same feeling again, I think everyone who knew him does too. Words cannot adequately describe Steve and the impact he has had on those who knew him. I want to express my deepest sorrow and send my love and prayers. I've always loved you Steve and I always will.

Stephen was a pretty good friend when we went to school together. I remember being on the same hockey team as Stephen. We weren't that good but we had a lot of fun. My dad would always tease me because I had a big crush on him for years and he would ride to hockey games with us so I never heard the end of it "oh guess who we are picking up for hockey. Stephen" in a teasing voice. But he was a great guy, kind to everyone. I will continue to miss him. I have been since he moved away. He was just one of those people that stick in your mind and he will be greatly missed!

Sending special prayers, thoughts and love to your family at this time.

Stephen was my locker buddy from grade seven until grade ten and we had the most special moments through our teenage years - whether it was stuffing sandwiches in the top of each other's lockers or writing see ya later notes.

He was a special friend to me, a kind soul and a true gentleman.
He will be remembered as a wonderful friend to all.

"You can shed tears that he is gone,
or you can smile because he has
lived.
You can close your eyes and pray that he' ll come
back, or you can open your eyes and see all he's left.
Your heart can be empty because you can't see
him, or you can be full of the love you shared.
You can turn your back on tomorrow and live yesterday,
or you can be happy for tomorrow because of yesterday.
You can remember him only that he is gone,
or you can cherish his memory and let it live on.
You can cry and close your mind,
be empty and turn your back.
Or you can do what he' d want:
smile, open your eyes, love and go on."

Stephen was a special child to teach and I remember grade one like it
was yesterday. His smile brightened everyone's day and he will not be
forgotten.

I am standing by the seashore.
A ship at my side spreads her white sails to the morning breeze
and starts for the blue ocean.
She is an object of beauty and strength,
and I stand and watch

until at last she hangs like a peck of white cloud
just where the sun and sky come down to mingle with each other.

Then someone at my side says, 'There she
goes! Gone where? Gone from my sight –
that is all.

She is just as large in mast and hull and spar
as she was when she left my side
and just as able to bear her load of living freight
to the places of destination.
Her diminished size is in me, not in her.

And just at the moment when someone at my side says,
'There she goes! ',
there are other eyes watching her coming,
and other voices ready to take up the glad shout :
'Here she comes!'

Forever grateful for your life,
Forever thankful that we were blessed to be in it,
Forever loved and missed.

It's amazing how some little souls just take hold of your heart and you know
immediately how special they are. That is how I have always thought
of Stephen. I can clearly remember that shy little boy who would come
and visit us in nursing school. He was always so polite and Kelly would
come back from her weekend and tell us all about Stephen's
adventures.
I was young but I knew their bond as mother and son was special,

maybe more special than anyone else's I have ever seen since. He was so proud of his mom and she adored him. I can't even begin to express the sadness I feel. I can only share with you that knowing Stephen and Kelly and seeing their love and family support had such an impact on
my own relationships. Many times when my friends and I discuss people that inspire us and amaze us, I talk about Kelly and little Stephen. It didn't matter that little Stephen was now a big, strong, handsome young man. He will be forever in my heart and Kelly in my thoughts.

Please accept my most sincere condolences for your sudden loss. Hold fast to the wonderful memories you experienced as a family as these are the fibers that will weave an eternal bond for you and all that had the privilege of know such a fine young man. Seek solace in your family and friends as these comforts will ease your burden. Know my thoughts will be with you as you gather in celebration of Stephen's life and accomplishments and for your journey back home. God Bless.

On our graduation day from Nursing School, 16 years ago. Stephen proudly and very LOUDLY stood and announced that, "That is MY MOM and she is a Nurse". Even at the gentle age of 7, he was so proud of his Mom. A gentle and kind hearted boy that grew into a wonderful, kind hearted man. "Gone Too Soon"

"Dream as if you' ll live forever, live as if you' ll die today" -James Dean

We celebrated Will's 21st. birthday in Raleigh with some of the hockey team guys and I'm so glad Stephen was there. We laughed, danced, and created a great memory. That's what hockey players do, they enjoy life. But the one thing that I will always remember about Stephen was his expression. He seemed to have a constant smile on his face and when he actually did smile it was from ear to ear. May his love for hockey always be an inspiration and may he continue to live in all of our hearts.

Driving to Cook-Out at 3 am
Watching Terrible Movies
Canadian Steve

Climbing Trees
Listening to Elliot Smith
Going to Farmer's Market

On the night of July 2nd, Steve and I walked back into the apartment to get my iPod stereo and we walked out blaring "Hey Jealousy".

He stopped at the door, turned around, and said "You know, I've been thinking about this recently, and you and I are a lot more alike than you think" I told him that I already knew we were. Despite how many great moments I've had with Steve, I never asked him exactly what he meant by what he said that night. Not asking is my only regret, besides not taking advantage of more time with him.

IPODS

As I opened his knapsack for the first time after being presented with Stephen's belongings, his iPod was one of the first things I found. I sat for what seemed to be forever and simply stared at it. This little gadget had spent more time with Stephen than most of his loved ones. He wore it when he was working out, working at our warehouse, mowing the lawn, and a multitude of other daily tasks. As I watched him, I would often wonder what he was listening to, as he ran like the wind, or cleaned his room. But, for some reason, I did not ask.

The next day, I tried to turn on the iPod, but it would not work. Funny things like that happened for Brady and I. With Stephen electronics, like his iPod and computer, it was as if he was deciding when they would work, and it would only be at a moment when we were ready for it. The funny thing was, instead of being upset about it, I immediately understood this and just accepted it.

Shoving the iPod in my knapsack, we took it with us to Newfoundland, hoping it would work when we got there. A few days after our arrival, the day before his funeral, I took it out, and held it in my hands. He had used it so much, almost every day, and the wear and tear was obvious. The dial was visibly well used, and from the look of it, Stephen had to press a little harder these days to make the play/pause button work.

I took out his Nike arm band, putting it to my nose to smell him, and collapsed in tears. I would see that on his arm more often than not, cradling his iPod, as his carried the music with him, on his arm and in his soul.

An iPod Playlist is created by that person for a special reason. Some make a playlist for exercise, for love, for fun. It is such a personal thing, and truly is a window into their soul.

Stephen's iPod gave me insight into the man he had become since going off to college and it was a beautiful thing. It was fascinating to me, because he had grown so much, but also still held on to his roots tightly. I could tell that through simple music.

His playlists were as eclectic as his varied taste in life and friends. Laughing, I realized that his music was a reflection of his soul. Everyone was welcome. From Dean Martin to Mozart; the Avett Brothers and Band of Horses to AC/DC. There were simple and old songs and tunes I had sung to him as I rocked him in my arms as a baby.

Of all the things that have given me comfort, this is a big one.

If you or someone you love has lost someone, and they have an iPod, take some time to listen. It will feel like you are dancing with your loved one, if only in your dreams.

EMAILS, TEXT MESSAGES AND LETTERS

I have shared some of the more intimate exchanges between Stephen and I with you in this book. I agonized about that, but decided that the only way to truly convey the relationship and the story was to open up the intimate parts of our life and let them be seen.

Our relationship was imperfect. It was beautiful. It was unconventional as parenting goes. It was magic. The emails reflect that.

The one email from the spring that I have referred to so often provided me with a turning point in my grief, and was perhaps the very thing that sparked my focus on gratitude. To receive confirmation that as a mother and child, we had said everything that needed to be said, well that is a gift.

But what is remarkable and beautiful are the emails that have been sent since his death.

The initial email, which I have written about in the book, was a back and forth exchange that I count my lucky stars for every day. I decided to really take some time to tell him my thoughts, to spend time right then speaking the truth, giving him encouragement. I can remember the day perfectly, as I was in fact, pretty busy with other things. I am so thankful I did that. I said everything I needed to say to him, as a mother. In fact, as I read those words just days after his death, I realized that I would not have said anything additional to him had I'd been given a chance by God before he died. And, to add to that, his response said it all right back to Brady and I. He said it, he knew we loved him and he loved us back. He knew that we would crawl over glass, spend our last pennies, die for him, and believe in him no matter what the situation. And, I exhaled. It was quite something, I felt an immediate peace.

As I continued to look through the emails and text messages, I received another gift. Not only had we said it in that one email, we had said it ALL THE TIME. We spoke our truth and our love every day. I am sure we seemed sickly sweet to onlookers. I found silly exchanges, exchanges about money (as any college student would send), emails about seeing each other, friendship, love, break ups, business, his brother, it was all there.

Although I had never received the instruction guide to parenting, maybe I had some things inherently right. It served as confirmation that indeed,

A happy family is but an earlier heaven.

-- JOHN BOWRING

We also found text messages, cards and letters. Simple words that were treasures for me now. I could exhale and have peace in my heart, with the knowledge of the fact that we had shared what mattered.

This has changed the way I parent, and it has changed every relationship I have, forever. I now understand that taking the extra few seconds to say what matters does make the difference.

In addition to finding the emails between Stephen and us, I also received so many messages from friends and family. Emotions flew over cyberspace, sending us words of comfort and love. I always thought that there was a great loss in our culture, with the demise of the written word, the thank you note, where people took the time to truly think about the words and the message. But what I found during this most difficult time is the words were not lost. There were simply being sent in a different forum.

Those who loved us poured out their souls. And in turn, I felt compelled to share with them my feelings and thoughts, starting with that email from the spring.

What resulted has been a beautiful blossom of love within my family and circle of friends. We have reconnected and we have started talking about what needs to be discussed.

iPod Playlists, Emails and Facebook. Prior to the evening of July 4th, I would have scoffed at the idea that those three things would carry me through the valley of despair following the death of my son. And, although early in my grief, I know they will continue to give me the solace and consolation on dark days, when I have to consciously look for one thing to get me through the day.

From those things, this book has come, from my soul, in the hopes I can adequately convey how he lived life and give others some points to ponder. For who he was, the credit goes to so many. Stephen was raised and molded by many people, and his spirit reflected their influence. Most of all, he was a child of God, and I can honestly say he lived each day, conducting himself with a grace that makes me proud to say I was his mother.

Conclusion

As the first months of my grief come to a close, so does this book. However, it is not the end of the conversation. I wrote this book in the hopes that perhaps someone who is hurting like me will take something positive from my words of gratitude. Perhaps others may be reminded of the fragility of life and live more aware of the fact that we only have a short time to live with purpose. We need to live the life of our dreams now, we need to parent as if there is no tomorrow. And, most importantly, life begins with love, kindness and gratitude. Going forward, I will be inviting people to have that discussion, with me, with their children, and with each other.

My grief does not end on the last page, it will continue. In fact, I am sure I will be grieving Stephen in some way until the day I die. He was just such a huge joy to me, and I will always miss him.

But, just as the grief will go on, so does my gratitude. I will be thankful for what I have right now, and for what this life changing event has taught me, has illuminated in my own life. I will be thankful for what Stephen's message can do, and will do, for others. I will be thankful that I have an opportunity to pass this message along, and maybe, just maybe affect positive change on someone who needs it. I will feel grateful for whatever allowed me to see the good in this. It has saved me.

For you, the reader, I hope you can take some tidbits from this simple tale. I hope that you can see, if, in this circumstance, I could find gratitude, you can as well. No matter what you face, if you look closely enough, there is beauty. Always. And you can find it. Death is not the end, just a change in the way we love. I will leave you with a poem I wrote to sum up the conversations I've had with God and my gratitude for Stephen's time and life with me.

The Deal

God came to the young girl, who was afraid and alone.
Crying in the dark, she had lost her way home.
Pregnant with not one baby but two, she thought
life was over, she knew not what to do.
I know it seems hopeless, but do not have fear.
These babies are angels, you will hold them dear.
They will be your sons, but your teachers as well.
Your time with them will be an amazing story to tell.
A tale of love and kindness, and of pure and simple joy.
A story of perseverance and innocence; a tale of a beautiful boy.
It will not be forever. Nothing is or could be;
But their presence on earth will change things, now and what will be.
One will come and go again, so fast it won't seem real.
But understand his time with you will change how you see and feel.
His presence is important, and will show you in many ways.
The impact of a life is not measured in simple days.
The second angel with stay with you, to grow, to love and in turn;

This very special angel will teach you all that you must learn.
He will show you the meaning of kindness, and will always have a smile.
He will be patient and understanding and will go the extra mile.
He will show you what can happen when you give your very best.
You will look at him and wonder why you were luckier than the rest.
But one day you must know I will need him to come Home;
When he has learned all his lessons, and taught you ones of your own.
His parting will be swift, but I want you not to cry.
His coming home to Me will teach you how to fly.
Your tears will flow like a river, running to the sea.
You will not understand, but you must trust in Me.
I have a plan to spread my love, not for you to live in fear.
I promise you, it is the truth, even when you don't feel Me near.
Your sadness and your pain will break open your heart and make it
ache. But, with that open heart, you will take the steps that you must
make. You will take all the hurt and make something special from the
pain. You will spread your angels love like a cloud spreads cleansing rain.
The young girl sat quiet; it was so much to contemplate.
It was such happiness with such sorrow; could she handle such a fate?
He was offering her wisdom, and love despite the pain.
Could she be strong enough to handle it, would it feel like love in vain?
And as the girl sat quiet, God showed her pictures of her life.
She saw her beautiful angels, but she saw the pain and strife.
God took her by the hand, and said with a soft and tender voice,

These angels are My gift to you, but you always have a choice.
How could I choose differently, how could I possibly say no?
You've shown me all the seeds that his precious life will sow.
And from his death, I see there will not only be the pain.
But the harvest of his crop to live on and on again.

"I only ask one thing, when it comes time for that painful
day. Help my heart stay open and keep the bitterness

away. Show me how to spread the love that his time here leaves behind. Keep love in my heart and gratitude in my mind."
"So, yes Father, please bring me my angel son. I accept with my heartfelt thanks, and say, "Thy Will Be Done".

For more information on this book, or Kelly's other works, please visit
www.kellybuckley.com

AUTHOR BIOGRAPHY

GROWING UP ON THE EAST coast of Canada in Newfoundland and Labrador, Kelly Buckley lived in a culture that personifies courage and resilience. She drew upon those childhood teachings to survive the death of her son, Stephen.

Buckley coped with her tragic loss by helping others with theirs. She has published two books about her experiences: *Gratitude in Grief* and *Just One Little Thing*. She has also launched a global Facebook community called Just One Little Thing. It helps people all over the world focus on giving thanks for the little things in life. This community has grown to over 125,000 "JOLT'ers" from over forty-five different countries. By sharing her story, she has sparked a conversation about life, gratitude, compassion, and resilience, helping others navigate through both the hills and valleys of their own lives.

Buckley also created the online community Strong Wise Women, which supports women coping with loss. She worked as a registered nurse and a health executive before becoming a full-time writer. Buckley lives in North Carolina, where she continues to write about the healing power of finding blessings in the little things.

Made in the USA
Monee, IL
20 November 2019